Love Valley

Love Valley:

An American Utopia

Conrad Ostwalt

Bowling Green State University Popular Press
Bowling Green, OH 43403

Copyright © 1998 Bowling Green State University Popular Press

Library of Congress Cataloging-in-Publication Data
Ostwalt, Conrad Eugene, 1959-
    Love Valley : an American utopia / Conrad Ostwalt.
        p.   cm.
    Includes bibliographical references (p.   ) and index.
    ISBN 0-87972-759-4 (cloth). -- ISBN 0-87972-760-8 (pbk.)
    1. Love Valley (N.C.)--History. 2. Utopias--North Carolina--
History--20th century.   I. Title.
F264.L68088   1998
975.6'793--dc21   98-23595
                                                                 CIP

Cover design by Dumm Art

*Dedicated
to the memory of
Conrad E. Ostwalt, Sr.
and to the life of
Doris B. Ostwalt*

Contents

Acknowledgments

Producing this book has taken years, and many have helped during the process of research and writing. The staff and research consultants at the following libraries provided invaluable assistance and access to holdings: the Iredell County Library, State of North Carolina Public Library, and Appalachian State University Library. Heather Sharpe, of the Iredell County Clerk of Court's office, helped locate archival information. In addition, Ellenora Barker, unofficial archivist for Love Valley, provided crucial assistance in the process of sifting through materials and tracking down obscure references. The Office of Graduate Studies and Research at Appalachian State University provided support for field work and writing during the summer of 1992 and for indexing. My graduate assistant during the summer of 1992, Stacy Suzanne Moffitt, checked notes and references and helped during the initial stages of writing. Pat Beaver, director of the Center for Appalachian Studies, assigned me a research assistant, Kathy Staley, who provided invaluable assistance during the final stages of manuscript preparation. Melanie Rice helped with final manuscript production. As usual, Christy Lohr added her keen insight to this work.

Grant Wacker and Peter Kaufman offered refinement during conversations with them concerning the project. Sam Hill offered his assessment of the manuscript in the beginning stages. David Ball was always willing to talk about the story, provided encouragement when I needed it, and offered countless clarifying suggestions. The Dean's office at Appalachian provided invaluable assistance at crucial points in the production of the manuscript: in particular, Dean Donald Sink, Sandy Sanders, and Sara Earp were especially helpful. Ruth Cook and Emily Farthing sacrificed their time to help with manuscript preparation. A special thanks to Ruth Cook for her patience during the times I dislodged her from her work station. From the Department of Philosophy and Religion, Debi Tibbett, Alan Hauser, and Jesse Taylor all provided support of one sort or another. As the manuscript neared completion, Mary Ostwalt read every word and made suggestions that greatly improved the book. And on a more informal level, friends such as Brad and Susan Berndt, Beth and Spencer Clary, Bryan and Michaele Haas, and Megan and Tom Lawson provided a sounding board.

Many provided interviews and unique insight on Love Valley, and these are mentioned in the notes. In particular, Tonda Barker Smith provided views that only a child of Love Valley could offer. She and her husband, David, were generous with their time and were major primary sources of information. In addition, Cyndy Allison offered her time and story, and I greatly appreciate her honesty and forthrightness. Pam Simon was especially gracious with her time and candor, and Butch Trucks volunteered his time when many celebrities were unapproachable. Special thanks to John Ogden in Atlanta and Kirk West in Chicago for their perspectives on the Love Valley Rock Festival, and Rory Knapton who provided an insider's look at life in Love Valley after the Festival. Love Valleyites demonstrated a remarkable patience with me during the process of writing, and to them, regardless of their role in the project, the guy wandering the streets with pencil, tape recorder, and camera offers his gratitude.

Several have granted permission to reproduce quoted materials in the book. Thanks to Loonis McGlohon for permission to reproduce the lyrics to the "Love Valley" song. Don Berg, who wrote the song, "Love Valley, U.S.A.," and Andy Barker, head of Love Valley Records, granted permission to reproduce the lyrics to "Love Valley, U.S.A." Timothy E. Dearman, publisher of the *Statesville Record and Landmark* gave permission to quote several items from his paper. In addition, the *Statesville Record and Landmark* has been an invaluable source for verifying information and stories through the years. This newspaper provided an indispensable record of Love Valley activities. My thanks to Timothy Dearman and the many reporters who faithfully recorded these activities. In addition, Thomas Blount, editor of the *High Point Enterprise*; Elizabeth Cook, editor of the *Salisbury Post*; and Elaine Tynan of the *Charlotte Observer* all granted permission to quote from their newspapers. Professor Melton McLauren, managing editor of *North Carolina Humanities,* granted permission to reproduce material that originally appeared in an article I wrote entitled, "Love Valley: A Utopian Experiment in North Carolina." Rory Knapton and Don Berg gave permission to quote "Flood" promotional literature. In addition, Andy Barker gave permission to use photographs from the Love Valley Archives. Virginia E. Hauswald gave permission to reproduce a photograph by Bill Ray that appeared in the *Winston-Salem Journal*. Marcus Green of the *Winston-Salem Journal* and Ann Bryant of the *Charlotte Observer* helped locate photographs. Finally, the editors at Popular Press, especially Barbara K. Solosy and Pat Browne, provided insightful work and critique to make this a better book.

Those closest to me provide support in one way or another—so to my parents, Conrad and Doris, who first taught me about love, I dedicate this volume. To Mary, my wife, with whom love has continued to blossom after more than 17 years of marriage, this work is a continued love note to you. To my brother, Mark, and my sisters, Donna and Angela, thanks for your support along the way. To Carrie, Amy, Jordan, Jacob, Kadi, Anna, and most recently, Jessica, thank you for adding perspective. To John, Martha, Mike, Marcia, and Emily, thanks for your patience. And to Louise Queen, thanks for making this work possible—I only wish you could have seen the completion of this work you helped start.

Finally, my greatest debt must go to Andy and Ellenora Barker. They opened their home, their lives, the town records, and anything else I might have needed. I rarely left their house without a gift, but then neither does anyone else. Thank you, Andy and Ellenora—thank you for Love Valley.

Boone, North Carolina, 1998

1

Introduction and Preface

This is a story of a small town—a town that has attempted to reach far beyond its boundaries. It is the story of a visionary builder and his attempt to found a community that would be a model to the rest of the world.

Growing up hearing about Love Valley, I gained several different perspectives of the small town in northern Iredell County and was intrigued by the place. The rumors and media coverage concerning Love Valley painted a biased portrait of the town that I wanted to test. Knowing that my wife's aunt, Louise Queen, had ties to the town, I quizzed her about the possibility of conducting a little research on the village. A short while later, she introduced me to Andy and Ellenora Barker and to Love Valley. What I found during the months of research that followed was a different view of the town—a perspective that I suspect is hidden to many people who are familiar with Love Valley as I was, through rumor and innuendo. My research grew in scope, and I soon realized an article would not sufficiently tell the story of Love Valley. In this attempt to tell that story, my goal is to allow Love Valley to shape its own narrative.

To do this, I depend largely on oral histories and tales that circulate among those associated with the Valley. In addition to circulating orally, some of these stories have been recorded in letters, diaries, newspaper accounts, town records, collections of reminiscences, and poetry. Whenever possible, I attempted to verify the stories with secondary or written sources and have noted the source of such verification. Nevertheless, verification was not always possible, and I have often depended on personal recollections. In addition, newspaper accounts were sometimes pejorative and not always reliable. In either case, I suspect exaggeration of some details has crept into the tradition as these stories have been told and retold and in some cases have achieved mythic levels and proportions.

This project is an oral history project but not in the sense that I reproduce individual voices. I have attempted to hear and present a community voice that has emerged from a collection of individual perspectives. What follows is a narrative history based largely on a growing oral tradition. I have tried to maintain the narrative quality of the story in the telling. My principal sources of information come from my own field-work and observations in Love Valley, from narratives and stories told by Love Valley residents past and present, from collections of written stories, from town files and records, and from local newspapers. The exception to this occurs in chapter 10, the conclusion to the study. Chapter 10 suggests characteristics of Love Valley that are utopian in nature and offers final reflection on the uniqueness of Love Valley as a utopian community.

It is appropriate to make some comments about narrative and oral history and about concerns for historical validity and objective historical writing. I am telling a community story, and this narrative history must be read from that perspective. Feelings about Love Valley are rarely neutral, and to try to tell the story of this town with neutrality would be to neutralize the vitality and energy of the town's history. I have often walked a tightrope, attempting to reproduce a factual and trustworthy account of actual occurrences and at the same time capture the significance of events from the perspectives of those who participated in the history. This is the curious nature of oral history and narrative history, but I have been encouraged by recent efforts at writing this type of history. In this case, oral traditions provide the backbone of this reconstruction rather than a secondary means of investigation. Similar to the method of David Kimbrough in his book on snake handlers, *Taking Up Serpents*, oral history is the primary means of collecting information and the result is a vibrant and vital history told from the perspective of the participants. Kimbrough quotes folklorist William Lynwood Montell to support the use of oral material as long as the reader understands the method.[1] Montell writes that "accuracy of local historical legends is not the most important question to be faced by the person who gathers and analyzes them, but rather the essential fact is that these folk narratives are believed by people who perpetuate them."[2] I am trying to reproduce the community folk narrative of Love Valley, and in this spirit I write this narrative history.

Andy Barker, the founder of Love Valley, is a hero to many; Andy Barker has also made bitter enemies. Some readers will look for me to either canonize or demonize the leader of Love Valley. I am trying to do neither—that task is for another writer at another time. Neither am I trying to tell the story with objective neutrality. Rather I am attempting to present the perspective of those who voluntarily participated in the Love Valley project. In the process, I have tried to be sensitive to the fact that I am writing about the lives of people who are still living.

This narrative history is taken up for several reasons. First and foremost, this story of Love Valley is offered as just that—a story of a unique and very interesting place, a cowboy town that grew out of Christian idealism. Historical documentation of this town has come only in bits and pieces until now. The purpose of this work is to provide the reader an overview of Love Valley's history and character as seen by the principals involved and to preserve this history and character in narrative form.

A second, less obvious goal behind this work involves examining Love Valley in light of the vision of America presented in the illuminating sociological studies, *Habits of the Heart* and *The Good Society*.[3] *Habits of the Heart* suggests that American individualism is so firmly entrenched in consciousness and so radically separated from the communitarian ideal that societal responsibility has become a rare, if not absent, quality in American life. Love Valley, as an intentional community, challenges the type of individual isolationism that *Habits of the Heart* critiques. Love Valley tests the assumptions of the study by sponsoring a type of communitarian lifestyle that promotes "the good society"—a lifestyle that suggests that community responsibility is requisite for the proper functioning of society.

Third, I hope to suggest some sense in which Love Valley fits the descriptive designation of utopia. Chapter 10 examines those characteristics of the American utopian impulse that Love Valley incorporates into its history and character, interprets the narrative in that light, and places Love Valley in the American tradition of utopian and social protest. Thus, this reflection, and the study as a whole, attempts to isolate various utopian ideals, to view the story of Love Valley in light of those ideals, and to ask the question, then, "Is Love Valley a utopian experiment?" My claim, of course, is "yes"; however, as I shall argue, Love Valley is no typical utopian experiment. Chapter 10 portrays Love Valley as a utopian experiment by highlighting themes and characteristics rather than through comparison of Love Valley to the many communities in America's history.[4] In this way, Love Valley's uniqueness as a utopian community emerges in all its eccentricity.

I will avoid the various distinctions and theoretical constructions of utopia (e.g., the divergent philosophies of Fourierism and Owenism) and concentrate more on the general ideas and assumptions behind utopianism as it has existed in the United States. The result is a general definition of the utopian impulse, a discussion of common characteristics of utopianism, and an examination of utopian types. My contention is that Love Valley fits the general definition of utopia, that it exhibits some, if not most, of the general characteristics of utopian experiments, and has at one time or another fit the description of various types of utopian experiments in America.

Finally, I hope to provide some reasons behind Love Valley's continued survival and success. The life span of most intentional communities is brief. Love Valley has enjoyed an extended existence and appears to be headed for an indefinite and promising future. The elements contributing to Love Valley's survival are numerous and include its flexible social boundaries and strong philosophical basis. But perhaps the key element for Love Valley, as for many communities, has been its ability to secularize its philosophy, to acculturate, and to amend its original vision to be more palatable to the larger society while still retaining its distinctiveness. It is this ability to change that makes characterization of Love Valley so difficult. Love Valley is not the product of a highly developed plan; rather, it is the result of idealism and evolution. This evolution of purpose and motive has allowed Love Valley to survive, and in the end, this is what makes Love Valley so interesting.

2

The Utopian Dream

On July 16, 1970, a trail of hippies in Volkswagen buses began to dot the small secondary roads of northern Iredell County in rural North Carolina. By that evening a small army of the counterculture free spirits marched toward the town of Love Valley, intent on a weekend of music, love, and fun. They came from everywhere. Before the weekend was over, their numbers swelled to 75,000 or more, and they quickly overflowed the little town with a population of about 75. Some of the hippies spread out into the surrounding farming community of North Iredell, slept in barns, defecated in the cornfields of family farmers, and copulated in the woods and backyards of local Baptists. They came to attend "The Love Valley Thing,"[1] a rock music festival that was hastily organized. When they vacated the community at the end of the weekend, they left behind drugs, trash, destruction, and the battered dreams of the promoter of the event, Andy Barker.

The Love Valley Rock Festival took place on a hot July weekend in the year after Woodstock. It brought local hatred, statewide scrutiny, national curiosity, and international mention to bear on the little town of Love Valley and its founder, Barker. The festival grew to proportions beyond Barker's imagination, and it nearly destroyed him, his health, his family, and his dreams. This event forever changed Love Valley, so much so that most people who know of the town know of it by way of the rock festival. "The Love Valley Thing" became the defining moment for shaping public attitudes about the town and its residents. Yet, even though the rock festival catapulted Love Valley into the public consciousness, it falls short in defining the character and the history of the town and the dream of Andy Barker. Love Valley existed for over 15 years before the rock festival, and it has continued for more than 25 years since. And while drugs, hippies, and outlaws might define Love Valley for many, there is much more to this town than one long, hot, frightening weekend in 1970.

Love Valley was founded upon the dreams of one man who envisioned a religion-based community organized around the ideals of civic virtue and communitarian responsibilities and values. Working with this basic utopian standard in mind, Andy Barker attempted to build a community based on what he perceived to be Jeffersonian democracy and Christian virtue. To place his unique stamp on this utopian enterprise, Barker drew upon mythic images from the Old West, believing as he did that the West embodied for mid-twentieth-century southerners virtues that had been lost—clear-cut distinctions about right and wrong, good and evil, honor and dishonor, loyalty and infidelity. The result of Barker's dream was Love Valley, a western-looking cowboy town built on the myth of frontier virtue, Barker's understanding of Jeffersonian doctrine, and the Christian admonition to love unconditionally.

Barker's dream has been severely challenged since the inception of his project in 1954. But, dreams die hard for a man like Andy Barker. At the beginning, Barker stood at the foot of Fox Mountain, surveyed the expansive valley stretched out before him and declared it to be the site of his "valley of love"—a utopian experiment built upon community cooperation infused with Christian goodwill.

Perceptions of Love Valley have varied throughout the years: a dude ranch; a tourist attraction; a western cow town; a frontier outpost; a haven for modern-day outlaws; a hippie love commune; a settlement for those dissatisfied with the modern world; a self-supporting village reliant upon all the members of the community. Yet Andy and Ellenora Barker did not leave a successful contracting business, an elegant Charlotte, North Carolina home, and a comfortable, stable future to pursue a dream for any of the above reasons. Love Valley was to be a community built around the church and based upon the Barkers' understanding of Christian virtue. Whatever else it might be, Love Valley cannot be understood fully without viewing the community with an eye toward the religious values and commitments upon which it was based.

Perhaps sensing the turbulence the sixties would bring to the youth and families of America, the Barkers sought to build a community that would provide wholesome opportunities for young people and reinforce the contention that the family, centered on worship, constituted the moral fiber of America. The little Presbyterian church, which overlooks the valley, the town, and the residents, was the first permanent building erected in Love Valley and continues for many as the focal point of the community. "I always thought that a community should be built around the church," commented Andy Barker as he removed his hat to enter the modest house of worship. It was from this building that the Barkers first reached out to the poor children of the area, providing summer camp experiences and church training for children who had few opportunities in the summer or otherwise. From the beginning, Love Valley was based upon the utopian desire to build a community separate from the outside world, which would, in turn, reach out to the world in order to make it a better place—a kingdom of heaven cut into the valley of love.

More than 40 years later, this dream still echoes across the the valley; however, few hear or see it. The Barkers and their valley of love have been misunderstood, praised, and maligned by family, politicians, clergy, the press, and the public. Now after four decades of existence, the valley is experiencing a quiet maturity and sought-for peace. Its critics are silent for the most part, its residents are settled, and its buildings witness the memories and harbor the stories that reach into a past era and generation.

When no one else could envision the dream that would eventually take shape, Barker carved out the little town of Love Valley as an extension of boyhood daydreams and a promise to God. Barker's utopia would ideally and nostalgically recreate a past laden with values and traditions of the pioneering spirit—independence, autonomy, and freedom balanced by virtue and communal responsibility.[2] For Barker, this utopia would be based on conservative but open-minded Christianity and the institutions of the church and local politics.[3]

The Love Valley story encompasses a utopian experiment—a visionary hybrid of idealism, myth, and religion that attempts to create a more perfect society. This enterprise promotes curiosity even to the most casual observer who wonders at the two phrases on the signs advertising Love Valley. One proclaims Love Valley as "Cowboy Capital" while the other simply states, "God Bless."

The exhortation "God Bless" symbolizes that Love Valley from the beginning was defined by the religious idealism and religious purpose of its founder. In this way, Andy Barker has existed as a spiritual paragon to some in the community. Barker's vision began with religious conversion and conviction and was transformed into a type of civil religious experiment incorporating biblical and patriotic principles as partners in building a perfect society. Barker's combination of biblical principle with the dream of recreating an American myth based on his hero figure, the American cowboy, defines Love Valley. This dream arises from such values as frontier independence, Barker's concept of biblical brotherhood based on the golden rule, and antiestablishment protest.

But Barker's vision also encompasses political activism and the creation of a supportive community where citizens can find healing and nurturing. Thus, Barker's dream community functions in different utopian roles. I will be envisioning Love Valley using a typology suggested by Rosabeth Moss Kanter in her insightful study on utopianism. Kanter argues that in America three types of impulses have initiated societal critique and the "impulse for the utopian search: religious, politico-economic, and psychosocial."[4] Love Valley has at various times in its history functioned as each of Kanter's types of utopian critiques. I will use this terminology throughout the book to describe Love Valley's utopian emphases.

This story of Love Valley is sometimes incredible, often sad, yet frequently inspiring. Most important, the story demonstrates an essential humanity shared through a place and a time, a human picture of community that I hope to preserve through telling the story as it was told to me. Of course the arrangement is mine, the analysis is mine, the decisions of what to include and exclude belong to me; however, the humanity and the stories of human defeat and triumph belong to Love Valley, and this is where the real utopia lies. Here are the people and the story of Love Valley.

* * *

During World War II, Jetter Andrew Barker, Jr. (Andy), crouched low in a foxhole in war-torn France and began to give substance to dreams he had harbored since childhood.[5] He pieced together images from the past as he recalled all the old western movies that first introduced him to brave, larger-than-life cowboy heroes. As the imminence of war shook the cobwebs from his memory, he recalled a day in the sixth grade when he transformed his reverence for those cowboys into a plan for his life. As part of a class project, students in Andy's sixth-grade class were asked to share their plans for adulthood. The often asked question, "What are you going to be when you grow up?" produced predictable responses for most, but not for Andy Barker. Young Barker stood up and announced, "I'm going to build me a western town right up in the middle of the mountains."[6] His classmates snickered, his teacher barely contained a smile, and Andy confidently sat down and endured the kidding of his buddies.

Barker thought of the days in his youth when he rode through the mountains on horseback, and his mind wandered to his horse, Clipper. He also remembered fondly the days at Brevard College where he played basketball and prepared for a career in Civil Engineering before war and military duty interrupted his plans. He thought of his father's contracting business in Charlotte—the business that would be his if he wanted it. And the thought of contracting reminded him with a smile of his precocious exploits in the construction business; how he subcontracted a project at 12 years of age and how he built his first house when he was 14. He began to lay plans to make his childhood aspirations reality.

Finally, from the depths of war, Barker gave his dream substance. On February 1, 1945, Andy wrote home to describe his dream:

Been in a fox hole all day—tonight I'm thinking and planning . . . my western town . . . best ideas yet since I've gotten my new partner, the Lord. I'm bound to make it. I know that with Him, my purpose and complete faith, anything is possible. My part of the bargain is to build a town, a Christian Community with clean recreation and strive to help people know more about God and His outdoors. I know I'd never make a preacher, but can build a church and help out personally in many ways. We can keep young boys occupied and out of trouble by letting them help run the place.[7]

The dream now had shape; it had substance. It had been transformed from a boy's daydreams of adventure and heroes to a man's vision of faith and service.

Barker's dream was uniquely his own; however, it was a dream based upon the particular circumstances of the United States, its foundation, and its settlement; it was an American dream of pioneering and living independently while maintaining a community, in Barker's words, "a Christian community," where everyone would be vitally involved with life. For Barker, this kind of community should also incorporate the values of family, community, love, and peace.

Over three decades ago, Sidney E. Mead published *The Lively Experiment*,[8] a classic study of religious traditions in America that described religion in light of the same myth of America. Mead ingeniously formulated a thesis for understanding religious liberty in America based upon space—a vast space that was seemingly infinite to seventeenth-century Americans. According to Mead, the early pioneers and settlers of the New World found themselves liberated by the expanse of land on this continent. The new Americans were no longer confined by the tight boundaries and crowded towns of their European world, and Mead suggested this contributed to the development of religious liberty in America.

Since Mead formulated his thesis, the idea of space as a catalyst for the development of the New World has been considered and reconsidered in various studies concerning American institutions. The notion that space represents freedom and independence is an idea that has played itself out in the mythology and legends of America. Today, many urban, suburban, and rural Americans equate freedom with having a space, no matter how small, where they can "do as they please." The visions of the frontier and its freedom have been ingrained into the American consciousness to the extent that the "West" still carries nostalgic images of the lone cowboy or the noble Native American or the vast, open prairie where one encounters nature with a most reverent awe.

Andy Barker was concerned with space disappearing. For twentieth-century Americans, there is no longer an unlimited western frontier, and there is only limited space for expansion. The idea that freedom is accompanied by wide open spaces is quickly becoming an unattainable dream for more and more Americans as rural America slowly disappears. Barker's dream was to preserve freedom by maintaining images associated with the western ideal and popular visions of the frontier. His visions were based on the image of the pioneer, who in Barker's mind lived in harmony with nature and neighbors and lived the heroic life of independence and freedom.

Barker built Love Valley from the ground up, not simply as a business enterprise, not solely for a residence, but to breathe life into the vision he held from childhood. And as this vision matured, it took shape as an intentional community based on Barker's Christianity, on faith as a witness, and on ministry to others (especially children). Love Valley was to be a town where the citizens would be free to do and believe independently, a town conceived and built because Barker is a man who is "tall on faith."[9]

The dream, shared perhaps by no one but Barker and God, gained an ally when Barker returned to the United States following the war. On February 15, 1947, Ellenora Spratt and Barker were married, and Ellenora accepted and worked to attain that dream with dogged determination. Ellenora's steadfast will has, as much as anything else, led to the realization of the dream. Years later, a daughter, Mary Tonda Barker (born January 5, 1948) and a son, Jetter Andrew Barker, III (born February 25, 1952) inherited the dream, the determination, and the hardship. When the children were six and two, respectively, the family moved to Love Valley where citizens and visitors would learn "about God and His outdoors" and where children would stay "out of trouble."

As Barker's dream was unconventional, so are Barker's life and the town that resulted from that dream. Perhaps the best example of this came with the 1970 Love Valley Rock Festival. Barker established immediate rapport with the young, rock festival followers of the late sixties who felt drawn to the town. When asked to comment on this unusual rapport, he explained it by claiming a camaraderie with the hippies because he was outside of the "establishment" himself and exercised a freedom from social convention. For Barker, this antiestablishment stance of protest can be a positive way to live.[10] Of course, Barker is not the only nonconventional resident of Love Valley. Some of those who appear in this story are only a few of the "last pioneers" who make up Love Valley and who are committed to keeping the American dream of independence (the American vision of the West) alive in the hills of North Carolina.

But the dream was not only one of space and independence. Barker's dream was also to preserve a time, an era, a symbolic period forgotten by many. Love Valley attempted to resurrect a time, perhaps the mid-nineteenth century, the era after which the town is modeled. From a mythical perspective, this was a time when family and community not only defined values but were valued in and of themselves; a time when love, understanding, and hope were more valuable and prevalent than indifference, intolerance, and desperation. Barker recognized his dream as idealistic but urged visitors to "give love a try." The name "Love Valley" itself was a shortened version of the original "Valley of Love," a name Barker coined because it expressed the love he hoped to model through his community.

Barker's dual dream of space (defined by independence) and time (defined by love) outlined his utopian ideal. This utopia was one where independence and love checked one another, where people were free to do what they wanted, but where individualism was tempered by social responsibility. It was a place where, according to Barker, the rules were few, where the only real rule was to treat others with respect.[11] Barker's utopian vision was summed up by the words of the song Love Valley inspired:

> LOVE VALLEY, Old mountains of hate all around you
> But here where the sun is shining, I am gonna stay. . . .
> All of those mountains of hate stand around you,
> In time they'll fall, and peace and hope for all will have found you. . . .
>
> LOVE VALLEY No weeds of intolerance grow here,
> The river of understanding runs deep and clear . . .
> LOVE VALLEY I've waited a long time to find you,
> As long as your sun keeps shining, I'm gonna live here.
>   ("Love Valley," written by Loonis McGlohon)[12]

Love Valley began as the manifestation of one man's dream. The dream was to build a Christian community founded on values that to him had virtually faded into the past—the values of family, love, and peace. The community started that way and has matured, evolved, and changed. Love Valley has been different things to different people at different points in its history, but it has always retained that original vision of community and traditional values—values undergirded by a "tall faith" and values that perpetuate, indeed, require faith.

3

Beginnings

This chapter expands the idea of Love Valley as religious utopia[1] by chronicling how Barker's vision was transformed into reality through the establishment of and building of his town—his "Christian town." Love Valley demonstrates many characteristics of utopia, but nowhere else is this utopian ideal more fully expressed than in Barker's church. This religious basis of Love Valley arises also from Barker's stated purpose for establishing the community. Out of fear of what society was offering families and children, Andy Barker attempted to establish a community that would provide a Christian atmosphere where families could enjoy wholesome recreation. Barker's theory of wholesome recreation is outlined here through the description of such planned activities for the community as county fairs, rodeos, and square dances. These events immediately drew religious criticism from outside of the community for various reasons, and the events themselves reflect a southern folk and civil religion based on patriotism and southern pride.

* * *

Ellenora fussed to herself as she guided the long, white Cadillac along what had to be the roughest road she had ever navigated, if you could call the path that Andy cut with a bulldozer a road. The dust rose from the tires so that as she turned around one hairpin turn, she was facing the clouds of choking dust she had just left behind. Up hills, around curves, doubling back, and down a slope, Ellenora drove on and on through what seemed to her to be miles of relentless cattle roads, separated from the paved road, which seemed itself a continent away from civilization.

As she pointed the Caddy down a particularly steep slope, for a moment she was so overcome by the beauty of the unspoiled land that she ignored the obstacle ahead. Suddenly, brought back to her senses, she brought the car to an abrupt halt. Ahead the road meandered down the hill to a stream, disappeared into the slowly churning water, and reappeared on the other side as a dusty, winding, ribbon among the weeds and fields and trees. This is the ford Andy had mentioned. The water was shallow, the creek was narrow, and the current was gentle, almost imperceptible in its movement. Andy drove right through the creek in his truck, but Ellenora's confidence in her Cadillac lagged as she reluctantly pulled the lever into gear, released the brake, and inched forward. When the front tires entered the water, she could sense the lack of depth. The water would not even muddy her hubcaps. The creek bottom was rocky and solid, and she was reassured. With renewed confidence, she continued on. Suddenly, as the long front end of the car emerged from the creek and pointed up the hill on the other side, Ellenora felt a terrible scraping from under the car. The clearance was too low and the front end had caught on the dirty, rocky incline of the creek bed. She could not continue forward unless she backed up and perhaps took a running start. Ellenora, now more angry than uncertain about the creek crossing, popped the car into reverse and started to back up—again the scraping occurred that was more felt than heard, and this time it came from the rear. Ellenora was stuck; she could go neither backward nor forward. The long, low Cadillac was hung on both sides of the narrow creek, stranding its passenger on a dusty country road that seemed to lead nowhere.

The better part of an hour later, sweaty and dusty from the walk on an unusually hot March afternoon, disheveled and fuming from frustration, Ellenora appeared at the door of Andy's temporary quarters. Andy had been waiting and was more than a little worried, but at the sight of his wife's silhouette in the doorway with her head tossed back in defiance, he could not help but let out a little snicker. "What happened to you?" was his involuntary greeting. Ellenora strode past him, smoothed her hair, drew herself a refreshing drink of water, sat down facing her bewildered husband, and said matter-of-factly, "The Cadillac is stuck in the creek. Let's go home."

Ellenora had been excited about the Love Valley project from the beginning, but on her first visit to the land with her Cadillac stuck between opposite sides of a creek bank, the thought of moving to the country seemed ludicrous, impossible, and unthinkable. All of the protestations from her family and friends began to sink in as the reality of pulling up roots and moving to northern, rural Iredell county hit hard. Andy shared Ellenora's feelings of uncertainty, but it did not cause him the same despair. His own anxiety had long since been eclipsed by the magnitude of his project, dream, and community. He answered her using the term of endearment that would insure a sympathetic response, "Mom, don't worry about our families. They might think we're crazy, but they won't desert us. We can't expect them to understand yet. You know they are just worried about us, about the kids. But we'll be okay. We're not losing family, we are a family—me, you, Tonda, and Jet. Ellenora, we have to do this together. I won't do it without you. You let me know, but don't let your family decide for you." Of course, Ellenora agreed to continue.

It seemed to the Barkers that the whole world ridiculed the project. Some madness had possessed them and caused them to leave security, success, and a good life for the uncertainty of a vague dream in a back-country place. Nevertheless, Andy Barker was not one to succumb to madness simply because the world declared him insane. What was back country to all his friends and business associates from Charlotte, contained hills of opportunity for him. His vision extended beyond the poverty of the mountain communities surrounding his land and included the community of his dream. That day, the Barkers made a decision they never again questioned. For good or bad, they would build the Valley of Love. Andy later took his tractor and pulled Ellenora's Cadillac from the creek, freeing their spirits along with her car. They would not be confined or constrained by anything but their dreams.[2]

* * *

A few months earlier, Barker had made a trip to North Iredell looking for lumber when he spotted the land on the south slope of Fox Mountain. He immediately knew this was the place for his utopia to become reality. The surrounding community first heard of his scheme through a short newspaper excerpt with a matter-of-fact report stating that a charter had been granted for Love Valley, Inc. The capital stock equaled $100,000 and was divided into 1,000 shares at $100 each. The actual transfers of land were made on February 25, 1954.[3] The land tract originally equaled 212 acres but at one time grew to include about 2,900 acres. Three days after this first report, Iredell County got its first description of Love Valley in the same paper. Love Valley was to be a "dude ranch," a fancy equestrian resort that would provide a much needed boost to Statesville and surrounding areas with increased tourist trade.[4]

This description was a far cry from what Barker had envisioned and suggested some of the future misunderstandings that would surround the little frontier town in North Iredell. It did not take long for the identity of dude ranch to wear off, and Love Valley became simply a cowboy town, an identity that much more closely matched its purpose and character. Barker worked to change the identity to reorient the public's perception of Love Valley as a community rather than as a resort. However, Andy

Barker much prefers a story that was told by D. L. Morris to describe why Barker disdained the designation, dude ranch. Once when Barker was travelling with a friend, the two visited his friend's elderly aunt. During the course of discussion, the mention of Barker's planned "dude" ranch prompted an abrupt reaction from their hostess. Upon inquiry, they learned that his aunt had mistakenly heard the men describing Barker's "nude" ranch and was shocked that such a thing would come to a community near Statesville.[5] Barker still chuckles when he tells the story.

The word was out and Love Valley created curiosity and some excitement in North Iredell and Statesville. The first few months of Love Valley's existence found Barker bulldozing and building, living in makeshift quarters while Ellenora and the kids commuted from Charlotte on weekends. At first, Barker lived in a tent, and later, after he built a small cabin, his family joined him. By the summer of 1954, the Charlotte house had been sold and the Barkers had committed themselves completely to the woods of North Iredell. In the process, Barker gave up a lucrative contracting business, and the family of four traded a large house for a one-room log cabin. For two years the family lived a pioneering life, making do without running water (without even an outhouse), cooking on an open fire, and living in little more than a hut. Their life was a far cry from the comfort they knew in Charlotte. But in these conditions the Barkers claim to have found something good and pure, wholesome and healthy. They still declare this was the happiest time of their lives. It was as if they were on a camping trip—the type that binds the family together and brings them closer to nature. But this was no camping trip—this was their future.

By June, Love Valley was in the local papers weekly, and the activities in the Valley received much attention. There were originally 69 lots available for residences, an adjoining business district, and the rodeo stadium. Barker also had planned picnic areas, playgrounds, and a rifle range. His "town" was beginning to take shape, and it was not long before a major North Carolina newspaper carried advertisements for land in Love Valley. The September 26 edition of the *Charlotte Observer* advertised "100 beautiful lots on mountain trails: Terms $100 cash and $10/month. Lots priced $450–$1000."

As Love Valley began to take shape, it was clear that the focus of the community would be family activities. Barker described the nature of Love Valley in the June 4 edition of the *Statesville Record and Landmark* by emphasizing that Love Valley would be a family-centered community focusing on "wholesome" activities for young people.[6] From the beginning, the catalyst for action revolved around philanthropic ventures aimed at children. The Barkers continued in Love Valley working with

Fig. 1. The Barker family during the first year of Love Valley's existence. From left to right: Andy, Jet, Tonda, and Ellenora. Love Valley photo archives, used by permission of Andy Barker.

young people, with civic organizations, and with volunteer groups as they had in Charlotte. That June 4 weekend in 1954 was when Love Valley became available to the world. The Barkers held a wiener roast for 50 kids in the North Iredell area and staged a free rodeo, with the Statesville Broken Spur Saddle Club, that drew about 2,500 spectators.

Throughout the summer, showdeos (a combination western show and rodeo) and square dances were almost weekly events; top cowboys became local celebrities; a Love Valley Queen was crowned at the First Annual Love Valley Stampede;[7] and Barker sponsored several events for the Statesville Lions Club. By August of 1954, some two months after the first free rodeo and a short six months after Barker first started construction of his town, Love Valley was sponsoring commercial rodeos, which routinely brought in 2,500–3,500 paying spectators, and benefit rodeos for organizations such as the March of Dimes and the Lions Fund for the Blind. The numbers of spectators were quite impressive for a rural farming community with only the small town of Statesville several miles down the road.

In addition to such activities, Barker pursued early in 1954 establishing a religious undertone to the community. In July he sponsored the first annual "Sing in the Valley" where churches could sell ice cream at the Saturday night festivities and keep their profits (many churches did this), and on at least one occasion, he was careful to postpone a Saturday night square dance until after revival services were concluded at a local Baptist Church. With this early interest in area churches, it would seem that Barker might have gained support from the local religious community for his venture, but this was not necessarily the case. What appeared as a minor exchange of letters in the local newspaper in August actually foreshadowed controversy that would trouble Love Valley in future years. In the August 27 edition of the *Statesville Record and Landmark,* a curious letter to the editor from a disgruntled resident of North Iredell appeared in the "Down in Iredell" section.

A nearby resident of North Iredell resented the implication that his church was involved with the Love Valley activities and made it clear that he did not approve of the Sunday amusements such as horse racing and dancing taking place at the town.[8] The next day, the same newspaper printed a response from Andy Barker, who defended Love Valley's activities as good, clean family entertainment and added that alcohol was prohibited on the grounds of Love Valley.[9] (It should be noted that originally the town was dry and Andy and Ellenora remain committed teetotalers. However, eventually the town voted to serve beer in the local saloon.) The August 30 edition of the *Statesville Record and Landmark* published one last addition to this confrontation in which the original writer replied to Barker.[10]

With that letter, the public controversy between neighbors died down; however, this exchange of letters demonstrated a basic misunderstanding and miscommunication between Love Valley's founder and the larger community surrounding the Valley. This misunderstanding would continue to haunt Barker and Love Valley in the years to come.

Amid the minor controversy of August, summer also brought Love Valley a bit of international attention and catapulted Barker into political circles. The Japanese ambassador to the United States (the second since the assumption of diplomatic relations with Japan in 1952) traveled the country with a United States senator. A local politician arranged a visit to Statesville for the ambassador from Japan, and while in the area, Barker arranged a free rodeo to be given in honor of the ambassador. The goodwill ambassador visited Love Valley while urging trade between the two countries and seemed to be genuinely taken by the little frontier outpost.[11]

In letters dated September 18, 1954, and February 8, 1955, the ambassador wrote the Barkers, thanking them for their hospitality and an honorary deed of land awarded to him by the Barkers in the miniature Love Valley Cattle Ranch. Such deeds were for a one inch by one inch plot of land and were awarded to dignitaries and celebrities by the Barkers as souvenirs and promotional tools. These deeds were awarded to many through the years, such as the foreign ambassador from Pakistan, who visited Love Valley in May of 1955 and Arthur Godfrey, who thanked Andy for his deed in a letter dated June 13, 1955. The Barkers even presented a deed to President Dwight D. Eisenhower, although the President returned the deed with a letter from his secretary saying he could not accept the gift for reasons of political ethics.

The visit by a United States senator and a Japanese ambassador seemed to push Barker into the political arena. Hardly a week went by without some regional or state dignitary dining with or honored by the Barkers at Love Valley. Barker said such activities gave him the opportunity to meet North Carolina dignitaries and high-ranking Democratic officials from the North Carolina Senate and the governor's office.[12]

October 1954 brought the last two events of the year to Love Valley: the First Annual Love Valley Fair and the Love Valley Fiesta. The Fair raised a reported several hundred dollars for a scholarship fund for the New Hope and Sharpesburg townships. But even more than that, these activities provided a clue as to how Love Valley organizers attempted to recreate a nostalgic vision of a past time and community orientation.[13]

The Love Valley Fair came with October and the harvest. Local farmers proudly displayed their crops from a summer of toil and sweat.

Indian corn, squash of all sizes, shapes, and colors, cucumbers, red apples, pumpkins, and sweet-smelling bales of hay lined the display case where farmers gathered to discuss the growing season, the lack of rain, and new tractors. In the livestock arena, champion horses, prize bulls, and heifers were groomed, pampered, and displayed.

The smell of hot dogs and candied apples wafted in the air as the women displayed their quilts next to the concessions stand. These mountain tapestries were handmade works of art—mountain craft that represented countless hours of painstaking cutting, stitching, and conversation in a group of four or five women. Next to the quilts were the pies (apple, peach, chocolate, and coconut), the baked goods (including, of course, persimmon puddin' and pound cake), and rows and rows of canned green beans, tomatoes, and pickles. Over to the side was an old woman with a bonnet and frontier attire working patiently at the spinning wheel while others watched her re-create her lost art.

Across the arena from the more sedate activities of the adults, the children had their own activities. There was the three legged sack race, the greasy pole climb, the banana eating contest, and the pop drinking contest for the older boys, while the younger boys tried to catch a greasy, squealing pig that was faster than lightning.

Following the fair, the "fiesta" included a weekend of square dances, horse shows, and the season's last rodeo. Caravans of horses and covered wagons promoted the event that concluded with the season's Showdeo championship. Barker concluded that hectic first year by serving as parade marshal for the Statesville Christmas parade and establishing himself as a visible figure in the community. Within nine fast-paced months, Barker founded Love Valley, sponsored regional entertainment, promoted the town as a political attraction for state Democrats, and established himself and Love Valley as household words in Iredell County. The winter of 1954-1955 brought a welcome and quiet respite to the Valley following the frenzy of summer and autumn.

* * *

In many ways, 1954 was the most remarkable year in Love Valley's history. It was certainly one of the busiest for the Barkers. And in many ways, 1954 set the course for Love Valley's future. Indeed, the two institutions that have been constant throughout Love Valley's history (the two institutions the Barkers pushed more than anything except Love Valley itself), the rodeo and the church, were founded in 1954.

The Barkers played a crucial role in establishing the popularity of rodeo in the Southeast. In 1954 alone, they sponsored eight rodeos in

Love Valley (two of them for charity), chartered the Silver Dollar Saddle Club, and formed the Southeast Rodeo Association. By 1959, the Southeast Rodeo Association was officially incorporated with Barker as president and Ellenora as secretary. The association was responsible for legitimizing rodeo in the Southeast and for promoting and producing professional and safe rodeo entertainment.

From its inception in Love Valley in the fifties, rodeo has changed very little. The cowboys bring with them the same hopes and dreams, they participate in the same events, and even some of the fans are the same. Cecil and Joy McCall from Ellerbe, North Carolina, have attended rodeo events in Love Valley from the beginning and rarely miss a rodeo. For the McCalls, as well as for others, there is something in Love Valley's dusty arena that draws crowds and creates much more than a show. In any event, rodeo has changed little, and a contemporary rodeo event mirrors the events of the fifties as rodeo remains one of the constants of Love Valley.

One such recent rodeo was held on August 30, 1991.[14] Like most August nights in the South, the evening was warm and sticky—had it not been for a hint of mountain breeze rustling the leaves and branches overhead, the humidity would have made blue jeans a bad choice for attire. As the spectators made their way along the dirt roads from the church to the arena, horses, buggies, trucks, and cars kicked up the dust around pedestrians. The dirt stuck to sweat moistened skin and gave it a gritty feel that made the humid air feel more uncomfortable. Many in the crowd met and spoke to Andy Barker on the way to the arena—he was directing traffic with a Stetson on his head and a six-shooter strapped to his leg. In 1991, at 67 years of age, Barker cut an imposing figure when he walked around town or simply directed traffic. A few of those who stopped sported baseball caps with "Andy Barker for Mayor" emblazoned across the front.

Once in the stadium, visitors followed a maze of fences and gates that led to the arena and to the seats. The rodeo arena itself was situated at the bottom of a steep embankment where the town once stood. Stone ledges were cut into the bank for seating, making the arena a natural addition to the landscape. As spectators ambled to their seats, they passed by a jewelry and souvenir stand and stopped to admire the handmade jewelry and belt buckles, all with a Southwestern flair. The smell of hot dogs, hamburgers with chili and slaw, and french fries filled the air and was coming from a small hut that served as a concession stand. Those who mustered enough willpower to pass on the hamburgers and fries walked on by and found their seats.

Before the rodeo began, most of the spectators, dressed in jeans and shirt sleeves, were milling around the food stand or the animals or simply the entrance gate where they had stopped to chat with a neighbor or friend. One young man sipped a beer until a marshal confiscated it—alcohol was not allowed at the rodeo. Finally, as the master of ceremonies began to test the public address system, spectators began to make their way to their seats, and it was clear that the show was about to begin.

The opening ceremonies began with tremendous fanfare. First on the agenda was the presentation of colors, and while many prepared to stand for the national anthem, Elvis Presley's voice thundered from the PA system with a slow, melodic version of "Dixie." With this, a female rider dressed in full confederate uniform guided her galloping horse through the South entrance of the arena. She carried the Confederate flag in an unabashed display of southern pride and heritage. After a few turns around the arena (this female soldier was obviously an expert rider), Presley's voice changed cadence and without missing a beat began a deeply moving version of "The Battle Hymn of the Republic." The Confederate rider was joined by a second female rider, who displayed just as much skill and expertise as the first. The second rider was dressed in a sequined, red, white, and blue, stars and striped leotard; she rode erect and proud with the American flag unfurled by her side and flapping in the wind. The two riders rode side-by-side around the arena in a symbolic fusion of cultures and an interesting display of civil religion. One got the eerie feeling that the presentation was an attempt to make peace for a war that was fought over a hundred years earlier.

With Elvis's voice silenced and the patriotic medley finished, the two riders stationed themselves stolidly in the middle of the arena, facing the crowd. The MC asked for quiet and for prayer. Hats came off and heads bowed. The MC, with the fervor and feeling of a revival evangelist, prayed for the protection of the rodeo participants and thanked God for the blessing of freedom.

After the prayer, all remained standing for the national anthem, this time the "Star Spangled Banner." In the space of a few minutes (20 at most), emotions ran the gamut from good times at the county fair, to ritualistic celebration of southern pride and patriotic fervor, to an old-style-southern revival meeting, and, finally, to a sporting event, the rodeo.

Once the rodeo started, it was everything one might expect. The crowd was appreciative of the riders' skills and showmanship. There were clowns who bravely protected the riders once they hit the ground. There were cowboys and cowgirls who participated in events commonly seen on television: bucking bronco riding, calf roping, team steer roping, barrel racing, and bull riding. However, a mere television experience of the rodeo could not attempt to match the emotions tapped by watching

Fig. 2. Charlie Hoover on a bucking bronco during an early Love Valley Rodeo. Hoover is a seven-time All-Around Champion of the Southeastern Rodeo Association. Love Valley photo archives, used by permission of Andy Barker.

the rodeo in person. The feelings of excitement over the contest of human brawn versus animal strength were almost overwhelming. When a cowboy successfully rode and dismounted a bull weighing up to a ton, the crowd cheered with excitement. Yet, they also cheered when the bull was able to dislodge the rider from his mount a bit early, and they laughed when a particularly ornery and stubborn bull refused to exit the arena after his time was up. It seemed as if the bull's nobility was at stake as he claimed the arena for his own and refused to leave until he was ready.

But all of this male bravado and machismo was balanced by the beauty and grace of the events for the cowgirls. The barrel racing was as exquisite as the bull riding was intimidating. The successful barrel racer demonstrated finesse and something akin to tenderness as she guided her horse through the figure eight course. Whereas it seemed the cowboys tried to dominate the beasts in their events, the graceful cowgirls worked to achieve cooperation with the animals, an understanding, a gentle force that was as beautiful to watch as a well-performed ballet.

The rodeo recalled and celebrated the archetypal American hero who was master of nature yet balanced by a cooperative spirit. A vanishing and rare breed, a western cowpoke in the Southeastern hills of rural North Carolina came alive that night and for a brief time reminded spectators of a shared American myth and dream. But the real spirit of the myth occurred after the two-hour show, after the ceremony, and after the crowds dispersed. This American dream was enacted when the cowboys "riding in slack" took over the arena. Almost every rodeo has more entrants than available slots for participants, so before each show, entrants draw straws to qualify for the paying events. Those unfortunate cowboys who are refused by the luck of the draw made the trip but are unable to ride in the show and compete for prize money. These cowboys "rode in slack" after the show—they stayed after the rodeo for their own, mostly private, rodeo. No one watched, no one paid, no one cheered, except when they cheered for each other, yet they rode and roped until the early morning hours. And all the time, they kept their own dreams alive. They rode to make it to the rodeo circuit that everyone would watch and that might pay a little money.

After the rodeo, the streets of Love Valley were quite rowdy and remained that way until the early morning hours. The dirt streets were lined with quiet horses tied to hitching posts, while the local saloon rocked with music and good-natured, beer-drinking cowboys. The wooden-planked sidewalks creaked and clopped under the weight of leather boots. An occasional six-shooter glistened in the light of the moon, but the weapon was always strapped safely in a holster, and somehow everyone was sure it would stay that way. A country-western band played bluegrass and country blues outside the general store while folks relaxed outside the stores to hear the music. Riders galloped by on their way to midnight trail rides or visits to neighbors in the Valley.

* * *

The rodeo is a constant in Love Valley, but equally so is the church. The little brown structure that is now the Love Valley Presbyterian Church was the first permanent building erected in Love Valley, reflecting Andy Barker's desire to build a Christian community centered on the church. And even before the current structure was built (the current building is the original structure along with an addition that was built later as a fellowship hall), Love Valley residents, workers, and neighbors met for services in a temporary building that served as the meeting place for a North Iredell Fox Hunters Club as well as the church.

The small, brown church sits on a hill overlooking the rest of Love Valley. On approach to the building, one climbs stone steps that are bordered by flowers, a rough handrail, and a hand-painted sign that reads, "Love Valley Presbyterian Church." The building is simple and inviting, and the steps lead up to a central weather-beaten pine door, which is always left unlocked. Upon entering, the worshippers find themselves in a small vestibule located under the bell tower. On the walls of the vestibule are pegs for hanging coats, hats, and revolvers.

When one enters the worship area, the old pine floors quietly creak in the small area that measures approximately 30 x 40 feet. The simple and stark building contrasts to the elegant and beautiful stained glass windows on either side of the sanctuary and immediately behind the pulpit. The windows were donated by Laws Stained Glass Studios and depict familiar symbolic scenes: a cross with a crown, the tablets of the law, a vine, the praying hands, the cup, a descending dove, and a large window behind the pulpit depicting Jesus in Gethsemane.

The pulpit itself is separated from the rest of the room by a low, oak rail that is just over two feet high and that traces a semicircle between the communion table and the pulpit. That rail, along with the kneeling bench, pews, and pulpit date to the mid-nineteenth century. According to the Barkers, these artifacts were saved from an old Methodist Church from Pineville, North Carolina, as it burned to the ground, a casualty of war.

When one faces the pulpit, familiar sights adorn the front of the church. To the left of the pulpit by the wall is a small table with a guest register welcoming the visitor who wanders in by the side door. To the left of the pulpit and in front of the rail is a wooden baptismal font bal-

Fig. 3. The Love Valley Presbyterian Church. This building was the first permanent structure erected in the town. This original building was constructed during the first two years of development. Photograph by author, 1997.

anced on the right side of the communion table by a single collection plate. Further to the right sit the organ and a beautiful, antique piano that boasts complex wood carvings on the front upright panel and that is in dire need of tuning. Behind the pulpit are two antique, leather-backed chairs, and in the pulpit rest an American flag, a tin of Johnson paste wax, a fire extinguisher, and an empty cup.

In the main section of the room, two sets of seven pews are divided by a central aisle and will seat about 100 to 125 people. The room is usually about one third to one half full. Those who attend are comfortable now because the building is serviced by a heat pump. However, for much of its history, worshippers huddled around a coal-burning stove that sat in the middle of the room.

The church employs a full-time preacher, but for most of its history, the church's pastor has been a student pastor, interim pastor, or part-time minister. There is no choir, and the music is led by an organist who sits to the right of the congregation. Worship is consistent and the service is a fairly standard Presbyterian one following a basic order that seldom varies. The Valley knows when church is about to begin because music and bells are played over a public address system from a record player in the fellowship hall. Once the service begins, there are invariably stragglers—Andy Barker being perhaps the most notorious (he claims he cannot get anywhere on time). The congregation appears as anything but uniform: one might find a local doctor, many cowboys, young people, or parents. The dress is even more varied: some dress in suits, dresses, and high heels while most opt for jeans, cowboy shirts, and cowboy boots. The informality of the service matches that of the dress, and often the worship is followed by a covered-dish lunch.

After lunch, a stroll around the church grounds reveals the stone foundation of the church (the stone was taken from the quarry in Love Valley), the simple tin roof, and the rough-hewn cross that tops the steeple. The fellowship hall of the church was built after the main structure and is joined to the church by a covered walkway. This peaceful setting of a small community church in a quiet valley on a Sunday afternoon also reveals the pain and suffering the community has endured —a pain made tolerable by the faith shared by the community and church. A few headstones scattered across the grassy knoll express a history of sorrow in the community.

When Barker first donated land for the church, he looked for support in erecting a building, and he found it. Friends and neighbors donated the labor, and the Reverend Eugene O. Cole, a retired Methodist minister, donated money, his services as minister (free of charge) and the pulpit, altar, rail, and pews. In many ways, the Reverend Cole built the little church in Love Valley and left a legacy for many years to people who looked to him as their minister.

Once the church was built, the leaders (at the time there were only about 20 people who took part in the services) set about to determine the future course of the congregation in terms of denominational affiliation. At first the desire to remain unaffiliated and nondenominational was strong; however, the Reverend Cole pointed out the likely difficulty the Love Valley Church would encounter in finding and retaining pastors and financial support if the church remained nondenominational. So the Love Valley congregation set out to explore the possibility of affiliation. After initial inquiries, local Baptists and Methodists expressed interest but balked at the idea of a competing church in Love Valley that would represent their denominations. Finally, the church petitioned the Concord Presbytery and the Presbytery was impressed by the concept of building a town around a church.[15] On September 2, 1956, the Love Valley congregation became the Love Valley Presbyterian Church;[16] however, in reality the church has retained its ecumenical spirit throughout its history because of the eclectic nature of the visitors to and residents of Love Valley.

The humble beginnings of the Love Valley Presbyterian Church boasted 25 charter members. Andy Barker's parents, J. A. Barker, Sr., and Elizabeth H. Barker, and Andy, Ellenora, and their daughter, Mary Tonda, were joined by 20 others to form the first church.

The oral history surrounding the events of the church and its leaders contribute significantly to the mythology of the Valley. The Barkers particularly like to tell one story about faith—faith that is for them the key to the whole Love Valley enterprise. In the summer of 1955, a divinity student from Union Theological Seminary in Richmond, Virginia served the church. The church had promised Dolphus Allen $600 for his services that summer, although members of the church were skeptical about raising that much money. Allen decided to serve even without the guarantee of the full amount and the church went ahead with the $600 goal a seeming impossibility. The church "proceeded on faith" that the money would be raised and by the end of the summer had saved only $488 for ministerial salary. On the last Sunday of Allen's contract, the church was $112 short, and church leaders, doubtful they could raise the entire amount, decided the entire Sunday's collection should go to Allen as a gesture of goodwill and intent. To their surprise, an exact amount of $112 ("to the penny" according to Barker) was collected that day. It is not surprising that church members still look fondly upon this event as an illustration of the power of faith Allen held for the intentions of the community and the faith the church members exhibited in committing beyond their means.[17]

One last church story still circulates about Love Valley as it could nowhere else.[18] Following Allen's tenure at the church, the group contracted with Davidson College for student supply ministers. One student minister, a Parson Baker, had a particular evangelistic zeal that led him to encourage the rodeo participants to attend worship services while they stayed in the Valley. Baker would go to almost any length to coax these cowboys to church. Apparently, one cowboy, weary of Baker's incessant urging, and being in a playful mood, was determined to rid himself of this pesky preacher. He made his wager: he and the other rodeo participants would come to church if the parson would ride a bull in the afternoon's rodeo. Not to be dissuaded, the young city boy from Davidson College agreed. The cowboys were in church that morning, and Parson Baker, true to his word, if not to common sense, showed up at the corral that afternoon.

The cowboys laughed as they watched the preacher approach, not thinking that he would actually uphold his end of the bargain. When they realized that Baker was serious, their merriment ended. Bull riding is the most dangerous of all the rodeo events. Not only do bones break when the bull throws its rider from his perch, but the greatest danger comes when the dismounted cowboy finds himself helpless on the ground with the maddened and unpredictable bull flinging itself around the arena. At best, the cowboy escapes to a high perch along the outer gates of the arena. At worst, goring is a distinct possibility. Parson Baker, undaunted by the cowboys' pleading and emboldened by his own missionary zeal and sense of duty, brazenly climbed into the chute, whispered a little prayer for his soul, and quivering, slowly straddled the devilish monster whose sole purpose was to throw his rider as quickly and as viciously as possible.

The bull snorted with all the ferocity of hell itself, charged from the chute, and with power and strength unimaginable to most, twisted, lunged, bucked, and catapulted his frightened rider with impunity. For a moment, as Parson Baker soared toward heaven, it seemed that he would meet his Maker early, at least he was closer to his heavenly home. Upwards and upwards the parson sailed, and for a second, time ceased to move, sounds were muted into a quiet, muffled hum, and the air rushed by with the furor of unrelenting winds.

And then that sudden sinking feeling, the kind that tickles the pit of the stomach when one goes too high in the backyard swing, overcame the parson. His bull ride was coming to an abrupt halt as he watched the earthen floor of the arena hurtling toward him. Impact was sudden as the parson disappeared into a cloud of dust. For a moment, he was dazed, and then, for what seemed to be hours he could not catch his breath.

Luckily, as the parson slowly gathered himself from the pit of the arena, he was out of danger because the rodeo clowns had done their job and escorted the proud bull from the arena. There were no broken bones and no gored bodies. The crowd cheered, and the cowboys had to swallow hard to get rid of the lumps in their throats and the bitter taste in their mouths. The parson quietly brushed himself off and struggled to breathe through the choking tears that were tracing muddy streaks across his dust-caked face. The parson walked from the arena a respected man in the eyes of the cowboys. Few people experience a bull ride, and he never would again. Needless to say, those cowboys attended church more regularly from that day on.

* * *

The rodeo and the church have been the two institutions at Love Valley from the beginning and the two institutions that have insured its survival. There is something foundational and pure about both, and as Parson Baker discovered, both can lead to transcendent experiences.

4

The First Decade:
Promotion

The whirlwind of activity that characterized the Barkers' 1954 establishment of Love Valley did not abate after those initial few months. However, the focus shifted somewhat through the first decade from an intense focus on religious utopia to religiously based political and social activism. Civil religion and Barker's Christian vision, which required him to reform society, led him to expand and promote the town as a year-round community and to enter into formal politics. The first 10 years of Love Valley's existence, which were celebrated in a 1964 July Fourth extravaganza, witnessed steady growth, development, and change. Three pursuits energized this development and change: promotion, philanthropy, and politics. The town's founder, Barker, refused to allow Love Valley to stagnate in the early years and was constantly promoting the area as a tourist attraction and horse-lover's haven. Barker, who likened himself to P. T. Barnum, staged some impressive shows during the early years to pique curiosity and interest in his development. A second characteristic of Love Valley during the early years was philanthropy. Not only were the Barkers constantly giving their time to charitable causes, but the contagion of goodwill seemed to mark the environment of Love Valley residents. Third, the first 10 years marked the entrance of Barker into the political realm and the beginning of Love Valley's official political status as an incorporated town. Promotion, philanthropy, and politics defined the early Love Valley and continue to describe the town today.

* * *

Andy Barker is "a dreamer, a promoter, a super-salesman. Indeed, Barker may be all three rolled into one."[1]

"I want to move the town." Andy Barker's words bounced off the walls and reverberated through the room as slack-jawed members of the board of directors stared incredulously at the founder of Love Valley. Asked to repeat himself, for no one believed what he had just heard,

Barker spoke slowly and tried to convince the board that the town must be moved to the top of the hill above the original location. Barker had formulated a plan to grade the top of the mountain, to move the town up the slope to the new site, and to enlarge and improve the rodeo facilities at the original site of the town.

The meeting of the board of directors of Love Valley Enterprises, Inc., erupted into confused chaos. Less than six months earlier, Love Valley Enterprises had just formally dedicated and opened the municipality of Love Valley, bringing an end to an extensive period of building and financing that finally resulted in a real working western town. And now this crazy man wanted to move the town and start all over. After five years to bring a dream to reality and about $200,000 to finance the project, what could possess Barker to suddenly decide to trash the progress? He explained that the original location was a mistake, that the top of the hill would be a more advantageous location, and that the new site would provide a better location for a permanent population. Barker felt that if Love Valley were to be more than simply a location for the rodeo, then they must move the town.

More moaning and near hysteria marked the meeting when the directors learned that the proposed move would cost an additional $200,000, that there was all of $67 in the Love Valley treasury, that Barker had already hired a bulldozer to level the mountain, and that Love Valley Enterprises would owe the earth-moving crew $10,000 in nine days. Of the board of directors, 14 of the 16 members resigned that night convinced of the lunacy of the founder of the town. But this was not the first time Barker had been called a crazy man, and this time as in previous times, Barker realized the fruits of his lunacy. The town was moved.[2]

The hesitancy of the board of directors was justified. Moving the town was a radical suggestion under any circumstances, but moving the town less than six months after officially bringing a major development stage to a close was unthinkable. Just a few short months earlier the town hosted a successful grand opening celebration, an event recounted in the following scenario.

It was a hot, dusty day on the streets of Love Valley (too hot for May 21), but at least it was not raining. And with any luck, by the 7:30 p.m ceremonies, the air would cool sufficiently for the comfort of all the spectators who would attend the official grand opening of Love Valley. It was 1960, Andy Barker had completed the major stages of his five-year plan, and Love Valley, even though it had been operating since 1954, was ready to be officially offered to the world. Barker busied himself all afternoon making sure that everything was in order for the ribbon cutting ceremonies.[3]

Fig. 4. Original town before the move to its present location, circa 1957. The shops of the original town followed a curved street around the rodeo arena. The rodeo arena still sits at this location. Photograph by Fred Harris. Love Valley photo archives, used by permission of Andy Barker.

The little place had grown in six years and by grand opening day enjoyed a national reputation among horse and ranch lovers. Love Valley had become much more than simply a rodeo site. By 1960, many people were so attracted to the carefree lifestyle promoted at Love Valley that they had either moved there permanently or had built vacation cabins in the Valley. Visitors on the weekends increased the number of people in the Valley tremendously; however, even during the week, the streets were filled with cowboys who dressed the part and who carried loaded pistols strapped around their waists.[4] By 1960, guns were a common sight in Love Valley. Andy Barker enforced the rule that guns *had* to be loaded, because, as Barker is fond of repeating, "A loaded gun is a respected gun. No one plays around with a loaded gun, and most accidents happen with guns that people assume are empty."

The town in 1960 included a main street that curved around the rodeo arena and sported such businesses as The Gold Nugget Cafe, a post office, a newspaper office (which published "The Smoke Signal," the town's weekly paper), a jail, a saddle shop, a motel, a general store, and the smallest Belk Department store in the company's chain, which specialized in western wear. The resident or visitor in 1960 might have stopped at the leather shop to watch the finishing touches placed on a custom-made saddle, or have watched the fine art of horse-shoeing, or have been fitted in a pair of stiff, pointed-toe cowboy boots. All the buildings were made of rough-hewn timber to conform to Love Valley's rule that all main street buildings must look a century old. Of course, the church overlooked the whole enterprise from its quiet setting on the hill above.

Perhaps the one difference between this little town and Dodge City was the absence of a saloon, although the cafe gave all the appearances of a saloon without the liquor. In 1960, as earlier, alcohol was prohibited and sobriety encouraged.[5] The deputy sheriff and Andy Barker, the justice of the peace, spent most of their law enforcement energies clearing the streets of the occasional cowboy who had over indulged from his private stock. For such a person, justice was swift and predictable. A couple of hours in Love Valley's holding cell, allowing the intoxicated offender to dry out, usually did the trick.

These images of the town must have come to mind for Andy Barker on that night in 1960 when he said it all had to go. However, any doubts were soon discarded from Barker's mind. He received funding to go ahead with his new venture. The fall of 1960 marked the end of the first stages of development and the beginning of a new chapter in Love Valley's growth.

* * *

From a cozy, one-room cabin in the middle of a snow-blanketed valley in early 1955, Andy Barker refined and announced a five-year plan for the development of Love Valley from a rodeo arena to a working and independent western town. The Barkers, of course, were the community's first residents, and Andy's parents, J. A., Sr. and "Mama Jib" followed soon after. The senior Barkers soon became stalwart figures in the community and were leaders in the early years after Love Valley's incorporation. Barker, Sr., like his son, was a community activist, and Mama Jib was nicknamed after the jib (the front sail) of a boat because she was the sure source of guidance for the family and community. However, Barker realized if the Valley was to be successful and to grow to anything beyond a vacation hideaway for family and friends, he would have to promote, and promote he did. He was so successful that after the first five years or so of development, he was able to claim completion of his working western town and to announce the removal of his town to another location in the above sequence of events from 1960. The events that carried Love Valley successfully forward from 1954 to 1960 were couched in Barker's successful promotion of the Valley.

The spring and summer of 1955 began much as the hectic summer of 1954 had with entertainment at the Valley providing much of the promotional strategy for Barker. There were bigger and better rodeos, fiestas, square dances, and shows. Barker also requested the help of such celebrities as Arthur Godfrey and Fred Kirby. By the beginning of the 1956 season, Love Valley boasted an improved rodeo arena for even bigger shows and had begun construction of a motel and cafe to serve the visitors who came to the Valley on weekends. The present church building had been added, three new houses were under construction, two store buildings had been started, and a new water system had been established.

By Love Valley's third season, the construction of a working western town was well underway; however, promotion relying solely on the rodeo and square dances was already becoming stale. Barker's promotional strategies branched out with the increasing awareness of the Valley throughout the Southeast. A wedding on horseback, complete with a horseshoe-shaped wreath under which the wedding party rode their mounts, a bride in a long, white wedding gown on horseback, and a justice of the peace who officiated with the preacher made news in several regional newspapers and increased curiosity about the growing western haven. Later, a buffalo was imported to the Valley and brought in additional tourists and curiosity seekers.

Fig. 5. Andy Barker (left) with Arthur Godfrey. Love Valley photo archives, used by permission of Andy Barker.

By 1958, Love Valley was making steady progress toward Barker's ultimate goals; however, promotional activities at the Valley had begun to receive less attention. The rodeos and square dances that had received major article space in local papers in 1954-1955 were announced in small columns tucked away in the middle of the newspaper by 1957-1958. This changed, though, as 1958 drew to a close and two promotional events sparked renewed interest in Love Valley. The first event was the annual Statesville Merchants Christmas parade; the second involved the revival of local legend and the events surrounding a new interest in the saga of Tom Dula (Tom Dooley).

In 1958, the Statesville Merchants named Andy Barker the parade chairman in hopes of promoting a bigger parade to attract area shoppers to downtown Statesville.[6] Barker, an acknowledged promoter, did not disappoint the Merchants Association and promised the biggest parade in Iredell County history. At the same time, Barker was able to use the parade to redirect attention to his tiny development in North Iredell. Numerous newspaper articles appeared in local papers promoting the parade, which promised to provide Barnum and Bailey kind of entertainment with glitter and gimmicks that would enliven the parade. Barker himself promised a longer parade with more floats and bands than any parade in Statesville's past. By early November, the surrounding community was anxiously awaiting to see Barker's holiday festivities.

Early promotions caught the attention of the captive Statesville audience. Barker promised to ride in the parade atop a manure spreader because he claimed to be the "biggest bull-shitter"[7] in Iredell County. He also planned to release 12 live turkeys into the crowd during the parade to be pursued, caught, and kept by those fast enough and crafty enough to capture the dozen luckless birds. Barker couched all these promotional activities in the theme of the parade that promised "an Old-Fashioned Christmas," and it was clear that organizers were attempting to promote the ideals of old-fashioned community values, ideals that Barker had been promoting for four years at Love Valley. In keeping with the theme, a post-parade community party was being planned where more turkeys would be given away during an old-fashioned community concert under the stars at the square in the town. Barker contacted dozens of beauty queens and organizations, and over one hundred entries had already committed to the parade by the end of November. While Barker was able to draw attention to the parade itself, he did not allow Love Valley's role in the proceedings to go unnoticed. He circulated handbills and posters around Statesville that pictured three desperate looking men in cowboy attire, holsters, and six-shooters to advertise the parade. The advertisement subtly reminded the excited community that Love Valley was behind what was going to be the best Christmas parade in the community's history.

Parade day came and, by Statesville standards, the event was spectacular. Crowd estimates ranged from 30,000 to 60,000 spectators, and the long parade stretched over two miles. The parade was marked by the usual floats along with some unusual reminders of Love Valley such as horses, buggies, and wagons from the Old West. In a post-parade party, Statesville Merchants basked in the glow of what they considered to be the most successful beginning of a Christmas shopping season. Barker was so successful with the 1958 parade, the Merchants asked him to organize and promote the 1959 parade as well. Barker accepted and produced a show that was even more spectacular than the 1958 parade.

Barker wanted to double the length of the parade in 1959 and enlisted the help of students in the high schools of Iredell, Rowan, Alexander, Davie, Wilkes, and Yadkin counties to reach his goals.[8] Schools from Iredell, Alexander, and Rowan counties decided to participate and promised some 44 floats between them. The schools also promised to provide beauty queens and bands to help produce what they hoped would become the largest parade in the two Carolinas. Pre- and post-parade entertainment was planned to boost interest in the event. Perhaps the most spectacular plan was to have Santa Claus arrive via helicopter before mounting his parade transportation, in this case a western stagecoach pulled by horses rather than a sleigh and reindeer. Barker arranged appearances by local and state beauty queens. The parade marshal was the North Carolina Parade Queen and the princesses were Miss North Carolina and Miss Statesville. The parade was a huge success with 256 entries that stretched an estimated four miles long.

With the 1959 parade (the theme was "Christmas for the Children"), the Statesville Merchants used the opportunity to express their unbounded pride in Statesville's growth and regional leadership.[9] Indeed, Statesville gained much regional attention with the high-spirited and enthusiastic promotions during the Yule seasons of 1958 and 1959; however, the big winner was Love Valley itself, because the promotional activity of its founder led to increased attention for the community and the progress it had made in four short years. In fact in many ways, the Christmas parades that closed out the fifties for Statesville illustrated a part of the Love Valley experience as Barker defined it: one could recapture an old-fashioned spirit, emphasize family and children, and have fun doing it.

The second event of 1958-1959 to spark a renewed interest in the western development occurred in conjunction with the legend of a North Carolina folk hero, Tom Dula. Two items affecting Love Valley appeared on the front page of the December 3, 1958, *Statesville Record and Landmark*. First was an article on the Christmas activities quoting Andy Barker on the incredible cooperation experienced in producing fund-raising for Christmas activities. Second was an article in the next column that described the efforts of the North Iredell Post of the American Legion to either refurbish or move the burial site of the legendary folk hero, Tom Dula. The close proximity of the two articles prefigured the intersection of Love Valley and the Dula legend.

In the summer of 1958, the Kingston Trio cut an album with Capitol records and became almost overnight sensations. Their recording of an old mountain folk ballad about Tom Dula, "The Tom Dooley Song," rekindled national attention for a short time on the fallen Civil War soldier. Iredell County was particularly excited about the renewed interest in the Dula saga because Dula had been tried and hanged in the Iredell county seat, Statesville. With the renewed excitement surrounding the national attention this local folk hero was receiving, the grave of Tom Dula was located in Wilkes County near Tom's home. The grave was covered with vines and weeds.[10] A local veteran's group proposed to honor the dead Civil War veteran by restoring his grave with a marker or monument or by moving Dula's grave to a more prominent site with a monument honoring all veterans in unmarked graves.

Almost immediately, Andy Barker offered Love Valley as a site for a new resting place for Tom Dula's remains. Dula's demise was a result of his love interests, and Barker seized upon the love theme to highlight Love Valley's interest.[11] There was initially quite a bit of support for the idea of moving Dula's grave to Love Valley, both for romantic reasons and because Love Valley was not far from the fateful route Dula would have taken from his jail in Wilkes County to his jail, trial, and execution site in Statesville. The community was quickly enamored with the romance of the Dula tale, visitors to the honeysuckle-vine-covered grave in Wilkes County increased in number, and news of the restoration or removal project spread to San Francisco and to Washington, D.C. papers in less than two days. For a brief moment, Love Valley gained national attention as part of a project to restore to mythic proportions a local folk hero. The story that so quickly fueled the imaginations of so many people bears retelling in order to understand the excitement.

Tom Dula, born near Ferguson, North Carolina, and filled with the romantic nature of most youth, enlisted in the Confederate States Army when he was about 17 years old. He apparently served honorably with the 42nd North Carolina Regiment. After a short period of training, Dula left for duty in Virginia in 1862 where he served for a short time before contracting typhoid fever. Dula and his regiment saw some fighting in and around Richmond before returning to North Carolina and back to Petersburg, Virginia, where Dula's regiment endured heavy fighting and where Dula was once again hospitalized. After returning to North Carolina, Dula's regiment happened upon federal troops. On March 10, 1865, Dula was taken as a prisoner of war with over 300 of his fellow Confederate soldiers. Finally, after the surrender of the Confederacy, Dula signed an oath of allegiance to the United States and was freed. This signature led to the variant spellings of the name Dula. Prison officials had spelled Dula's name, Thomas C. Dooley, and to avoid a disagreement, Tom reportedly signed his name "Thomas C. Dooley" and then wrote "Dula" over the signature.[12]

In light of Dula's undistinguished military career, how did he attain folk hero status? Tom's notoriety began with his return home. When

Tom left to serve in the war, he apparently left behind two lovers who would lead to his downfall. The first was Laura Foster, the enchanting daughter of tenant farmers in Caldwell County. The second was Ann Foster Melton, Laura's first cousin and a beautiful woman who had married while Tom was away. When Tom returned, he apparently rekindled a relationship with both women—while carrying on an adulterous relationship with Ann Melton, Tom and Laura planned to marry. Something happened, and history has yet to satisfactorily explain what. Laura Foster was stabbed to death, Tom fled the county and was later apprehended, and Tom and Ann were both implicated in the murder of Laura Foster.[13]

With local sentiment firmly against Tom, his lawyer, Zebulon Vance, had the trial changed to Statesville. However eloquent and powerful Vance might have been during the trial, his demeanor did not prevent the jury from convicting Dula, who was convicted and sentenced to die by hanging. The public execution took place in Statesville on May 1, 1868, when Dula went to the gallows proclaiming his innocence. Many people believe now that Dula was innocent of the crime and that he protected Ann out of a sense of chivalry or perhaps love.[14]

An eyewitness account of the execution by a *New York Herald* reporter helped to solidify Tom's heroic status. The report described a carnival atmosphere and a large crowd that had gathered near the railroad depot by a temporary gallows to witness Dula hang. By this reporter's account, Dula calmly accepted his fate yet refused to admit guilt or to implicate Ann Melton.[15] Thus, the life of Tom Dula was ended quite tragically on a hangman's gallows, the victim of love and, perhaps, prejudice and hysteria. That his romantic life and death were immortalized in song and story is no surprise. Neither was it surprising that the romantic Love Valley would want to immortalize the memory of such a folk legend.

Nevertheless, as appropriate as the Love Valley location for the final resting place of Tom Dula might have seemed, the relocation of the body was not to come about. Response from Wilkes County was swift. Prompted by the public discovery of the poor condition of a hero's grave, Wilkes citizens restored the grave site as an honor due to a hero but also expressed strong sentiment against moving the grave.[16] This did not eliminate the possibility of a Love Valley site for the monument; however, with that sentiment, the chances of Love Valley becoming the final resting site for the North Carolina folk hero were all but buried.

On Sunday, December 7, an Iredell County delegation traveled to Wilkes to make one last appeal to move the grave of Dula to Love Valley. The delegation met with the owner of the land where Dula's grave was located, who unequivocally stated that the grave could be restored but could not be moved, and the issue was decided. The grave site would be restored at its original location. With the decision, the owner of the land and the delegation walked down a small pathway that had led thousands of visitors during the revival of interest in Dula's story to the nondescript grave. The valley was undisturbed and peaceful on that Sunday afternoon, and the small delegation discovered a fitting scene when they arrived at the grave site to pay their respects. There, standing by the grave, was a cowboy in a ten-gallon hat singing the lonesome, heart-rending mountain ballad that immortalized the fallen lover. The cowboy's voice carried through the valley, reverberated off the hills, and sadly assured poor Dula that his resting place would not be disturbed.[17]

The fascination with Tom Dula did not go away quickly. In January and February of 1959, an artist from Ferguson toured North Carolina with her art exhibit containing some 38 paintings and etchings depicting the life of Dula. This, coupled with the arrival in Statesville of the Kingston Trio in early March, kept the Tom Dula saga in the news through early 1959. But Love Valley's role in bringing the story national attention quickly faded from view. Nevertheless, Love Valley, for a brief moment, captured the romantic imagination of a county and state, if not the nation, and promoted a story that epitomized Love Valley itself. Romance and honor were virtues associated with Dula and virtues re-created in Love Valley's own mythical cowboy heroes.

* * *

The years 1959 and 1960 were years of preparation for Love Valley—preparation for the formal opening of the town in 1960, preparation for business ventures, and preparation for promoting the town as a leader in the Southeast for equestrian activities. Early in 1959, the state agreed to improve and maintain the road leading to the Valley. This set the stage for increased business interest as evidenced by the April incorporation of Iredell Enterprises, Inc., a contracting and building business that set up shop in Love Valley. Later in 1959, a charter was granted allowing a motel to operate in Love Valley. These modest development plans signaled a future that would see many businesses prosper and others fail in Love Valley. But by far the most successful business ventures established in this period prior to the grand opening of Love Valley were those associated with the equestrian element of the community.

In April of 1959, Andy Barker and a small group incorporated the Southeastern Rodeo Association, an organization responsible for promoting rodeo in the southeast. Consequently, the SRA has probably done as much to promote Love Valley as anything, except for the gregarious personality of Andy Barker himself.[18]

The connection of Love Valley with horses was present from the beginning, and it may be that the horse epitomized Love Valley better than any story or single episode from its history. This was even more pronounced in light of the incorporation of a nonprofit organization by Andy and Ellenora Barker and Jim C. Taylor in November of 1959, the Chickasaw Horse Association. The Chickasaw breed is not the only horse to be found in Love Valley. The Barkers and Love Valleyites have owned and trained everything from Tennessee Walkers to Appaloosas and Palominos. Nevertheless, the Chickasaw was especially important to Love Valley because the breed had begun to die out in the early 1800s due to cross-breeding. The establishment of the Chickasaw Horse Association saved this breed from virtual extinction by reviving interest in and providing a registration service for the breed. Love Valley helped save an endangered species, and at the same time, the Chickasaw became a symbol for what Love Valley tried to emulate.

According to Ellenora Barker, the Chickasaw is known as a durable, independent, and tough creature with a proud ancestry, much like the human residents of Love Valley.[19] The Chickasaw horse, an American breed that evolved from Spanish stock, was famed on the frontier among the Native Americans who gave them their name.[20] Known for speed, durability, and general utility, this remarkable and beautiful animal found a home in Love Valley in 1959, some 440 years after the horse was first introduced to North America.

But this "horsy" atmosphere in Love Valley did not appeal to everyone. A series of articles and letters appeared in the *Charlotte Observer* during August and September 1959, that reminded everyone that it takes a certain type of person to enjoy equine company and that not everyone would find something to love in Love Valley. An article in the *Charlotte Observer* extolled the virtues of "western traditions" found in the North Iredell community.[21] The article elicited an interesting letter that appeared several days later under the title, "So What's to Love in Love Valley?" The author of this letter challenged the notion that Love Valley "even remotely resembled 'western traditions' and 'western-style life.'" The author described the Valley "as a mule swapping ground in Georgia" and suggested that the Valley was "as thoroughly unattractive and uninviting as a hog pasture in wet weather."

Approaching this desolate looking area a stream must be forded, then you bounce through a series of gaping ruts and holes that more befit a logging trail than a road. The "rough hewn buildings" surrounded by rocks, weeds and other unsightly undergrowth, would better qualify as dilapidated huts. Adjoining these shacks is a corral fetlock deep with offal and stable litter, and emitting a stench that is sickening.

Facing this foul-smelling bog, and located only a few paces away, is the unimposing shack called a cafe, where those with strong stomachs may imbibe coffee amid the polluted air from the corral.

The traditional covered wagon displays a torn cover, rotting side boards, rusting hardware and a missing wheel, to say nothing of the flies that buzz incessantly and feast on the human flesh.

Anyone who could see anything comparable to "western-style life" at Love Valley certainly must be credited with a strong imagination but a very weak sense of realism.[22]

Of course, the letter prompted response in defense of Love Valley. Some responses defended the offending characteristics of Love Valley as being truly western, including the horses. One humorous response to the letter apologized for the horses' lack of inhibitions. Others defended the hearty fare at the cafe, the invigorating aroma of nature, the beautiful natural setting, and the comfortable homes in the valley. But far and away the most common defense of Love Valley in response to the offended letter writer came in the descriptions of the Valley residents. Stories were offered lauding the people of North Iredell for their hospitality, friendliness, courtesy, and caring.[23]

All the printed controversy engendered by that letter was revisited in a September 3 article in the *Charlotte Observer* entitled "It's Hog Pasture or Paradise Accordin' to Who's Lookin'." The article emphasized a point that Andy Barker and the residents of Love Valley had been trying to make all along. Love Valley was not your ordinary main street in small-town America, so it should not resemble the paved, tree-lined, sidewalk-bordered street with closely manicured lawns leading up to white painted houses with picket fences nor the well-groomed television set western town. The emphasis was on authenticity.[24]

Andy Barker's response to all of this attention was predictable. Always the promoter, Barker responded to the offended letter writer, "Why, that was just about the best publicity we coulda got anywhere. Do you know that sixteen carloads of folks drove up from Charlotte last weekend just to see how miserable things are here? . . . After seeing our layout, one man shook his head and suggested, 'That lady has lived in the city too long. The stench she mentioned must have been this good, fresh country air.' "[25] This was not the last time Barker would take criticism and turn it into an opportunity to promote Love Valley.

* * *

As the time for the official opening of Love Valley drew closer, it became clear that with thousands of people flocking to the Valley during the summers, law enforcement was necessary to keep order. So, in May of 1959, Love Valley received its first deputy sheriff. Law and order came to the Valley just in time to deal with exciting events leading up to the grand opening of the western village. Occasionally justice had to be administered, and it was done quickly and without hassle. On the rare occasions when troublemakers would arrive at a square dance or rodeo, the deputy sheriff and justice of the peace Barker would round them up. In extreme cases, Barker carried a sawed-off shotgun to ensure justice. As soon as the deputy sheriff could round up troublemakers, justice of the peace Barker would dole out justice and punishment, and misbehavior was stemmed before it escalated. However, confrontation with actual lawbreakers took up very little time. For the most part the Valley was tame, and the deputy sheriff's main job was to handle the minor emergencies like the following that were a constant to life in Love Valley.

The rodeo was about to begin.[26] It was 7:00 p.m. and the last of the spectators were finding their seats or just pulling into the parking lot. As with all the rodeos, there was a hint of excitement in the air as the fans anticipated watching cowboys face and conquer the threat of danger.

Before the announcer had a chance to introduce the national anthem, loud noises and a crash rippled through the stadium bringing the crowd to a hushed silence. Had a grandstand collapsed, was there a car accident, had someone been hurt? The confusion and commotion that followed masked for a short time what had actually happened; however, soon enough, the story filtered through the crowd. A huge Brahma bull had crashed through the gate of his holding pen. When his owner realized what had happened, the bull lowered his head and headed straight for him. Luckily he was able to leap to safety and grasp the upper rail of the fence surrounding the arena just as the infuriated animal crashed through the lower rail and off an embankment into the parking lot below.

The Brahma's landing was not a soft one—the 1,500 pound animal crashed onto the hood of a parked car and in his scramble to regain his balance ripped an open door from the side of the vehicle. The car had been occupied by some latecomers to the rodeo, who were in stunned panic trying to escape the carnage and managed to jump to safety. After freeing himself from the twisted wreckage of the flattened vehicle, the liberated animal pranced off into the woods.

If one angry bovine roaming the hills and valleys were not enough, a second attempted to join his brother later during the same rodeo. Near the end of the bull-riding event (the last event of the rodeo) an irritated bull threw the poor cowboy who was trying to ride him. Refusing to leave the arena, as the bulls sometimes do, he charged at one of the rodeo clowns. The clown artfully dodged the bull's attempt to gore him, but the frustrated animal continued charging and crashed through the retaining fence into the crowd. Pandemonium struck, spectators scrambled for safety, a man and a woman fainted, and the big Brahma, seemingly satisfied with the fear he had instilled, trotted off into the night.

With such chaos and danger at hand, the Love Valley Law took charge to remedy the situation. A posse was formed as the deputy sheriff quickly organized a group of men to track the escaped four-legged offenders. Several cowboys rode into the night, only to find that protecting and defending against human criminals might be easier than tracking and capturing runaway bulls. The posse tracked and cornered but could not steer the bulls back to the corral. However, they did rescue a group of girl scout campers who had huddled in a van after one of the bulls crashed into their campsite. Finally, the next morning, the first bull, perhaps tired of his stint of freedom, returned to the herd on his own. The second, however, required the expertise and bravery of the posse. Eventually, exhausted by their search, the men apprehended the fugitive as a posse in the old West might have apprehended an outlaw and returned him unhurt to the corral.

But as every six-year-old imaginary cowboy knows, the real test of the law comes into play when the good guys come face to face with the bad guys. Most of the time there were only occasional minor episodes that ended with Andy Barker's sentence of a couple of hours in jail. So for Love Valley to be a working western town, it had to manufacture work for its sheriff. In what became an annual event at Love Valley, a genuine "badman" was crowned and honored as the meanest, toughest, and roughest looking cowboy after a week of trail riding and camping out without the benefits of toiletries or bathing. The year's badman was the symbolic bad guy so that the law enforcement officers of Love Valley could earn their keep.

These contests began with 50 or so cowboys riding out from Love Valley for a week-long adventure. For the experienced and older men, this was a time to experience and prove masculinity—men communing with men without creature comforts or the domesticating influence of women. For the younger, inexperienced boys, these trails became a rite of passage—a time of male bonding, of initiation and acceptance within the male fraternity. With these trail rides, boys became men and men became manlier. Sometimes women were included in the trail party, but they were never full members of the expedition, for they found sheltered accommodations at night while the men slept under the stars at places like Devil's Den or Goat Hill—places that unmistakably bore masculine names that connected these campers to the earliest settlers and roamers on this land.

The days dawned early and gloriously for the hearty riders; for others dawn transformed night terrors to reality. The trail disillusioned even some of the most romantic dreamers. One by one, some dropped out to return to the comforts of home. Others sought the nearest farm-house during the first rain shower or retreated when conditions became unbearable. But for the few who remained, dawn was the best time. The ground was moist from the summer dew, but the dew was cleansing rather than a nuisance. The sounds of the camp coming to life increased as bird song and horse whinnies gave way to men rustling, gathering wood, and building the morning fire. Soon after the flames caught hold, the air was filled with the aroma of bacon frying and coffee boiling—strong, black coffee that rolled slowly down the back of the throat and was so hot that tears welled up in the eyes. Before the sun had a chance to burn off the dew, the horses were saddled, the provisions packed, the gear stowed, and the men readied. The trail began once again as it had the day before and as it would the next, with the sun low and the heat beginning to hint once again that it was summer.[27]

A week or so of this and the most persistent returned dirty, tired, saddle sore, and bow-legged, but somehow renewed, revitalized, and sitting taller in the saddle than when they left. The meanest looking was the honorary badman. Covered with dust turned to mud from the last rain and sporting the scraggly beginnings of a beard, this unlikely hero was honored by his fellow riders for reasons only they could understand. And perhaps like the marshals from the Old West, even the Love Valley deputy sheriff paid homage to this badman, for badmen and good guys always respect and understand one another, even as do boys playing in the fields with a couple of sticks and a cap pistol. The unspoken bond between these men transcended the barriers between law and lawless-ness.

Over the years, Love Valley has enjoyed the able service and fine leadership of many good deputy sheriffs. However, perhaps the most unheralded of these men, yet in many respects the most important, was Harry Nance. Nance for years was a marshal to the town in every sense of the word. Harry first showed up in Love Valley in 1955, so from the beginning he was a part of the project and a close confidant of Andy Barker. Love Valley became a part of Harry and affected his life in many ways. Eventually Harry fell in love with and married Juanita, and the two lived for three or four years in a small cabin in the town. The pair is still as much a part of Love Valley as anyone, and for years, when the couple lived in Troutman, North Carolina, they maintained a vacation cabin in Love Valley and spent their weekends there. Harry recently retired from his plumbing business, sold the farm, and the two now live in the Valley full time.

When Harry was law enforcement officer for the community, his role stretched far beyond the confines of a jail and mayor's court. Harry understood his role as sheriff in terms of public service. When he was not enforcing the law, he was running errands for friends; when he was not functioning in his official role as sheriff, he was functioning in a number of volunteer roles throughout the town. If it needed to be done, Harry was more often than not the one doing it. For years he kept up the water system and volunteered for most every job that came along. Never in Love Valley's history have the residents been served by a more genuine and trustworthy person.

And Harry and Juanita are still indispensable to the town. Their loyal service to the community still finds them at the heart of every church and community event; people still clamor for a piece of Juanita's pound cake at community dinners; and when regulars visit the Valley, they always look for the faces of the Nances. Sheriff and public servant—to Harry, the two were synonymous, and to Love Valley, the pairing symbolizes a creed that embodies the philosophy of the town: Citizenship involves responsibility, and public service is the due for individual rights.

* * *

Soon enough, 1960 had arrived, the town was dedicated, Love Valley opened its own post office (this station would receive tons of mail around Valentine's Day so lovers' mail could receive the "Love Valley" postmark), new buildings and businesses were opened, expansion plans including a swimming pool and other recreational facilities were conceived and announced, and Love Valley connected itself, tenuously, to the outside world and to the twentieth century as Barker constructed a 2,000-foot airstrip to serve the town. The strip served as a promotional tool, because Barker wanted increased access for people with limited time and unlimited resources. The "airport" was built on land adjacent to Love Valley, and Barker planned to run a shuttle service from the strip to the Valley. Pilots flying into the valley would buzz the village once or twice, and Barker would send someone over the mountain to pick up the visitors at the airstrip a half mile away. All visitors coming to Love Valley were promised excitement, but Barker's air tourists would experience the added bonus of landing on an airstrip that bisected a state road bringing unique air traffic control complexities at the intersection of a state road and "Air Love Valley."[28]

The planned airstrip for Love Valley demonstrated Barker's dedication to promotion and expansion of his Love Valley project, so his surprise announcement to move the town some six months after its official dedication perhaps should not have come as such a shock to stunned directors. The move, after all, was to be done to allow for further growth of the development. Despite proceeding on little more than Barker's own faith that the job could be accomplished, the move of the town was successful. Plans for the move were formalized and acted upon during the winter of 1960-1961.

Of course, the major aspect of the renovation and expansion project was the removal and relocation of the town itself to the present site on top of a graded knoll. The grading itself was a mammoth undertaking, and the new town was built on both sides of a street providing more room for expansion. The character of the original town was retained: the street remained unpaved, rough wooden boardwalks continued to run the length of the street, hitching posts lined the street, and motorized vehicles were banned. This part of the renovation was planned to be completed early in 1961; however, weather conditions delayed grading and work for a good part of the winter.

The second major phase of renovation resulted in extensive improvement to the rodeo arena, including building a quarter-mile race track and a 5,500 seat arena. Further plans for the arena area included a swimming pool and horse stables. These expansion plans were also hampered by delays and problems; however, by June of 1961, Love Valley was able to sponsor the first races on its new quarter-mile track. The expansions were nearly all completed eventually; however, weather delays, Barker's foray into the political world, economic realities, and the immensity of the project slowed the development during the years 1960 to 1962. By 1962, Barker withdrew from a North Carolina senatorial race to devote more time to bringing his expansion to fruition. Nevertheless, despite delays and setbacks, the expansion was successful, and the never-say-die promoter had achieved another milestone.[29]

The whole purpose of the renovation and relocation was to promote Love Valley as a year-round community rather than a summer resort. To do this successfully required a stronger business base, and Love Valley received further investment support in response to Barker's expansion plans. In February and March of 1961, the Love Valley expansion plan gained a substantial boost when three investment firms made investments in Love Valley, Inc. The new investments led to initiation of a new

Fig. 6. Main Street Love Valley, early '60s. The three riders on horseback are from left to right: Jet Barker, Andy Barker, and Ellenora Barker. Used by permission of the North Carolina Department of Travel and Tourism.

firm, Love Valley Homes, Inc., for the purpose of mass production of shell housing, mainly for vacation and resort homes. The industry would be housed at Love Valley, would be managed by Andy Barker, and would utilize materials from the North Iredell area. With three new major investors and a new business in Love Valley, Barker's plans for expansion had the financing that was not present when he first announced the move, and the relocation and reorganization proceeded slowly.

During the winter and spring of 1961, the town was moved and the expansion began to take place. By the opening of Love Valley for the 1961 season, it was apparent that Barker had initially underestimated the amount of time required to complete the expansion. Still, the Valley had changed quite a bit from the last season. In addition to its new location, Love Valley had added an opera house for square dances, a general store, and a newly expanded saddle shop; Barker had renovated the rodeo arena and built a race track and grandstand around it; the town began to plan for recreational facilities such as a swimming pool, bowling alley, and recreational buildings; and new houses and improved roads were popping up everywhere.

During this period of expansion, Love Valley drew the interests of entrepreneurs such as Jack and Helen Laws. The Lawses were mainstays in Love Valley from early on and were particularly active during the years of greatest growth. The Lawses were always active in community events and were great promoters of early rodeo events, but undoubtedly their greatest contribution to the community came in the form of a business base. At one time or another, the Lawses owned, ran, or initiated several businesses in Love Valley. In the early sixties, they built a hotel in Love Valley, they bought many of the buildings on main street and filled them with businesses such as a gun shop, a boot shop, and a novelty shop. They ran their most successful business out of Love Valley, Laws Stained Glass, which grew to the largest stained glass studio in the United States.

Jack and Helen Laws made a huge economic impact on Love Valley; however, they demonstrated their belief in community responsibility and were constantly using their business base to contribute to life in the community. Perhaps their most lasting contribution can be found in the Love Valley Church. The church boasts exquisite stained glass windows, and all of them were donated to the church by Jack and Helen Laws. These windows continue to inspire worshippers at Love Valley, but even more importantly, they demonstrate a constant principle of Love Valley—the rights of citizenship require responsibility and contribution. As the Lawses and other businesses made their impact on Love

Valley's appearance and shape, Love Valley was preparing itself in the early sixties for the fondest period in its history. As 1961 got underway, Love Valley was ready for its grandest year yet.

* * *

Love Valley was at no time more a re-creation of American mythical space and a remembrance of Americana from a previous era than in the 1961 Fourth of July weekend. The events surrounding that celebration reinforced all that Love Valley embodied: patriotism, the central role of family, a lost innocence centered on harmless fun, and a combination of southern and western values—values of community, chivalry, courage, and heroism. That weekend demonstrated Love Valley's symbolic power as a microcosm of society and as a metaphor for the nation's idealized civil religion. This metaphor was seen across the country in July the Fourth rituals and comprised a mythical, religious response centered on civil values and couched in Christian terminology. Such a curious civil religion celebrated God and country, deified traditional American families, recreated a lost sense of communal existence, and hailed conservative values. And in the sixties when such values and traditional beliefs seemed to be disappearing, the Love Valley enterprise sought to become a symbol of an era on the verge of disappearance.

The big weekend of the Fourth actually began in June (Friday night, June 30) and continued through July 8, 1961. On the inaugural eve, campers, weekenders, city dwellers, and suburbanites flocked to the Valley in search of their mythical America. That search began with quiet strolls down the streets of the newly renovated town. For some visitors, this weekend afforded them their first view of the town since its move over the winter. By early evening, visitors made their way to the new opera house to partake in an American folk art form that evolved from an English country dance—the square dance. And although the dance seemed scripted and structured, it maintained the spontaneity, sensuality, and religious and social characteristics found somewhere deeply imbedded in its roots.

The participants of the square dance made up four couples to a team and formed a hollow square that enclosed some imaginary object—perhaps the long forgotten memory of an ancient fertility symbol, a maypole, or some other sacred object that carried with it the well-being of the social group. In response to the caller, the participants began to slowly encircle the object, which was then present only in the collective consciousness of the group. The communal nature of the dance was obvious with each group of eight moving harmoniously and consonantly with the other groups in patterned and ritualistic motion. The resonance of the dance predominated as the tempo increased to a feverish pitch while couples changed partners and instinctively merged as a single unit operating with mutual purpose. The dance floor was filled with the movements of a group of diverse people and personalities who celebrated a communal unity that was absent in their modern, impersonal, and individualistic society. The square dancers participated in a ritual that reaffirmed the communal yearning of humanity.

It was appropriate for this celebratory weekend to begin with the ritual of the square dance, for the dance extinguished the intrusive elements of modern society that destroy community and depended on mutuality and cooperation. With the initiatory rite complete, the group settled in for the celebration of its American heritage. The long weekend was marked by the ritual of the rodeo with all of its laudation of southern values and cowboy virtues. But the rodeo, at least on this weekend, was only a prelude to the real commemoration of the high-holy day in American civil religion.

The Fourth of July festivities began as one would imagine Independence Day celebrations in a small, rural community in the sixties. Swimming, horseback riding, and fishing brought the community together in the morning with recreational activities designed for every age and interest. Of course, all of these activities prepared the crowd for the community picnic to take place at noon. The promise of home-baked goods, fried chicken, potato salad, fresh vegetables, and plenty of sweet, iced tea kept the sporting enthusiasts close to home as the sun crept higher in the sky. After a tremendous spread where the food was plentiful and the appetites insatiable, many dozed under shade trees while others prepared to revive some old-fashioned sporting events to round out the afternoon.

About 2 p.m., with the full sun blazing through the valley, Love Valley olympians gathered to test their athletic prowess and sporting skill in a bevy of games and contests. The strong and the powerful warmed up for the test of strength known as the tug-of-war. Meanwhile the fast and quick prepared to compete in the greasy-pig catching contest or the egg race. Others lined up to compete in the frying pan throwing contest, the slick pole climbing contest, the watermelon eating contest, the egg throwing contest, the husband calling contest, or the more mundane activities such as horseshoe pitching. As the afternoon wore on and the contestants grew tired, the community assembled to hear a speech on "Americanism" and to view the newest addition to the Love Valley arsenal of entertainment—the horse race. As Love Valley visitors made their way to the arena, the day's tenor changed from a lazy day of eating, napping, and playing, to a rousing day filled with patriotic themes and ritu-

Fig. 7. A Love Valley Square Dance from the late '50s or early '60s. Photograph by Fred Harris. Love Valley photo archives, used by permission of Andy Barker.

als, to an exciting evening filled with the grace and speed (not to mention danger) of the horse race.

The newly expanded arena was buzzing with excitement as contestants readied themselves to test the speed and agility of their animals in concert with the skill and expertise of riders. To usher in the race, horses and riders carrying flags paraded by the stands to the strains of patriotic music, and a full team of horses and a covered wagon joined the parade to symbolize the pioneering spirit that built the country. Soon the parade of horses and patriots was over, the covered wagon was parked just outside the gate, and cowboys settled in to watch the races.

As the first heat was announced, the starter readied the contestants. Suddenly, the starter's pistol fired into the air and the horses exploded from their starting gates. But the race horses were not the only animals to catapult into action. The team of horses hitched to the covered wagon, which had been carelessly left unattended, was startled and broke into a frenzied dash away from the gate surrounding the track. The chaotic sprint lasted only about 30 yards when the startled but unhurt team and wagon all crashed into a deep creek. Meanwhile, those spectators who had not watched the crazed flight of the symbolic pioneers followed the riders into the first turn. They watched as the riders disappeared into a cloud of thick dust and then reappeared as the horses headed down the backstretch. The observant spectators noticed that one fewer horse and rider emerged from the turn than entered it—one of the ponies had jumped the outside fence, and continued a frightened sprint toward the creek. The rider, a little frazzled by the unexpected turn of events, must have had the most exciting ride of his life. The rest of the race evening was uneventful by comparison, and at the end of the day, Love Valley visitors and residents were tired, happy, and proud.[30]

* * *

As the first ten years of Love Valley's existence began to wind down, not much new happened on the promotion end of the business. Further expansion continued through 1964, and land and lots were being sold in Love Valley. Excitement was generated over rumors about the possibility of locating an automobile race track at Love Valley. But plans did not materialize, and the Charlotte Motor Speedway eventually provided a racing outlet for Piedmont North Carolina.

Big change did come, though, in 1963 when Love Valley became a political entity and was incorporated as a town (Love Valley's incorporation will be covered in chapter 5). By its 10-year anniversary, Love Valley had grown from a couple of hundred acres of rough backwoods hills to 1,742 acres of riding trails, roads, developed lots, an incorporated town, and a working western village that served as a vacation spot for rodeo and cowboy enthusiasts from across the Southeast.

This steady growth was possible because the town's founder and developer was a tireless promoter. Andy Barker, whether planning a Christmas parade, honoring a dead civil war hero, sponsoring a motorcycle rodeo, or moving the town, always had promotion of Love Valley in the back of his mind, and he promoted it well. On the eve of the 10-year anniversary, Andy Barker glanced back only briefly to the humble origins of the Valley in 1954, and looked ahead to 1974 with optimism and hope for growth.[31] Love Valley may not have been "the Greatest Show on Earth," but it was not from lack of trying.

5

The First Decade:
Philanthropy and Politics

From Andy Barker's religious vision emerged the belief in the perfectibility of society and the impulse to reform the social order. His religious purpose evolved to provide a model of reform that would lead to social change. Barker's strategy for social reform based upon a religious foundation created the necessity to espouse a political agenda and to work through the political realm for positive change. Love Valley was never an isolated community cut off from the rest of the world. Rather, Love Valley sought to be involved in active reform movements centered in political and economic ventures.

Love Valley's political activism was best symbolized by the community's becoming chartered as a town. The incorporation of Love Valley immediately raised the need for local government, a government that Andy Barker has dominated for most of the town's history. This creation of a political entity also gave Barker a base from which to launch his state senate and gubernatorial campaigns. Barker hoped to extend his reform movement beyond the stables and modest houses of Love Valley to a wider audience through state politics.

Barker described his politics as philanthropic and instituted reform projects in Love Valley through such agencies as the North Carolina Mobility Corps and I CARE. He based this vision of political reform on what he called Jeffersonian democracy. By that designation Barker meant that government should exist to provide for its citizenry freedom, rights, education, religious freedom, and the pursuit of happiness. Barker believed that government should exist in partnership with the citizenry but that most governments were antagonistically related to citizens. Thus, reform of government was necessary, and his antiestablishment support for rural concerns added a Populist stance to his political platform.

The base for Barker's political philosophy and religious underpinning is philanthropic venture—the political arena simply provides an avenue for promoting human welfare. In fact, Barker sometimes defined the two concepts in the same way. Both philanthropy and politics provide for a greater good to a greater number of people. Barker's political activity was based on the assumption that government should exist solely for the purpose of providing that greater good and should, therefore, by definition be philanthropic in initiating and sponsoring humanitarian ventures.

During Love Valley's first 10 years, the growth of the Valley was marked by unrelenting promotion of the town as a tourist attraction. However, to focus only on the commercial aspects of Barker's ventures would highlight only a small portion of the story. Love Valley existed for much more than its commercial value. The guiding force behind the Barkers' dream from the beginning was the desire to build a Christian town and to revitalize the communal spirit—a spirit that symbolized what was for them a lost American virtue. The Barkers' goal was to use the community base and resources as a springboard for Christian charity. From the beginning, the Barkers viewed their enterprise as a vehicle for promoting goodwill among God's creatures and as a tool for helping those in need.

But Andy and Ellenora were not the only Love Valleyites to attempt placing the biblical exhortation to charity into action. Their benevolence was quickly recognized, and humanitarian zeal was passed along to the community with ease. The community turned to the Barkers and to one another in times of distress—there were few crises in the Valley that were not shared. A strong communal sense still exists more than 40 years after the town began, but the expression of its communal spirit had been felt in those first 10 years.

Two characteristics of this communal emphasis arise again and again in Love Valley's history. First, the Valley, its residents, and its neighbors have experienced more than their share of hard times and tragedy. Tragic deaths, heroic rescues,[1] and life-threatening events have highlighted this undercurrent of the tragic element in Love Valley's life span. Second, it was during these hard times that the uniqueness of Love Valley was best experienced. When someone experienced tragedy in this community, the community responded with help and aid. The people who lived in this area made neighborly philanthropy a way of life.

The philanthropy and benevolence of the Barkers were evident from the beginning of their venture in the North Iredell woods. In January of 1955, only a few short months after the Barkers moved to Iredell County, Andy was chosen to head and direct the 1955 Cancer Crusade. Barker's charitable work with this organization ironically foreshadowed the tragic way this disease would affect his own family in the years to come. Not only did Barker plan various fund-raisers for the crusade, but he used Love Valley as a source for raising money for the fund. For example, all proceeds from a Love Valley Showdeo in May went to the

Iredell County Cancer Fund. Of course, this type of benevolence was not new for the Valley. Rodeo and Showdeo proceeds had been donated to charity during the first year of events, 1954.

The Barkers envisioned Love Valley as a center for more creative philanthropic activities and began to use the facilities and activities to reach out to children in need. In the summer of 1956, the Love Valley Church sponsored its first vacation Bible school with an emphasis on providing opportunities for mountain children in surrounding areas. By the second year of its operation, this Bible school averaged an attendance of 125 children, who were taught and fed at the Love Valley cafeteria. Dolphus Allen, the minister instrumental in helping begin this school, remembers covering miles of mountain roads to pick up and drop off children who would otherwise not have been able to attend the school.[2] The school enlisted the help of young people from Statesville and was so successful that it sparked interest in pursuing an outdoor camp venture for Love Valley.

Outreach to children developed as a natural extension for the Love Valley enterprise. When pressed to describe the community in the early days, Barker consistently answered that Love Valley was designed for children.[3] Eventually, some area judges recognized the potential of this place for kids and sent Barker young boys from their courts who were in need of rehabilitation. Some parents heard about Love Valley's programs and sent boys who were discipline problems at home. The proponents of Love Valley claimed that a tough program of riding, discipline, and outdoor survival training thoroughly reformed many of these young men who became productive citizens. Through the years, over 50 boys found their way to the Valley.

News of Love Valley's successful work with children spread quickly and several experimental programs were initiated at the Valley. For example, the North Carolina Mobility Corps, funded in part by the Federal Government and the Ford Foundation, sponsored a relocation program for disadvantaged Native Americans in Robeson County.[4] Love Valley invited 50 young Lumbee men to the town, housed and fed them, and trained them for skilled jobs. The program met with varied success; however, in the end, a large number of the program participants returned to their homes before finishing the training. Barker speculated the participants were too young to benefit fully from the opportunities they were being offered, but despite the relative lack of success of the Mobility Corps' efforts, the Barkers continued in their outreach efforts to young people.

Aside from their informal "adoption" of many young people, the Barkers continued to found and sponsor innovative new programs

Fig. 8. The Love Valley Bible School and Summer Camp, 1956. A large, framed, colorized version of this photograph hangs in the fellowship hall of the Love Valley Presbyterian Church. Ellenora Barker is in the middle at the very back. The man, fourth from the left on the back row, is Dolphus Allen, the student minister at the time who ran the school. Photograph by Fred Harris. Love Valley photo archives, used by permission of Andy Barker.

directed at the problem of poverty and the rehabilitation of troubled youth. The Barkers helped start I CARE, Inc., a successful Iredell County organization designed to help disadvantaged youth and a precursor to such programs as Head Start. Barker worked with the organization until he felt it had become too bureaucratic with too much money going to administrative costs. Later, Barker operated a heavy equipment school for government sponsored programs where disadvantaged and troubled young people could work for low wages and learn technical skills that would lead to economic opportunities and betterment.

The Barkers' work in these areas was so extensive that state and local leaders began to look to Love Valley as a model for social programs. Perhaps this perception was best described by an inscription found in the front of Barker's copy of Allen Gwyn's book, *Work-Earn and Save: Observations on Crime and Correction* (1963). The inscription read, "To: Andy Barker, North Carolina's leading layman in our war against poverty and crime; a real champion in the art and service of rehabilitating youthful offenders; whose pattern is worthy to be emulated throughout the nation. . . ." The Barkers were using Love Valley as they had intended. They had built a community that operated on the precept that all people had a responsibility to contribute productively to larger society. In this case, and in its own way, Love Valley was attempting to wage a war on poverty and crime.

Andy and Ellenora Barker involved themselves with many social programs through the years, and they searched for any means possible to use Love Valley as a haven for young people and as a place for assisting youth to become more productive citizens and adults. The idea of a camp for such a purpose seemed to be a natural extension of the Love Valley enterprise. In January 1957, the first such camp was begun at Love Valley. The Barkers enlisted the assistance of the popular cowboy star Fred Kirby to begin Fred Kirby's Junior Rancho, Inc., a western-style camp for young people. The camp featured recreational activities including horseback riding and swimming.[5] Later, in 1958, the Patriotic Order, Sons of America of Pennsylvania established a camp in Love Valley where young boys could learn the "western ways."[6] The creed statement of the Patriotic Order, Sons of America, and their interest in a camp at Love Valley reinforced the ideals that Love Valley represented, namely that there is something patriotic, good, and wholesome about a place that emphasizes traditional values and love of God and country. This, of course, embodied the social utopian impulse as Barker envisioned it.

Perhaps Barker's greatest contributions to charitable causes came in his ability to translate promotional techniques and political savvy to raising money and gaining attention. For example, when chosen to serve as March of Dimes chairperson in 1959, Andy responded with the zeal and enthusiasm he used to promote his Love Valley enterprise. Barker immediately enlisted the help of area Boy Scouts and high school students and set a goal of $12,000, which was more than twice the amount raised the previous year. Typical fund-raising efforts were initiated (sale of lapel buttons, restaurants donating all receipts from coffee sales on "Coffee Day," competition between schools, a benefit fashion and talent show, the mother's march, etc.); however, with Barker as chairperson of the drive, a particular western flair was inevitable. The North Iredell Post 113 American Legion supported the drive by sponsoring a county-wide square dance and by donating all the proceeds from the dance to the drive. However, perhaps the most unusual and "western" fund-raising event to take place for the 1959 drive was the "chuck-wagon" race conducted by rural high schools.[7]

At first, Barker did not announce the wagon race but only promised a rural "surprise." The strategy of silence worked well to create curiosity, and the event stirred up considerable interest when it was finally announced and conducted. High School teams from Central, Union Grove, Harmony, Cool Springs, Unity, Troutman, Celeste Henkel, and Scotts sponsored western wagons drawn by tractors and navigated by FFA (Future Farmers of America) students. Each team traversed a different rural route, based on a distance of 15 miles, with their destination the Statesville town square. Students canvassed houses and businesses along their respective routes, and each dollar they collected allowed them to move the wagon 250 yards forward. Prizes were offered for the team that traveled their route in the least amount of time and for the team that raised the most money. Despite a wagon breakdown with the Central team, the race went well, and the Troutman team rolled into the town square ahead of the rest after just two hours and 10 minutes of collecting. The successful race raised $1,050.52 for the March of Dimes, but even more important, it provided a means for rural communities to become involved in a fund-raiser that had before been concentrated in the town of Statesville.[8]

Similar strategies originated from Love Valley that ultimately aided charitable organizations. In 1961, Barker planned a Labor Day extravaganza to benefit the Cancer Crusade. Not only did he donate all the proceeds from Love Valley events that weekend, but he concocted some drawing cards to make sure the proceeds were substantial. First, Barker built an "artificial moon" to shine over the Valley for the three-day weekend as a curiosity seeker's exhibit and as an inspiration for all those who took the name "Love Valley" seriously. The moon was a lighted fiberglass globe that sat on top of a 60-foot pole on the crest of a mountain and was visible from everywhere in the valley.[9] The soft glow of the "moon" was quite inspiring, according to those who fell in love under its influence, and Barker hoped that such an inspiring aphrodisiac would also kindle the generosity of visitors and residents.

Nevertheless, Barker's real drawing card for the Cancer Drive weekend turned out to be celebrity cowboys. Rex Allen, television and movie star, the hero of *Frontier Doctor*, the "Voice of the West," and famous singing cowboy, was contracted to visit Love Valley and to perform for the crowds with proceeds going to the Cancer Fund. In addition, another television cowboy, Bob Carson, planned to appear at Love Valley as the Valley's acting mayor for the weekend. Carson arrived in the Valley riding shotgun on a stagecoach full of local personalities, was sworn in as mayor for the weekend, and sealed his political future by promising "no new taxes." Carson spoke about the importance of supporting the campaign with the hopes of speeding research toward finding a cure. Carson's own family was tragically affected by the disease, and he was able to give a first-hand account about the importance of continuing the fight against the killer. Later in the weekend, Rex Allen appeared to perform, and the presence of both stars helped to ensure the success of the drive.[10] On a hot, sticky Labor Day weekend in 1961, two stars and a soft moon kept vigil over the Valley to remind everyone why Love was in the town's name.

Love Valley's philanthropy was not all outwardly directed, however, and when tragedy struck the community, there was more than enough goodwill to help each other in the community through the difficult circumstances, thus actualizing Barker's utopian vision for his community. Through the years, Love Valley residents depended on the communitarian spirit that assured them if a son or daughter were in trouble, the parents would not face the challenge alone; if a spouse died, the bereaved would not grieve alone; if a home burned, the family would not face that tremendous loss alone; and if trouble or pain of any kind afflicted any member of the community, it afflicted all in the community.

Love Valley's goodwill reached many people both directly and indirectly through the years; however, the benevolence of the people of this small town was not limited to human beings. According to town residents, everything in God's creation was subject to the goodwill engendered by the community feeling of this town, and residents would go to great lengths to care for animals as well as humans as the following story demonstrates.[11]

The late March snowstorms had created frightening weather in the Brushy Mountains. The temperatures were frigid and the winds, howling as they sometimes do, added dangerous wind chill factors for all living creatures who happened to wander outside for too long. But as the winds pounded the side of the house and seemingly threatened to rip the roof off the top, the Barkers sat cozily in their living room, surrounding the coal-burning stove that helped to create one of the warmest houses in the county. Days like these, with the weather simply unbearable, made the Barkers more thankful than ever for the old coal burner. The peacefulness of sitting with family in a warm home while the wind whipped cold air outside lulled the Barker family into a sense of quiet contentment on winter evenings.

A phone call changed all that. The call was from northern Wilkes County near the Ashe County line where the Barkers had 11 horses grazing. The caller had bad news for the family—two of their animals had wandered off from the rest of the herd and had been cut off from food supplies during the snow storms. Someone found the two horses nearly starved to death and frozen from exposure to the severe weather. Upon receiving the news, Barker called for help and immediately headed for the Wilkes County farm and found the animals. One of the horses was fine; however, the other was nearly dead from exposure and starvation.

Barker and his helpers worked quickly to help the animal. They loaded her on a sled, hauled the mare through the woods, and sped her home toward Love Valley. Meanwhile, a Statesville veterinarian rushed to Love Valley. It took seven men to unload the animal, and faced with what to do with the dying beast, the veterinarian said that her only chance for survival (and those chances were slim) was for the horse to be moved to a warm place. Barker remembered the embracing warmth of his living room before he received the emergency call—he remembered the quiet contentment his coal-burning stove always seemed to create for those who shared its warmth. Why wouldn't the stove bring the same sort of contentment to an animal? The seven men carried the frozen body into the Barker's living room—this seemed to be the horse's only chance for survival.

The horse still could not stand, so Barker rigged up a metal scaffolding frame and suspended the horse from the frame with blankets. Ellenora and the Barker kids nursed and encouraged the horse and tried to feed her warm milk and hay. Finally, after about four hours, the mare could move her head, and for the first time, it appeared the horse might survive. Eventually, after vigilant care from the Barkers, and after recuperation in the living room for the better part of a week, the seven-hundred pound, two-year-old mare was munching hay right by the old coal stove just as if she belonged there. The horse was unnamed, but when it became clear the mare would live, Ellenora suggested the name Snowbound.[12]

This episode is a prized story for the Barkers. The horse was not a thoroughbred, a special animal to the kids, or of financial importance to the family. But the Barkers' and their friends' efforts to save the animal represented to them the same respect for life that led to most of the philanthropic activities that took place in the Valley. The respect for life and human responsibilities concerning the preservation of life saved that mare during a late winter snow storm in 1960. According to the Barkers, it also saved the lives, or improved the lives, of many others along the way.

Philanthropy was a mainstay of Love Valley's utopian venture whether it resulted in heroics or dangerous rescues, creative and fun-filled activities, or simply goodwill. This story chronicles only a few of the charitable acts performed by Love Valleyites throughout the town's history. Their countless acts of helping are a way of life in the small, close-knit community they share. When Barker stockpiled far more coal than he could use so he could share it with others, or when Ellenora prepared 100 pounds of turkey so everyone would have a place to eat on

Thanksgiving, or when one of Barker's helpers chopped wood for a neighbor, it was simply another example of the town's attempt to establish a civic body organized around the utopian desire to support others in the community.

* * *

As suggested earlier, the philanthropy that characterized the Barkers and Love Valley developed hand-in-hand with Andy Barker's political ventures and with the establishment of Love Valley as a political entity, a town. Barker likes to describe himself as a Jeffersonian Democrat, emphasizing government's responsibility to provide for benevolence, happiness, inviolable rights, religious freedom, egalitarianism, and an informed and educated citizenry. In addition to his Jeffersonian ideals, Barker might be described as a new Populist in that he has (through most of his political career) opposed the political establishment, attempted to appeal directly to people for support, and kept rural areas and concerns foremost in his political agenda.

Barker fought for these ideals during his political forays and always viewed his political efforts as an extension of his humanitarian and religious interests. In many ways, he emerged in the mold of other southern lay leaders, like A. W. McAlister, who spoke on the basic tenets of religious liberalism, the social gospel, and political progressivism while remaining squarely within the southern evangelical tradition.[13] And because of Barker's leadership, Love Valley evolved as a pocket of Jeffersonian idealism and Populist themes in a rural southern setting.

Barker's political philosophy was based in part on his belief that the United States citizenry had lost confidence in the political system and in the politicians who ran it. He pointed out that some officeholders, political candidates, and elected officials were tainted in some way, corrupt, untrustworthy, or unethical. Barker believed the political machine of the United States had deteriorated to the point of gridlock, and he blamed the decline on the loss of the art of politics based on the barter system. If gridlock and dysfunctional government were to be overcome, claimed Barker, the political barter would be a part of the process.[14]

As Barker described politics, he recounted a time when the art of trade was alive and well in rural America. The exchange of goods and services was based upon the idea that a person's labor and possessions were actually worth something—that a person's work and the products of that work had some intrinsic value. Gradually, the practice of trading became cumbersome and complicated as society became increasingly isolated and specialized. With increased urbanization, industrialization, and privatization, the ability to trade time, labor, or goods became impractical if not impossible. One's time and work no longer had intrinsic value but symbolic value, which was more or less arbitrarily evaluated. According to Barker, one's possessions were assigned a monetary value that separated the worth of something from its intrinsic value. The worth of one's time and possessions was externally separated from the intrinsic value of the person or service itself. This separation caused a radical change in the way people in society conducted business with one another and related to one another. With the decline of the barter system, one's time and possessions were assigned external and symbolic value, and the way one would employ another or obtain a desired object was by purchase rather than by trade. In other words, according to Barker, with the decline of the barter system, things and people could be bought and sold.[15]

According to Barker, politics, at its best, should be based upon the art of bartering—an art that locates and understands intrinsic worth and values objects, ideas, and services based upon that intrinsic worth. With the barter system dead, politicians no longer recognize intrinsic worth; they no longer understand the difference between what is valuable and what is desirable (because worth and value have been separated); they no longer understand how to barter, compromise, and trade in order to obtain goals. With these tools no longer available to them, politicians know only one way to achieve their goals, through buying and selling, and this is where most of the perceived corruption in government originates. According to Barker, politicians attempt to get what they want, whether their intentions are good and honorable or not, by buying and selling, by resorting to monetary exchange, and by handing out political favors. And with the loss of the ability to barter came the loss of the art of compromise. Thus, the loss of the barter system has led not only to corruption in government but to stagnation as well. Nothing gets accomplished because no one knows how to barter, to trade, to compromise.[16]

Andy Barker epitomizes the art of the barter. He is a master trader and has employed the art in his business as well as his political endeavors. He will trade boxes for apples, watches for guns, ancient log homes for land that he will trade for metal conduit that he will trade for building materials—he will trade for almost anything that might be of future value to someone else. One time he even traded for a truck load of coffins. Barker envisions himself as a politician born in the wrong era. A barterer by nature, Barker believes he has been politicking on the basis of barter and exchange while the political world around him was looking for political favor and handout. To understand the politics of Andy Barker and of Love Valley, one must understand two things: Barker's

Jeffersonian position that the political arena is the forum for humanitarian benevolence, and the art of bartering.

Several stories of Andy's skill at bartering circulate and have been recorded in Love Valley.[17] Invariably, these stories portray a man who trades for the sheer pleasure of the competition. Barker's trading style involves strategic maneuvering, a practiced indifference, a shielded caution that veils his intent and purpose. Barker can call upon his best poker face during a trade as skillfully as a card shark can bluff an opponent. Feigning apathy or excitement as required, Barker trades with a passion.

Often these trades are for small items that Barker doesn't really want. But he has a difficult time passing on the opportunity to trade. Many of these trades take place with friends, and the process can be a way of forging a relationship. Some trades take hours: Barker and his partner might discuss the trade, make offers and counter offers, puff on a pipe, walk around town, talk about items not even remotely related to the trade, and finally reach some sort of agreement some hours later. Invariably, both traders claim they were "taken" by the other—neither will admit to making a good trade, because they do not want to be indebted to the other in case another trade becomes imminent.

The trade is a game often played by friends and usually carried out in good-natured contests of will. Money is rarely exchanged except in nominal amounts to make up some perceived difference in worth. By and large, the trade takes place based on an item's worth, and an item's worth might vary significantly from person to person. This is what makes trading so unpredictable and also powerful. And this is why Barker enjoys it so.

The process of trading and bartering is politics as Andy Barker practices and understands it, but it proceeds with a language that too few people understand. The art of bartering is a secret ritual that only the initiates understand. The two barterers approach each other with suspicion regardless of their relationship otherwise. The barter itself requires artful dodging, deception, and cunning. The key is to always hold something back—once the trader offers something, he has lost, because the trader has lost all bargaining power and is left exposed and vulnerable. This is the way traders communicate—they hold back because to divulge everything is to become vulnerable. This is the art Barker wants politicians to relearn.

* * *

From the beginning of Love Valley's existence to the present, political maneuvering has been a constant force in the town's growth and in

Barker's leadership. Early on it surfaced in the various dignitaries who visited Love Valley (often at the prompting of a state political leader) or in correspondence with political figures in Washington or Raleigh. Later the political workings in Love Valley came with actual activity in the political realm and the establishment of the Valley as a political entity. Nevertheless, in every case, Love Valley's involvement in the political realm was tempered with the quiet hospitality symbolized by Love Valley and recognized by the foreign ambassador from Pakistan after his visit to the Valley. The ambassador thanked the Barkers for their "southern hospitality" with its western flair.[18] The same sentiment was expressed by a French envoy after a visit to Love Valley in April of 1963. He expressed thanks for the hospitality of Love Valley and for the western, cowboy experience.[19]

In the early sixties, these relaxed political liaisons were formalized with the entrance of Barker and the town into the political realm. The first hint of official political activity in Love Valley came with Andy Barker's announcement in January 1962 of his candidacy for the North Carolina state senate. Barker's intention was to run in the May 26 Democratic primary for the 25th district senatorial seat. Barker's announcement caught Democratic leaders by surprise and apparently shook up the establishment enough to force consolidation of strategy and to revitalize interest in the race by other Democratic potentials. Barker outlined a simple platform, foreshadowing issues that would continue to energize his political goals in the future. Barker's agenda included 1) upgrading state secondary roads (This constituted a much needed improvement that Barker knew all too well since Love Valley was accessed by rural secondary roads.); 2) educational reform (Barker opposed consolidation plans that were being considered and later outlined plans for education that specifically focused on problems of rural schools.); and 3) developing the state's natural resources (Barker opposed tax increases and proposed increasing tax revenue by expanding the tax base through development and promotion of natural resources.).

Barker's early political platform revealed his developing Jeffersonian tendencies and Populist themes and charted the future course of his political endeavors. Nevertheless, 1962 would not witness the fruition of these ideas, for Barker withdrew from the race just before the May primary date, citing business demands as conflicting with his campaign. The campaign corresponded to a crucial stage in the development of Love Valley, and wet spring weather had hampered plans for the 1962 opening of the resort town. Thus, vowing to run again in the future, Andy Barker dropped his plans for a senate run in 1962 and turned his attentions once again to the promotion of Love Valley. Nevertheless, his political activity was far from finished and took on a more symbolic nature during the fall of 1962, as the following story suggests.[20]

The afternoon air was tinged with a brisk autumn bite of October in 1962. In a small baseball stadium in Statesville, North Carolina, excited local Democrats (and probably a few Republicans, too) were anxiously awaiting the arrival of the first vice-presidential visit to Statesville in the twentieth century. Andy Barker shifted nervously in anticipation as his stage coach, the handsome Tennessee walking horse, and the cowboys in dazzling western apparel were all ready for the vice-president's visit. Cowboy Barker was responsible for making the big Texan feel at home, and the stage-coach limousine was the trick. Lyndon Baines Johnson was about to come to town on a campaign tour to support local Democrats in the Mecklenburg and Iredell regions. Johnson was stopping in Statesville and Charlotte to stump for North Carolina Democrats, and Iredell County Democrats turned to Andy Barker and other local talents to insure a rousing rally in Statesville.

The stadium began to fill well before 3:00 p.m. even though Johnson was not scheduled to arrive until 4:00 p.m. The stadium was hardly recognizable to those who frequented the arena for local baseball games—the stands were free of the hot-dog wrappers and drink containers that marked baseball events and the dugout areas were neat and free of all the signs of the summer pastime. The setting was perfect for a political rally.

The mayor of Statesville and a local minister chatted anxiously as they waited to help meet the dignitaries and introduce them to the assembled crowd. Democratic officials had managed to pull the massive rally together and anxiously hoped that all would go smoothly, while scores of volunteers worked feverishly to insure the event would proceed without a hitch. Technicians double- and triple-checked the public address system to make sure the vice-president would be heard without the irritating feedback that seemed to inevitably plague such gatherings—the familiar "Testing . . . 1, 2, 3 . . ." echoed through the rapidly filling stadium until the crew got the volume just right.

As 4:00 p.m. approached and the crowd of 3,500 became more and more fidgety, word quickly spread through the stands that the vice-president had been detained in Salisbury and would be arriving in Statesville later than expected. A collective murmur began to grow in intensity and volume as expectant Statesvillians learned they would have to wait indefinitely to glimpse and hear the celebrity, and perhaps the thought crossed everyone's mind that LBJ would not show at all. Nevertheless, the nervous crowd was quickly diverted as the assembled local bands stepped in and took advantage of the lull in activities. Band members and local school personnel inspired the vigilant crowd, and the stadium was transformed into a giant pep rally.

Finally, as 5:00 p.m. approached and as the shadows of late autumn afternoon began to lengthen on the field below, a flurry of activity was followed by the musical strains of "Yellow Rose of Texas." The crowd's anticipation froze, the knot in Andy Barker's stomach tightened, and everyone sensed that the theophanic moment had arrived. Fathers strained their necks to catch a first glimpse of the vice-president; mothers stood on tiptoe to see over hats and between bodies; children peered through their parents' legs or sat astride their shoulders in order to witness what their parents told them was a once-in-a-lifetime event. To the delight of the crowd and the pride of Andy Barker, the vice-president made his entrance into the stadium riding shotgun on the Love Valley stagecoach. Passengers on the stage included Lady Bird Johnson, senators Sam Ervin and B. Everett Jordan, and candidate Hugh Alexander. Governor Terry Sanford followed the stagecoach in an open wagon with a parcel of exasperated looking secret service agents. Once inside the stadium, the big Texan bounded from the coach only to mount a handsomely outfitted Tennessee walking horse provided by Love Valley. Governor Sanford cautiously mounted a second horse. To the amusement of the crowd, Johnson sat tall and straight in the saddle (as an experienced Texas rancher would), and he pranced gracefully around the stadium while a hapless secret service agent saddled up and attempted to stay close to the cantering equestrian.

As Johnson finished his ride around the stadium, he dismounted, and once again leaving bewildered secret service agents behind, made his way along the edge of the stadium, shook hands and greeted strangers in the crowd as if they were close acquaintances, and climbed onto the speaker's platform with gusto that would be repeated in the words he had to share with the voters of Statesville. After ceremoniously receiving the key to Statesville, Johnson repeated the speech that was his repertoire for this campaign trail, rarely referred to notes, pounded the podium for emphasis, and preached the Democratic gospel to a congregation primed to shout "amen" at every pronouncement. His sermon was punctuated by plenty of homespun humor and analogy to make his points clear. The anecdotal sermon worked. The crowd loved him and cheered loudly as the vice-president made his way from the stadium and back to the campaign trail.

The vice-president of the most powerful nation on earth had just visited the little town of Statesville and was off in a flash. He did not stay long. The preparations for his visit took much more time and effort than his actual appearance, but his influence and effect were long last-

Fig. 9. Andy Barker (left) with Senator Sam J. Ervin (center) and Senator B. Everett Jordan (right), two of the Democratic dignitaries entertained by Barker and Love Valley. Love Valley photo archives, used by permission of Andy Barker.

ing. Johnson seemed at home in Statesville's high school baseball stadium. Perhaps he even felt at home as he pranced around the stadium on one of Love Valley's finest. He might have just as easily been riding the boundaries of his ranch or the trails of the mountains surrounding Love Valley. Nevertheless, regardless of what went on in Vice-President Johnson's mind, the rally made for good politics, and Love Valley helped put on the show. And when the show was over and the horses put up for the evening, the entourage of Democrats moved quite easily from the informality of a town pep rally to the elegance of a state dinner in Charlotte to honor Senator Ervin with a speech by Johnson. Judging by Andy Barker's inclusion in such events and by his ease in functioning in more than one world, it was becoming increasingly clear that Barker was well connected in North Carolina political circles and ready to inaugurate the remainder of his political goals. And even though some of those goals were destined to remain unrealized, the frequent stream of personal notes and letters from prominent North Carolina Democrats suggested the political potential that once resided at Love Valley, North Carolina.

By the end of 1962, with Love Valley's development back on track and with his close brush with Washington still vivid in his memory, Barker put his 1962 state senate bid behind him and outlined his remaining political goals. First, Barker would seek the incorporation of Love Valley as a town, thus granting his development political status. Second, Barker would run for the state senate in 1964. Third, his final goal was to seek the office of governor of North Carolina. By the turn of the new year, 1963, Barker had begun to work on at least the first two of those three goals.

By early April 1963, Love Valley's incorporation as a town had been approved, and plans were under way for Love Valley's first election, to be held May 18 at the Love Valley post office. Ellenora Barker was named registrar. At the time of incorporation, the new municipality included 77 residents and 52 freeholders, an official population that has remained relatively constant through the years.[21] With the incorporation, changes in the administration of the Valley took place. For example, the financial entity, Love Valley, Inc., was dissolved as the town's sole owner, but a corporation entitled Love Valley Enterprises, Inc., was formed to operate most of the town's business. And of course, the most important change was the advent of political office for the community. The leadership of the new town included the offices of mayor and five town commissioners. Iredell County's cowboy capital was officially referred to as "The Town of Love Valley."

Love Valley's first election represented an idyllic small-town America envisioned by Barker's utopian ideal. Friends and neighbors ran against one another with good-natured political posturing. The race began with rumors concerning who would run for mayor. The early favorites were Andy Barker and Jack Laws, one of the leading business-men in town as owner of the Lazy L Hotel in Love Valley and Laws Art and Stained Glass Company. Nevertheless, Barker had something else in mind, and Jack quickly denied rumors that he would run. But rumors quickly gave way to reality as candidates began to step forward and announce their intentions. (There were very few secrets in a town of 77.)

The first election was marked by political posturing, spirited debate about the future of the town, and a couple of husband-wife teams on the ballots. Progress, development of adequate water and sewer systems, and a paved road leading to Love Valley were favorite themes for candidates for the town commission. The mayoral race produced two conflicting visions for the future of Love Valley. One candidate made development and progress a priority and advocated improving town services with revenue generated through increasing the commercial and industrial activity of Love Valley. This vision and platform included development of an industrial base for the town.[22] The vision of Love Valley based on industrial and commercial growth failed to capture enough support for victory, perhaps because some residents seemed to fear that such development would hurt the small-town, communitarian lifestyle they enjoyed at Love Valley.

Of course, anyone would have had a difficult time winning the election in any event when the very popular J. A. Barker, Sr. (Andy's father and a seven-year resident of Love Valley) entered the race for mayor. Barker, Sr., was a veteran of World War I, a member of the board of directors and a stockholder of Love Valley Enterprises, an elder of Love Valley Presbyterian Church, and was credited for much of the success of Love Valley. To many of the town's residents, Mr. Barker embodied the traditional values and rugged individualism that for nearly 10 years defined the community symbolically. The election results were hardly in doubt from the moment of his announcement to run. Mr. Barker, like many of the candidates for commissioner, supported improvements in the town that would allow for modest growth. Improved roads, water, and sewer systems would not only make some growth possible, but would improve the lives of citizens of Love Valley. In addition, Barker supported strong law enforcement and pledged to make town govern-ment responsive to the citizens. Echoing some of his son's Jeffersonian ideals, Barker said the town should be governed by the valley citizens rather than by a powerful mayor or town government. Finally, perhaps to separate himself from a vision of aggressive growth and development, Barker committed himself to continuing the direction the Valley had taken up to that point and to continuing wholesome entertainment for citizens and visitors. Barker won easily, and the town citizens demonstrated their support for their current lifestyle rather than embarking on a program of development of Love Valley as a commercial and industrial site.

As the calendar approached May 18, the political story in Love Valley became more complicated and more interesting. No one else ran for mayor, but eight candidates ran for five seats on the town commission. Most of the candidates supported a vision including infrastructure improvements to the town while maintaining the western atmosphere of main street and its buildings. Five of the candidates were elected to commission seats, and the first governing body of the town had been selected.[23] On May 21, 1963, this group, headed by Barker, Sr., met at the Long Branch Cafe for their first official act of government. The town board was busy that night setting the town in motion. A regular meeting place had to be established, and no one could think of a better place than the Long Branch. Strong law enforcement had been on the platform of Mayor Barker, so a chief of police was chosen. The group chose a law firm as the town attorney, a commissioner as mayor pro tem, and a local bank as depository for town funds.[24] The beginnings of the town as a political entity may not have been momentous for anyone outside of Love Valley; however, this event did chart the future direction of the town as the residents chose one vision of the town over another, and the incorporation of Love Valley and the town's first election fulfilled another of Andy Barker's political dreams. There were at least two left, and Barker spent a good part of the following 20 years pursuing them.

By the early part of 1963, it was no secret that Andy Barker planned to run for the state senate in 1964, and he began to outline his political agenda of reform long before he officially announced his candidacy. Again, his platform included Jeffersonian ideals and Populist themes. Barker emphasized his Jeffersonian idealism as the route to social reform.[25] Yet he balanced this with a special concentration on his rural constituency by touching Populist sympathies and by emphasizing rural needs. Barker's general Jeffersonian idealism was most obvious in his campaign literature and was summed up succinctly in a letter Barker penned after his defeat in the Democratic primary.[26] The following excerpt from that letter demonstrated Barker's basic political philosophy and promised that he would continue to fight for his political reforms. In the letter, Barker portrayed himself as the leader of an antiestablishment political libertarianism that would certainly catch on as more and more people became aware of the movement's philosophy:

When entering this campaign I was one and alone in the fight. Now I have several thousand dedicated loyal supporters who are not committed to either gubernatorial candidate nor to "the machine" or any special interest group in the field of politics in our state. My campaign card read "to be your humble servant." It did not read "if elected." This pledge I still keep.

I pledge to the following program:

1. To work for general improvements among the senior citizens of our 27th district and the state of North Carolina also.

2. To begin a program for heavy equipment and industrial schools for high school dropouts in our district and in our state at large.

3. The preservation of R.E.A. in sensible ways that are good for all concerned.

4. The improvement of life for the small "dirt Farmer" of North Carolina.

5. To improve working standards of all factory workers in our state.

6. To work toward secondary roads general improvement.

7. To work for the correction of grievances for our State Highway Patrol system employees.

8. To strive for the state employee to receive time and one half for all his overtime work.

9. To work for the elimination of large billboards on our Interstate Highway system.

10. To always work for a better educational program for our children.

11. We stand for a strong remodeling of our whole structure of taxation.

12. We are for a general survey of our North Carolina Highway safety program and for immediate improvements of Highway safety marking signs.

How will I begin this program?

Not being committed to any candidate, I and my dedicated supporters are in position to do some political horse trading to give more life to these basic needs of the people and the programs we support.

These needs for these thousands of voters must be recognized by any candidate for any office before he will qualify for our support.

My dedicated supporters have proven that they cannot be bought by "the machine" or any other political faction. We are the people's people. We are not new dealers or fair dealers because in the dealing someone always gets dealt out. We are Jeffersonian Democrats who are dedicated for the betterment of life for all people. . . .[27]

Some of Barker's proposals were mostly idealism with only incipient practical plans while others were well developed and thought out. For instance, Barker's educational proposals demonstrated a developed plan of implementation and practicality and at the same time exemplified his concern for the needs of his rural supporters. In the early sixties, mobile units for classrooms solved many of the needs of school systems facing shrinking budgets and increased facilities demand created by increasing numbers of students. The experiment was successful, and in many cases, mobile units still provide classroom space for youngsters across rural North Carolina. Barker took the idea, revised it to benefit rural and poor school systems, and submitted the concept to the Iredell County School Board. His goal was to provide equal opportunities to school children in the rural areas of Iredell County, who had fewer facilities, without implementing a full scale consolidation and building program, which he believed the county could not afford.

Barker's plan involved taking the mobile units and making them truly mobile and transportable from school to school. One mobile unit could be outfitted for a subject requiring special equipment (such as chemistry or typing) and then transported from school to school throughout the county on a rotation basis.[28] According to Barker, this plan would eliminate the need to transport students long distances to a consolidated classroom (and would thus provide more time on task for students), the mobile classroom plan could be ready for implementation almost immediately and at half the cost for building a consolidated classroom, and the traveling teacher could use transport time to plan or simply relax and prepare for the next class. Barker outlined a detailed plan that comprehensively addressed problems of school spirit, community schools, sports, summer school, lighting, and more.[29]

Barker's revolutionary ideas even attracted the attention of a professor of administration in the Department of Education at the University of North Carolina at Chapel Hill, who suggested that Barker's proposals had merit and should at least be explored.[30] Nevertheless, his concept received little attention, and the Board of Education continued with consolidation plans that ultimately resulted in new schools and some of the ills Barker feared such as long travel times for students. Like so much of what Barker proposed through his political idealism, the mobile classroom concept was born of practicality with an eye toward the preservation of rural communities and the rural way of life.

* * *

The first 10 years of Love Valley's political life culminated with the beginnings of a town, yet its founder had still not realized two of his political goals, becoming a North Carolina senator and North Carolina's governor. Andy Barker did not give up on his idealism and refused to stop believing that the political arena was the stage for philanthropic activity. He did not give up on his dream of becoming governor, either. Toward that goal, Barker began the second decade of the town's existence with Love Valley as his base and with political connections refusing to let him rest. An invitation to Andy and Ellenora to attend and participate in the January 20 inauguration of Lyndon Baines Johnson as President and of Hubert Horatio Humphrey as Vice President started their 1965 off on a political trek. Later that year, in May, Andy Barker ran unopposed for the mayor of Love Valley after his father decided not to seek reelection, and his long tenure as mayor began.

The first decade of Love Valley had come to an end, but the promotion of the Valley, the philanthropy of its residents, and the political activity that suggested an era long since past continued, and still continues.

6

Controversy and Change:
The Love Valley Rock Festival

"The show must go on" is a phrase that suggests the inexhaustibility of the human spirit and the determined perseverance of those who continue in the face of tremendous adversity. It is a phrase that Andy Barker is partial to and that aptly describes Love Valley from 1965 to 1975. Change and controversy plagued Love Valley during those years—some of the changes were causes of joyous celebration; some caused immense pain and distrust; some simply signaled the incredible upheaval that American society was experiencing in every nook and cranny of a vast country. After 1965, Love Valley retained its unique position as a harbinger of foregone values and community life, but the values were sometimes obscured and the community changed face, at least to those outside the Valley. Change and controversy became the major themes of Love Valley during its second decade, and nowhere is this seen more clearly than in the 1970 Love Valley Rock Festival.

Barker's political philosophy informed the character of the town and the political independence of the town's citizenry during much of this decade. This philosophy even extended into economic organization and experimentation at various points in the town's history through reform experiments such as Barker's heavy equipment school. The town also tried to initiate a nonprofit corporation to sponsor social and educational reform.[1] This experimental economic venture grew directly out of Barker's religious vision and political aspirations. Of course, this interesting combination of religious belief, political ideology, and economic programs makes up part of the utopian impetus of Love Valley. Love Valley as a political and economic utopian experiment can be seen in the growing communitarianism of the town during the sixties, especially with the influx of counterculture hippies before, during, and after the 1970 rock festival. This event provoked ire among Love Valley's neighbors in surrounding communities, aroused suspicions, and suggested deviance to its neighbors.

By the end of the rock festival, life in Love Valley was in such turmoil and was so fragmented that a new era in the history of the town began. Although the religious element was still present and the political and social critiques would later result in Barker's running for governor twice, Love Valley had lost momentum in these areas. The religious and political influence of Barker and the town were forever damaged by the adverse effects of the rock festival.

* * *

Love Valley's second decade began where the first left off—political aspirations, philanthropic ventures, and promotional activities marked the spirit of the town. Nevertheless, these activities brought new faces to the Valley, and instead of presenting the town in a positive light, these ventures engendered controversy from the larger Iredell County community. Even when controversy was absent, change for the Valley was inevitable. By 1965, Barker and Love Valley sought to implement its populist political and utopian religious goals by turning to government agencies and focusing on economic betterment for North Carolina communities. At first the move met little resistance. However, eventually the programs initiated by Valley residents roused incipient frustrations based on racial tensions and the civil rights movement of the sixties.

The first of Barker's economic betterment programs caused little controversy because its goals were never realized. Nevertheless, as much as any of his previous ventures, it reflected the social utopian goals of the community dedicated to political activism, economic opportunity, and religious grounding. In April of 1965, Barker formulated plans to organize and conduct a heavy equipment school in Love Valley and was seeking support from North Carolina political leaders and monetary support from governmental agencies. The plan received considerable attention, but, like so many other ideas, it eventually faded from lack of funding.

Barker planned for the town of Love Valley to run a nonprofit, two-year training school for high school graduates that would be the equivalent of vocational training or college credits for on-the-job experience. The goal of the training would be to produce graduates capable of operating construction equipment and supervising in all phases of commercial construction (including design and maintenance). Such a goal would provide a promising career future for high school graduates who otherwise might not have continued their education.

In addition to Barker's goal of providing a means to better the economic potential of those who would attend his school, he envisioned a second goal of his school that went beyond vocational training and that mirrored his dream of a utopian society. The students of the Love Valley school would also be tutored in religion, recreation, education, and physical fitness. Such a program of instruction would be tightly monitored by a preacher and a housemother who would supervise the students in the attempt to build character and self-confidence as well as teaching a skill. Thus conceived, the heavy equipment school would continue the utopian goals of Love Valley itself by seeking to instill community values through an ethic based on work and traditional religious values and beliefs.

Barker presented the plan to governmental leaders and to North Carolina Governor Dan K. Moore. Moore noted that not only would the participants benefit but that the school would also provide a boost to the "mountain area."[2] After receiving verbal support from several politicians and from the Bureau of Apprenticeship and Training in Salisbury, Barker began searching for financial backing. Efforts with government agencies produced exuberant praise but no dollars, and funding sources consistently turned a deaf ear to the project.[3] Apparently, suspicion over Barker's motives for establishing the school undermined his efforts among politicians who feared Barker would be the one to gain from the venture. Finally, after a government inventory of equipment and a bill of good health cleared away some suspicions, Barker received necessary approval for the school. It began with 5 females and 23 males. According to Barker, government red tape made the venture impractical, and after operating on a limited basis, the construction school was abandoned. Nevertheless, the populist and utopian goals behind the project continued and were resurrected in other programs.

Later in the year, Barker continued to try to implement his utopian social vision in a way that would have an impact on an area beyond the town limits of Love Valley. In September of 1965, Barker announced that the Love Valley Town Council had approved a "non-profit corporation" for social and educational reform. The goal of the group was to organize an Iredell County Community Action Program making use of funds from the Economic Opportunity Act of 1964 (EOA), an anti-poverty governmental program that provided revenue funds to communities with an organized community action program.[4] Under the EOA, the federal government would provide funds to either state, local, or non-profit private organizations to pay for programs and education designed to better economic conditions in poverty stricken areas. The community would pay for 10 percent of the total cost with the federal government funding up to 90 percent of the program's budget. The plan seemed to be a noble one, and Barker set out to garner support for the 10 percent of funds the community would contribute. This is where the controversy began.

Apparently, after approaching members of the county commission individually, Barker was convinced that the commission would not support the Community Action Program. Barker sought support from others including leaders from some county-affiliated groups and from the NAACP. Barker put together a committee of 16 people in December of 1965 to organize the group. A field representative from Raleigh attended the meeting and provided some startling statistics about Iredell County to convince the group of the need of federal assistance in combating rural and urban poverty and illiteracy. According to his figures, one-third of the families in Iredell County lived off an income of less than $3,000 per year. The economic picture was bleak: joblessness and substandard housing affected substantial percentages of the county's population. Moreover, the statistics suggested a problem with educational levels in the county. Of county residents over the age of 25, the equivalent (or less) of a fifth-grade education characterized 4,600 of them, while over 22 percent of 16- and 17-year-old students were not enrolled in any school.[5] These figures persuaded the group that they should seek EOA funds; however, the procedures for seeking funds became a source of contention.

Several within the group felt uncomfortable pursuing the organization of a community action group without first approaching the county commissioners. Barker tried to convince the group that he had been stonewalled by individual members of the commission. Eventually, the president of the local unit of the NAACP moved to incorporate a group and to petition the federal government for funds under the EOA. The group voted for incorporation with 14 yes votes and 2 abstentions. Barker informed the group that the Love Valley Town Council had voted to pay for the papers of incorporation and to support the non-profit effort.[6]

The controversy that ensued involved a newspaper article and subsequent letter to the editor by Barker. Certain comments in the article attributed to Barker apparently alienated some county commissioners, and those comments, in addition to the NAACP presence at the meeting, left the impression that the community action group would become a special interest group or an arm for the local NAACP. Such impressions raised racial suspicion and threatened to destroy the program, and in order to allay such fears, Barker backed out of the organization (but Love Valley retained a representative) while the group took their plan to the county commissioners. The commissioners were assured that the organization would be made up of a diverse collection of interests and that no single group would exercise undue influence.[7]

In addition, Barker tried to calm suspicions that might influence public perceptions by writing a letter to the local newspaper to try to clear up comments attributed to him by the press. Specifically, he stated the meeting was not an NAACP rally and the committee included representation from a variety of groups and concerns in the county. Barker said, "It was a meeting of people who . . . are dedicated and interested in doing something for their community and the color of their skin, religion, or politics makes no difference." Barker went on to clear up misunderstandings concerning quotes that appeared to be derogatory toward the commissioners and commented that the group harbored no ill will toward the commission. He ended his letter by stating that "this program is a good program, a worthwhile program, and I have worked hard to try to get it into operation within the county, working without prejudice, without discrimination, and without ill will."[8]

Faced with the discontinuance of his heavy equipment school and the controversy concerning his community action venture, Barker continued to push for social reform and to use Love Valley as a religious, political, and economic base for such change. Late in 1965 and into 1966, Barker implemented an experimental economic program at Love Valley for Lumbee Native Americans. During a meeting with the North Carolina Fund's Mobility Project at a Raleigh convention, Barker was intrigued by the fund's attempt to transplant Lumbee Native Americans from Robeson County to the more prosperous and economically sound Piedmont region of the state. The Lumbees in the program were generally tenant farmers or part-time mill workers who managed to eke out an existence on less than $1,000 a year, and the Mobility Project attempted to find the participants more promising work and better housing. Barker loved the idea and immediately confronted the fund about helping with the program.

Barker learned that governmental grants paid to relocate families and provided loans until they were established in a new job and that the project's responsibilities included finding jobs and housing for the newly relocated families. The jobs were easy to find throughout the Piedmont, including Statesville; however, low-cost housing was at a critical shortage. Barker provided land and helped to arrange the acquisition of governmental surplus marine trailers to act as temporary housing for newly relocated Lumbees until they could get started and find permanent housing. In addition, Barker invested considerable money preparing the lots and providing plumbing for the trailers. His hope was to attract many new residents from poor areas, to help them situate themselves with good jobs in the Statesville area, and to assist them in securing land, perhaps in Love Valley, for permanent homes. In addition, Barker provided transportation for workers from Love Valley to their jobs in Statesville and surrounding areas and gave free training to some of the younger men in construction techniques and heavy equipment operation. What Barker was unable to achieve through his heavy equipment school he was able to provide to a few of the Lumbee Native Americans who found their way to Love Valley.[9]

The North Carolina Fund's Mobility Project was only partially successful, and Love Valley housing and training played a large role in the transition of several families. Some did not make it through the program—they moved home because of homesickness or the frustrations that temporary housing and isolation could bring. However, others persevered, worked hard, learned skills, became involved in the community affairs of Love Valley, and eventually blazed a new life for themselves. The limited success Barker experienced with this project helped ease his disappointment over the heavy equipment school and the controversy generated by the community action organization. However, even though the disappointment was eased, the controversy continued to brew under the surface. Suspicions already raised against Love Valley were being heightened by the uncertainty of the new residents the Valley was bringing to northern Iredell County, and there were minor episodes of violence stemming from these tensions. These suspicions would simply not go away and were vented in several different ways.

In addition to the suspicions created and controversies generated by Barker's social programs, concern from the surrounding communities was expressed frequently about the type of people and activities that some thought characterized the Valley. During the early sixties, Love Valley began to attract motorcycle enthusiasts. Love Valley even began to sponsor motorcycle rodeos and events, and it was not uncommon for motorcycle clubs to frequent Love Valley. The existence of these clubs and events were directed as any other event in Love Valley, and many of the events were sponsored to help charities. For example, the Blue Angels Motorcycle Club sponsored a fund-raiser in the Valley for the North Carolina Chapter of the Multiple Sclerosis Society. For a while, Love Valley became a curious mixture of horses, cowboys, iron machines, booming Harleys, and motorcycle enthusiasts. Nevertheless, the public perceived these motorcycle groups as "gangs" and their activities as less than honorable. This was perhaps an unfair but common assumption to make in the mid-sixties.

Barker and the community suffered the ire of several disgruntled neighbors because the perception of Love Valley as a gathering spot for outlaws and motorcycle thugs was growing. One letter to the local newspaper summed up the growing discontent. A frustrated neighbor wrote complaining about the noisy motorcycles in Love Valley interrupting church services nearby. The letter writer referred to Love Valley as "a little Sodom and Gomorrah" and accused Love Valley of negatively influencing young people.[10] During the late sixties, what was one person's religious and social utopia was quickly becoming others' "Sodom and Gomorrah."

Meanwhile, amid the growing community discontent with Love Valley, Barker and the town tried to carry on business as usual. The town newspaper became a weekly paper, the Double M Stables opened in Love Valley, Barker traveled to Greenville and paid a visit to City Hall on horseback. He continued his relationship with state Democrats, he was reelected mayor in 1967 by unanimous vote, and Ellenora Barker became the justice of the peace the same year. None of the Love Valley antics that made this town unique abated as Love Valley continued to play host to foreign dignitaries and ambassadors.

Nevertheless, the controversy ensuing during the late sixties led to change in the little town—social programs failed, economic ventures went sour, local press and publicity became increasingly more hostile, and development of the town was slowed. In short, Barker's development of Love Valley as a social and economic utopia began to slowly fail. These failures became evident during a series of events from 1967 to 1969. The first hint that controversy had slowed development came with the failure of a real estate venture instituted by Barker. During the summer of 1967, Barker planned a land rush for Labor Day at Love Valley. Barker included 800 acres in the land rush, and for a $200 fee, participants could claim a 75 x 150 foot lot for building a cabin. The lots would be claimed on the basis of who could outrace the competitors to the most desirable locations in the tradition of the old land rushes. The competitors would be assembled at a common spot a few hundred yards south of the land up for grabs and would be allowed to race for their preferred spot only by means of horseback, in horse-drawn buggies, or by foot (no motorized vehicles or bicycles were allowed). The land in question was described as scenic with woods and streams and was promoted as prime vacation or residential property.[11] Nevertheless, the 1967 Great Love Valley Land Rush proved to be a colossal failure. There was no race for lots because there were no potential purchasers. Barker was unable to muster even the least bit of interest in the event, presumably because the land was too remote and because interest in Love Valley was fading. The failure of the land rush would not have worried the promoter of Love Valley had it not come at a time when other promotions were going sour as well. What probably would have been a roaring success 10 years earlier (or even 5) was in 1967 a dismal failure, and it caused Barker no small concern that interest in the community was dying out. Amid worries that his social and recreational experiment was experienc-

ing the beginnings of a slow death, Barker worked even harder to promote the town with new ideas to generate interest.

One such promotional venture initiated an atmosphere of excitement during the spring and summer of 1968. In March of 1968, Twentieth Century Fox announced plans to film a movie, *John Brown's Body,* in
and around Statesville. The plot of the movie called for a depiction of
life during the Civil War era, and scenes called for, among other things, a
nineteenth-century Tennessee town. Of course, this proved to be a natural invitation for Love Valley to get involved and to promote the town
once again. Andy Barker arranged for remodeling of the town to specifications of the film crew, and the producers of the movie decided to shoot
several of the scenes in the mountains surrounding the western town. A
production crew with Twentieth Century Fox visited the Statesville area
and left with high praise for Barker and the spirit of cooperation that pervaded Love Valley and surrounding areas. By the middle of March,
excitement ran high, and Barker seemed to have hit upon the promotional tool that would once again boost Love Valley's profile to the
public.[12]

As spring gave way to summer, the Iredell County area buzzed with
enthusiasm at the prospects of Hollywood coming to the small, rural
community, plans were being laid and finalized for site preparation,
Love Valley and its role in the production of the movie were in the news,
and Andy Barker was his old self, busy building, directing, planning,
reconstructing, and adding life to his North Iredell community. By June,
the film studio had leased land from Barker for shooting and had contracted Barker as the local contact man responsible for finding "extras"
for the movie.

In addition to locating 400 or so people from Iredell and surrounding areas, Barker was also working to ensure enough horses, mules, and
wagons would be available for the scenes to be shot in and around
Iredell County. Many of the workers would camp at Love Valley and
most of the horses would be boarded there during filming.

With the help of the Statesville Chamber of Commerce, the film
executives chose several sites in Iredell and Wilkes counties and began
constructing sets. Split rail fences were erected, reconstruction of a farm
house was begun, and a bridge was constructed. Andy Barker was designated to reconstruct one set, which would depict a farm and homestead
from the time period. He began the project with his usual earnest zeal for
authenticity. The set, to be built on his property, called for a cabin, barn,
cornfield, and split rail fence. Barker obtained a cabin that dated to the
1830s, repaired and restored it in detail, right down to the handmade oak
shingles on the roof. A well with windlass was added, a barn was recon-

structed, and the corn was planted so the stalks would be growing during the shooting of the movie.[13] Barker and his son, Jet, worked tirelessly on the set to meet the standards of the film crew. They used a nineteenth-century method of stonework, employing mud for the adhesive; they recreated a haystack as it would have appeared before the advent of baling machines; they built a chicken coup to nineteenth-century specifications. In short, the Barkers reconstructed a farm of museum quality.[14]

Throughout the late summer and fall of 1968, numerous delays in filming occurred but did not dampen the spirits of the local people who worked to bring the film industry to Iredell County. Even into the early months of 1969, Barker and others still planned for the film to be a big boost to the area. Then, suddenly in June, Twentieth Century Fox canceled the project. The cancellation was a blow for Barker, who had worked as hard as anyone to make the filming a success. Abandonment by Hollywood added one more disappointment to a run of bad luck for the visionary and his town. Nevertheless, the disappointment Barker felt for the town was somehow muted by the positive changes he felt from his family. His children were becoming adults, and those changes added a bit of perspective to the upsetting events of the recent months.

On May 13, 1969, the picture of a young bride ran in the local newspaper—the bride was Mary Tonda Barker (Tonda), Andy and Ellenora's first child, and she had married David Haynes Smith four days earlier. This bride was the same girl who ran her own business as a teenager and who was as beautiful on horseback in western clothing as she was in a wedding gown. It seemed only a short while earlier that David had wandered into the Barker's kitchen, and suddenly he was a part of the family, having long since become part of the Love Valley family. David was one of the young men who came to Love Valley with a Wake Forest University fraternity looking to become part of the movie project. But long after the excitement of the movie had died down and the fraternity made its way back to the Winston-Salem campus, David Smith stayed in Love Valley, fell in love, and married into the "first family of Love Valley."

Jet, as well, was growing up and becoming increasingly involved in Love Valley Enterprises. It was clear by this time that Barker's plan was to groom the teenager to follow his father's footsteps and continue the Love Valley experiment. But Jet's plans did not exactly coincide with his father's vision. If he had ambitions of continuing the Love Valley dream, it was clear his own dreams would come first, and this included years later caring for his own family. Through all the years and changes Love Valley was about to witness, Tonda and Jet provided a stabilizing force in the community. After all, Love Valley might have been the vision of the elder Barkers, but Tonda and Jet were children of Love Valley who sacrificed much for the dream and who in many respects gave that vision substance.

All of these events, negative and positive, signaled change for Love Valley. A generation was coming of age; change was inevitable; the town was about to lose its innocence. And this overwhelming tide of transition ushered in by numerous and unavoidable changes was symbolized perhaps most poignantly in September when the state closed down the Love Valley jail because it did not meet state standards. The closing of the Love Valley jail posed no threat to security in the town; however, it did bring to close another era in the town's history. Barker's tie to history was slowly being severed, his promotional activities were being overshadowed, and the town's uniqueness was quietly being compromised. With the closing of the jail, only the stories were left of the law breakers and the long arm of the law that brought them to justice. But Love Valley residents still had their memories of frontier justice, including a tale of a jail break where the buddy of three prisoners roped a horse to the window bars and pulled the wall down to free his friends.[15]

The closing of the Love Valley jail seemed a minor event at the time, but in retrospect, the jail closed an era in the history of the town. Gone, at least for a time, were the carefree days of playing cowboy and practicing frontier justice—gone, at least for a time, was the relentless quest for a pristine past when the difference in right and wrong was clear. And with the demise of the jail came the blurring of the lines of justice and rightness. Love Valley was about to enter the most difficult period of its history—friend would be pitted against friend and neighbor against neighbor as the quest for utopia changed to the quest for survival. The next few years would be difficult ones for Love Valley, would test the mettle of everyone associated with the town, and would lead to reevaluation of the purpose and direction of the community.

It started one evening after dinner.[16] Tonda, David, and Jet were chatting with Barker when news of a rock festival came on the television. Andy's eyes gleamed; Jet's lit up. Jet turned to his father and asked a very innocent question, "Daddy, can I go to Georgia to the rock concert?"

What inspired Barker to respond to Jet in the way he did is a mystery. Perhaps he sensed the tide of change that had overtaken his family and town and wanted to control it. Perhaps he thought he could promote the town and make some money. Perhaps he envisioned a way to seek the ideal his experiment had fostered from the beginning—the ideal of family-centered wholesome activity for young people. Barker had just finished hosting the visiting ambassador from South Vietnam[17] and was

Fig. 10. The Love Valley Jail. The jail has been closed since 1969, but the building still stands. This photograph is from the 1960s. Love Valley photo archives, used by permission of Andy Barker.

looking for another challenge. Probably all of these things flashed through Barker's mind in an instant, and he responded in characteristic Andy Barker style: "There's no need to do that. We'll have one here." By the next morning, some four weeks before the festival would occur, David made a few phone calls and preparations were under way.

The time was early 1970, Andy Barker knew absolutely nothing about rock concerts, and his knowledge of music barely extended beyond the classical strains that played constantly on his radio. He was naive about the existence of drugs and had barely heard of Woodstock. All he knew was that he could promote and that he could provide some entertainment for the kids while earning some money for the town. From the beginning when Barker jumped head first into the concert promotion business, he had two objectives in mind: He wanted to stage a rock festival that, like his other promotions, would provide a wholesome environment for local youth, and he wanted to raise enough money to provide a sewer system for the town. He achieved neither objective, and the rock festival turned out to be the gravest mistake in the history of Love Valley. The Love Valley Rock Festival capped off a series of bad-luck ventures for Barker and the town and almost destroyed Love Valley in the process. What would he do differently, now? "I would not do it," he responded. "It was an exciting time, but there will never be another rock festival in Love Valley."[18]

* * *

Responses to the Love Valley rock festival ran the gamut. The festival-goers reveled in the spirit of love and goodwill. Many local residents were appalled by hippies swimming naked in the local pond, by the ragged clothes of festival goers, and by the rumors of unisex showers. Some festival goers considered Andy Barker to be one of them, an "anti-establishment" hero they could trust. Some local residents called upon God to send down righteous judgment on Barker and his Sodom and Gomorrah. Some were envious of Barker's project, others incredulous. Most of all, people were shocked: from the surprise of the sheer numbers of attendees to the utter disgust over public nudity and sexual intercourse in local farmers' cornfields.

Whatever the impressions, they were lasting and they brought a storm of protest from the surrounding communities of North Iredell and Statesville. But much of the vehemence expressed toward the little town came not simply from the festival. Rather, the festival provided the opportunity for venting frustrations and concerns about Love Valley that had been building probably from the beginning of the town and from at least the mid-sixties. Love Valley's second decade was marked by controversy and change at every turn, and this culminated in the Love Valley Rock Festival.

The festival had its genesis with Jet's desire to go to Georgia to a rock festival that was scheduled for a small rural community south of Macon. Byron, Georgia, was the site of the second annual Atlanta Pop Festival to be held July 3-5. Jet and Tonda were interested in the festival because of their interest in a southern rock group, the Allman Brothers Band. That interest eventually evolved into a friendship with members of the band, especially guitarist Dickey Betts and a drummer, Butch Trucks.

A scant three weeks before the event, David was able to book several bands to come to Love Valley. He and Tonda both had experience booking bands to play at college events at Peace College and Wake Forest University, but they had never undertaken anything of this magnitude. Nevertheless, David was able to work with an agent who had connections with Capricorn recording artists and contracted such bands as Wet Willie, Johnny Jenkins, and Big Brother. But by far, the real accomplishment was booking the Allman Brothers Band as the headline act. The Allman Brothers Band was already known throughout the Southeast and was beginning to command a national audience—they were sure to attract a crowd. When some of the band members visited Love Valley just before the festival, they fell in love with the place.

Eventually, some members of the band and some roadies began to make Love Valley a stopping off place, an unofficial escape from the rigors of the road. They rode horses or used the solitude of the place to hone musical skills without distraction. The band members were caught up in the whole cowboy persona and were accepted immediately by residents of Love Valley. Andy Barker treated the band members like royalty as they made their own climb to success and celebrity.[19]

As the festival date rapidly approached, David planned to travel to Byron to the Atlanta Pop Festival so he could learn how to plan for the Love Valley event. The Byron Festival was a huge undertaking bringing together artists like the Allman Brothers, B. B. King, Jimi Hendrix, John Sebastian, Procol Harum, Jethro Tull, the Bob Seger System, and Johnny Winter. About 400,000 to 500,000 people attended the three-day event, the heat soared around 100 degrees, and problems with drugs and some violence erupted.[20] So, in the midst of planning for the Love Valley event, which was only two weeks away, David, Tonda, and Jet crowded into the family station wagon with a tent and sleeping bags and headed for Byron. What they saw magnified the enormity of the task they had ahead of them.

The Byron experience was an eye-opener for the youngsters from Love Valley. On the one hand, they found themselves backstage with artists like Jimi Hendrix, B. B. King, and the Allman Brothers and could not have been happier. On the other hand, they were confronted first hand with the problems associated with hosting a rock festival. As the Byron festival wore on, the heat encouraged public nudity and short tempers among festival goers. Drugs were rampant, and medical care was scarce. The sights and sounds of naked young women and men and rock and roll music flabbergasted 18-year-old Jet, whose life in Love Valley had been fairly sheltered. Meanwhile, David circulated through the crowd, held business meetings with bands and sound crews, took care of some last-minute details, and suddenly realized that in two weeks, Love Valley was going to become a city overnight. After listening to a mesmerizing set from singer John Sebastian, the three Love Valleyites headed back to North Carolina, barely ahead of the crowd from Byron.[21]

Within a day or two after the Atlanta Pop Festival, festival goers began to arrive at Love Valley. As the time for the festival approached, a Hollywood film crew arrived as well. David and Tonda had arranged for a film crew from Hollywood to take footage of the concert for a movie. In the days before the festival, David was on the phone practically 24 hours a day, Barker hired a drifter who wandered into the town to help with last minute arrangements, Barker himself was everywhere at once, Jet was building a stage in the stadium, Tonda was busy cooking for the film crew, and the film crew was busy turning an old log cabin into a sophisticated sound studio. Organizing the concert was fast paced and furious, but it worked, and David and Tonda efficiently planned an event of great magnitude. They had planned for every contingency, and everything might have gone smoothly had it not been for those things that were beyond their control: the behavior of the crowd and the reaction of local residents.[22]

As these preparations were taking place, news of the Byron concert filtered up to North Carolina and people around Love Valley began to get nervous. Reported incidents of drug use, public nudity, and questionable moral behavior made their way to the town and some residents began to balk at the idea of the same thing happening to the rural community around Love Valley. Reports from Byron indicated that most of the 7,000 persons who were treated during the festival by medical officials were treated for drug overdoses, that marijuana smoke filled the air, and that couples copulated openly and freely. Barker, however, was determined that Love Valley could promote and host this event without the trouble associated with Woodstock and Byron. He maintained that he could provide wholesome entertainment for young people by establishing a controlled atmosphere. Barker blamed the problems at Byron on two factors: "shyster promoters" and the incredible heat of Byron, Georgia. He felt he could combat those problems by providing a shaded arena, by holding events only in the cooler evening hours, and by keeping the promotion of the event free from greed. In the end, Barker's naive faith in "the kids" who attended the festival led to his undoing. In an interview, Barker expressed his complete confidence and trust that concert attendees would behave out of goodwill.[23]

Amid uncertainty about what would happen, the weekend of the show came quickly. Just before the concert date, the film crew was ready to shoot. This added to the already high level of excitement that pervaded the town. Tonda and David leased the Lawses Motel to the film crew and Tonda fed the crew, while Ellenora's kitchen was turned into a restaurant for the other workers associated with the filming and with the concert. The spirit began to rise as July 17 approached, almost all the preparations were completed, the film crew was ready, Barker and his workers put the finishing touches on the stage just hours before the first band was to play, and the festival goers began to arrive in the Valley—and they kept coming! No one knew how many people would come to the Love Valley event, but Barker projected a few thousand would come, a number comparable to the number of visitors on a big rodeo weekend. But more than a few thousand made the journey to Love Valley. Despite its hasty organization and very little promotion, the word spread quickly, and no one was quite prepared for the number of people who descended upon the little North Iredell town. On the weekend of July 17, 1970, the population of Love Valley soared from about 75 to about 75,000! Estimates ranged from 75,000 to 250,000, but even with the conservative number, North Iredell was busting at the seams.

By Thursday night, July 16, estimates of visitors topped 5,000 and gave a feel for what was to occur during the three-day festival. State Bureau of Investigation agents had arrived on the scene because of the likelihood of illegal drug activity, and by early Friday afternoon, there had been 12 drug-related arrests involving marijuana, LSD, and speed. The highway patrol began stopping cars and searching them as they entered Love Valley. As word spread, festival goers simply started parking their cars on the side of the road and walking to Love Valley. The result was bottlenecked traffic for miles and disgruntled farmers whose fields were trampled by hippies on the hoof. Traffic jams plagued the roads from Love Valley to Statesville as young people continued to find their way to the festival.[24] To exacerbate potential problems, the weather was hot.

By Friday afternoon, it was clear that more people than anyone expected would show up for the festival. Still estimates were conservatively placed at 30,000 to 40,000, and these numbers sent David and Barker scrambling to try to deal with the problems such numbers would cause. Several first aid stations were set up in the camping area, and a temporary medical service center was established in the town. Barker put out a call for doctors who would volunteer their services during the festival, while people with injuries and health problems flooded the aid stations to be treated for problems ranging from minor cuts and abrasions to hepatitis and venereal disease.[25] Before the festival even started, Barker's idealism was shattered.

By Sunday morning, at least 75,000 people had packed into Love Valley, one person was dead, another suffered a serious gun-shot wound, a rape had been reported, some claimed that rampant violence and drug use went unreported by the media, and the Iredell County jail was busting at the seams. But worse than these confirmed reports were the rumors that circulated concerning the activities at the festival.[26] The rumors included stories of public nudity and sexual intercourse, babies being born, Andy Barker being beaten by drug-crazed hippies, Andy Barker being dead, and on and on. Obviously, some of these stories were baseless, others were exaggerations, some were true. Nevertheless, what was happening in this tiny little town was very interesting, and it was attracting a lot of attention.

A 21-year-old Fort Bragg soldier died of heatstroke during the festival, and a shooting occurred on Saturday afternoon. A deputy marshal at Love Valley was involved in shooting a festival-goer with a shotgun. When the incident occurred, the deputy was carrying a can of mace, a pistol, and a 12-gauge shotgun. The shooting stemmed from an argument over tickets; however, the details of the events leading up to the confrontation were sketchy and the stories did not coincide. Friends of the victim claimed the deputy approached them about tickets, threatened to shoot them, and then pulled the trigger. The deputy maintained the victim and his friends circled him and the victim tried to wrest the gun from him. During the struggle, the gun fired and hit the victim in the right arm.[27] Finally, a reported rape (a charge that was dropped a few days later) convinced local residents that what was going on in Love Valley was violent, immoral, evil, and a plague upon the community. These stories and others of violence quickly spread to surrounding communities and an orgy of bad press surrounding the festival had begun.

While tensions were heating up in Love Valley itself, some of the 75,000 young people necessarily spilled over into the rural community surrounding the town and even into Statesville. Confrontations between

Fig. 11. The scene at the Love Valley Rock Festival just before the thousands began to arrive. The rodeo arena was transformed into the main stage for the festival. At bottom right is the stage area. At the height of the festival, crowds packed the arena area and overflowed back up the hill (upper left) into the main part of town. *The Sentinel* photo/Bill Ray. Copyright 1970 Piedmont Publishing Company, Inc. All rights reserved. Reprinted with permission. Courtesy of *Winston-Salem Journal.*

farmers and festival-goers who were camping in cornfields, barns, or even yards were not uncommon. Charges that hippies were raiding private gardens or using the farmers' fields as bathrooms or for sexual activities were favorite complaints. Hard stares greeted longhaired visitors on the streets of Statesville, and surrounding communities experienced a mixture of curiosity, revulsion, and fear about how long they might stay and concern over how much moral and physical damage they might do while they were there.

From various accounts, the descriptions of Love Valley for the three days of the festival ranged from "war zone" to "love-in." But it became very clear that outsiders held a very different perception of the event than did those who attended the festival.[28] A newspaper article attempted to highlight the positive aspects of the festival, and this theme was immediately picked up by hundreds of those who attended the event.

Many of those in attendance highlighted the harmony and goodwill of the festival. Was the festival marked by harmony or chaotic amorality? Based on countless eyewitness accounts, photographs, movies, and written descriptions, it would have been something like this:[29]

Those lucky enough to negotiate the traffic and make it to Love Valley during the festival were greeted by an array of longhaired young hippies from the moment they turned off highway 115 until they parked their cars and walked the rest of the way into the town. Even before reaching the town's limits, young people were everywhere, strolling about arm in arm, spread out on blankets in the shade of trees, discussing topics of importance to them such as Kent State, police brutality, civil rights, or just sleeping in the sun and swaying to the sounds of the music in the background. Tents were everywhere, although most of the festival-goers brought little more than a sleeping bag and camped out under the stars. One could hear the music long before reaching the amphitheater and stage area, loudness being a prerequisite of rock 'n' roll music.

The town sported a great variety of dress and hairstyle.[30] The endless traffic of people increased in town—so did the loudness of the music, for the stage area was located just below Main Street in the natural, dirt amphitheater. The streets were packed with people shoulder to shoulder, moving not as individuals but as part of a larger organism. When asked, these hippies insisted that everyone was operating on the principle that all were brothers and sisters and you should not harm a loved one. Indeed, there was uncharacteristic racial harmony and cooperation during the festival at a time when racial tensions were inflamed elsewhere. Perhaps festival-goers were listening to the promoter of the event, Andy Barker, who kicked the festival off by announcing there was only one rule in force for the weekend: the golden rule.

The happenings at the stage area caused the most concern. Standing on the edge of the arena, the site of rodeos and western shows in the past, one was confronted with a sea of people, packed into the stadium as tightly as could be imagined. Beer bottles were strewn everywhere, and a major cause of injury occurred when bare feet encountered broken glass and other litter. Drug use was common and seemed mostly confined to marijuana; however, LSD and harder drugs were used as well.[31]

As dusk fell on Friday night, the music cranked up a notch and the featured bands took the stage. Campfires began to dot the landscape along the periphery of the performance area as people settled in for hours of music, love, and sharing. The stage itself was a masterpiece of workmanship, lit by arc lights that illuminated the crowd and the performers. Psychedelic lights permeated the night's darkness, and a screen above the stage flashed images from old cowboy films to add the Love

Valley signature to the event. People everywhere swayed with the music, danced seductively with new friends, and frolicked gaily in their huge playground. Friday night had a magical quality to it, everything was under control, and the festival planners rested for a few hours. This was to be the last restful moment for the remainder of the weekend.

Saturday dawned hot and balmy, people were still arriving, tempers flared, and conduct began to get out of hand. The shooting may have been one of the few confirmed acts of violence, but many more went unconfirmed throughout the day on Saturday. The town took on an almost surreal atmosphere. Young people listened to music, loved one another, stayed high, and wandered the streets. One young lady stripped naked and danced through the woods above the town scattering marijuana seed like some 1960s Johnny Appleseed. Motorcycle gangs terrorized some of the visitors to the valley and reports of theft were common. Andy Barker was a common sight in town as he roamed the streets with his double-barreled shotgun to keep the peace.

There were few havens where one could escape the heat, the bodies, the drugs, and the mobs. One such place was Tonda and David's room in the hotel. According to David and Tonda, Saturday afternoon found them in their apartment with some of the members of the Allman Brothers Band and their family members. Saturday afternoon baseball was on the tube, and the band members relaxed in the air-conditioned comfort of the Smith's apartment, in part resting before their next set and in part escaping from the craziness on the street. A phone call interrupted the lazy afternoon, at least for David.

Tonda answered the phone—it was her father. Andy Barker was seldom a man of few words, but this time it was different. The harried voice at the other end of the line announced simply, "Tell David to meet me on the street, quick!" When Tonda relayed the news, David scrambled to his feet while the band members looked at each other with concern. They, more than the others, knew what type of trouble this sort of gathering could bring.

After slipping on his boots, David rushed into the street into the throng of hippies and young people. The street was packed, people were shoulder to shoulder, and the heat was unbearable after the air conditioned comfort of his apartment. Somehow, he and Andy ran into each other. Jet was at his father's side, and the elder Barker grabbed David's arm and said simply, "Come with me." David had no idea what was happening, but as the three men made their way through the crowd, he suddenly found himself in an opening. The crowd parted, and for good reason. For the first time, David could see why Andy had made the frantic phone call.

In the street ahead, the crowd had dispersed, and lined up on either side of the street were two rival motorcycle gangs. The gangs were poised for a rumble as they held tight to homemade weapons they had concealed in their jackets. They spewed curses at one another across the street, and the only thing restraining them from all out warfare was the lack of a signal from their leaders. Those leaders were squared off in the middle of the street. Two huge, hairy, bearded, tattooed warriors were face to face, eye to eye, nose to nose. One of the men clutched a logging chain in one hand while the other sported a medieval-looking ax. They seemed moments from splitting each others' heads open when Andy walked up to the two. Jet and David followed. The two bears refused to take their eyes off their opponent as Andy started talking. "Look, these folks are here to have fun, and we're not going to have people like you creating problems. If you want to behave yourselves, you are welcome to stay, if not, get the hell out of here." Andy turned to David and said, "You take the ax, I'll take the chain." For the first time, David realized that Andy did not have the shotgun. Of all the times to leave the gun in the house.

Tonda and her guests watched the episode in horror from the second story window of the hotel. They and other witnesses wondered why they did not split Barker's head wide open. Perhaps Barker's status as folk hero to 75,000 young people held sway over the two warriors as they grimaced one last time. David, not knowing what to expect or do, held out his hand to the six-foot-five-inch monster who was holding the ax. He quietly handed him the ax while his opponent handed Andy the chain. Andy said, "These will be in my house. You can pick them up when you leave town." From that point on, there was no trouble from the motorcycle gangs. In fact, they even helped police the event and keep the peace.[32]

Saturday was a long day of a long weekend. The evening brought some respite and more good music, but the troubles were still there. Sunday brought hope—early morning rain showers encouraged some of the festival participants to leave early; others ended up in the Love Valley Church; still others sponsored their own religious service from the concert stage. The stage service went over well. It combined elements of conservative Christianity, New Age religion, and reincarnation hope. Sunday afternoon began in a spirit of play. The dirt floor of the stadium had become a mud arena from the rain and from earlier efforts to cool off the crowd by hosing them down. People frolicked in the mud and made human chains that were whipped around through the gunk.

The Allman Brothers Band took the stage for the last time and created the most excitement as they enthralled the crowd with searing favorites such as "Statesboro Blues" and "Whipping Post." As the crowd grew more excited and agitated, so did the playfulness in the amphitheater. Suddenly, some of the mud began to fly through the air onto the stage and threatened to end the music.

The crowd reacted in disbelief and tempers began to build. Sensing trouble in the making, Barker (who seemed to be everywhere at once during the festival), took the stage to try to bring order to the unruly crowd. After Barker calmed the audience and talked to Duane Allman, the music began again to cheers and laughter, drifting into the afternoon with a calming effect on those who were listening. Potential chaos had been averted, violence had been avoided, and the festival once again took on the appearance of brotherly love and peace. Other performers such as Blood, Big Brother and the Holding Company were still around and helped to keep the good vibes going, and the festival wound down as it began—with "fun and music, a lot of music."[33]

Unfortunately, by this time, the strain had become unbearable for Barker. He collapsed on the front porch of his home. Those close to him immediately suspected a heart attack, but a persistent Barker was able to convince his family otherwise. A doctor on the scene confirmed that he was exhausted, and Ellenora whisked him away sometime Sunday afternoon. Tonda and David were left to close out the festival and to face the initial community reaction.

In the middle of all this was the movie company, with lights and cameras everywhere. The images obtained from that crew were important even though little of it has been released. The footage contained one of the few existing motion pictures of Duane Allman playing the guitar, and it demonstrated how revolutionary his slide playing was. John Ogden described the importance of the film to understanding Duane's style, agility, and control as a slide player by quoting Arlen Roth from *Guitar Player* magazine.[34]

Finally, Sunday evening came and went, the crowds began to disperse leaving mounds of litter and marijuana crops in their wake. The arena resembled a war zone—much of the surrounding countryside was trampled and littered. Drugs were strewn everywhere, collected, and destroyed. About 30 or 40 of the hippies volunteered to stay around and help clean up the place. Barker was recuperating in some undisclosed location. The Iredell County Sheriff's Department, the North Carolina Highway Patrol, and the State Bureau of Investigation breathed a collective sigh of relief. David, Tonda, and the community sat back to wait for recovery and reaction. Recovery took a while—reaction was swift and immediate.

So ended the longest weekend in Love Valley's history. Andy Barker already regretted the event, but he had nothing but good to say about the young people and how they conducted themselves. And even though there had already been negative publicity from every newspaper in the area and from every major news network, Barker was unprepared for the onslaught about to occur from the community. The hatred was perhaps most explicitly found in the barrage of letters that choked the local papers and expressed venomous contempt for Andy Barker. In articles and letters, local people vented their rage at Andy Barker, at rampant sin and immorality, at the counterculture revolution, and at the people who were responsible for the destruction or vandalism of personal property.[35] Area residents accused Barker of misrepresentation and greed, and they lashed out at the festival goers for trespassing, polluting streams, their "filth," leaving behind trash and feces in fields and yards, nudity, fear of disease, drugs, sex, and alcohol.[36]

Of course, not all the letters received by the local papers were negatively disposed toward Barker, the festival goers, and the festival. A few wrote in support of the event by recognizing Barker's ingenuity in trying to raise money, by comparing the crowd control to other public events such as county fairs and football games, by criticizing religious bigotry on the part of those who spoke out against the festival, by comparing the crime rate at the festival to any city of 75,000, by praising the young people at the festival for their overall feeling of goodwill and cooperative spirit, and by using scripture and religious argument to stress the importance of tolerance.[37] Others pointed out that there were many "hippies" in the Love Valley Church that Sunday morning or that Barker had lost money on the event by letting people in free and by the town raising money to feed those who had no money for food.[38] Nevertheless, the overwhelming response from the surrounding community was negative while the overwhelming response from Love Valley residents was one of relief.

By far, Barker's most ardent public support came from an unexpected source, which also testifies to the extent of national coverage the rock festival achieved. Norman Cousins, of the famed *Saturday Review,* heard of the festival, paid a visit to Love Valley, and included an editorial in *Saturday Review* entitled, "All Hail Andy Barker." Cousins began the article by suggesting Andy Barker be named "man of the year." Cousins went on to praise Barker for his "wisdom" and restraint in handling the entire situation.[39] Throughout his interview with Cousins, Barker refused to have anything but praise for the young people who visited Love Valley referring to them as visitors he trusted and believed in and from whom he could listen and learn. Cousins was taken with this great respect in light of the trouble those visitors had caused Barker in the community, and he ended his article by praising Barker's humanistic morality, virtue, and openness.[40] But the article was little read and less noted by the folks Andy Barker had infuriated, and the festival would ultimately take its toll on Love Valley.

The festival would not go away easily. According to Barker, in the months that followed, he was not only harassed by local residents but had to deal with State Bureau of Investigation agents (who were looking for drugs), with the state tax people (who investigated possible profits), and with other promoters who wanted to bring another rock festival to Love Valley.[41]

The fallout came down to this: exhausted and embattled Love Valley residents did not want to sponsor another rock festival, and the community surrounding the town pledged to make sure they never sponsored an activity like the festival again. Before the town had a chance to catch its breath, a group of angry citizens gathered legal representation, law enforcement representation, and state government representation and met to determine how they could legally prevent such a scene from recurring. Calling themselves the North Iredell Betterment Association, a group of over 500 people met July 20 at the Central Community Building to discuss the situation and to call for a plan of action. There were heated discussions and some threats, but for the most part, the meeting remained peaceful.[42] Eventually, legal action was taken with a bill that would grant counties regulatory powers over gatherings exceeding 25 people who would meet for more than 24 hours. The proposal carried stiff penalties for those who violated the regulations. The bill became known, at least in the Iredell County region, as the "Rock Festival Bill."[43]

The Love Valley Rock Festival actually brought to a head ill feelings harbored toward the town since its beginnings. Suspicions surrounding Barker, the rumored communitarian lifestyle of the place, the activities that took place there, and the parareligious grounding of the community had grown, festered, and with the rock festival, exploded. Love Valley would never be viewed by the public in quite the same way as before the festival, and those July 1970 events virtually ended Barker's hope to establish a working political utopia. The controversy and change of the late sixties leading up to and including the festival altered the public perception of Love Valley so much that the public never quite forgave Mayor Barker for that hot July weekend. From July 1970, Love Valley had either enemies or supporters—indifference was a thing of the past. For those who were not sure about the community, the festival pushed them off the fence, and for most people outside the town, the Rock Festival became the premier event in defining the town's existence and population. A few of the festival goers remained in Love

Valley after the concert was over, some bought land, and others wandered off around Iredell County. However, by 1972, most of those who had made their way to Love Valley via the counterculture had drifted on to somewhere else. And despite all the controversy surrounding this time period, Love Valleyites persisted in pursuing their lifestyles. Nevertheless, for a few years in the early seventies, Love Valley was a curious mixture of cowboys, longhairs, and tepees.

7

Tepees and Longhairs:
Communal Utopia

The aftermath of the Love Valley Rock Festival brought criticism, hatred, ruptured relationships, controversy, and cynicism. Love Valley's tenuous relationship with the outside world for a short time became antagonistic. Those beyond the streets of Love Valley were more convinced than ever of the deviant nature of Andy Barker and his experimental community. The town teetered on the brink of collapse, many moved away, and outsiders vowed to destroy the remnants of this Christian, cowboy community. The old faithful and the new residents (some of the hippies who stayed behind) were left to salvage what was left of Andy Barker's dream.

The first item of business was personal healing of those who had invested so much in the success of Love Valley. The town closed ranks, turned a deaf ear to outside criticism, and rediscovered the communitarian spirit that aided in healing disrupted relationships. From the new residents, the town learned the importance of the unity of body and mind and the imperative of brotherhood, respecting others for their humanness. From 1970 to the present, Love Valley has established informal social structures to serve the primary purpose of supporting the physical and emotional needs of residents through extended family networks and community consensus. Although this was present from the beginning, it became much stronger in the wake of societal backlash in the late sixties and early seventies.

Following the rock festival, the population of Love Valley changed for a short time. Festival-goers who stayed to make Love Valley their home brought new ways of viewing relationships, new ways of defining family, new ways of understanding communal arrangements, and new ways of understanding religion (many considered themselves Jesus freaks). The focus with these new residents was inward, toward a greater understanding of, and development of, self. Many of the hippies who stayed after the rock festival stayed to "find themselves," and in fact, many of the long-time residents of Love Valley, including Andy Barker, embarked on the same journey of self-discovery. To the extent relationships in Love Valley supported this journey of self-discovery, Love Valley became a psychosocial utopia.[1]

This inward focus and the need for psychic healing among some members of the community were compounded by a series of failures and tragedies that affected many in the town. Andy Barker's two gubernatorial bids were unsuccessful; the Barkers lost their son to cancer; Joe Ponder was nearly killed in an accident; a shooting death shocked the community—all of these difficult and tragic events multiplied the isolation of the town as Love Valley continued to turn inward in the attempt to heal itself. Part of that healing provided residents the opportunity for self-expression, which is still evident in the main activities of Love Valley at the present, arts and the rodeo.

Yet, even though the community turned inward, even though it endured hardship, it did not fold, and because of the psychosocial functioning through support structures, the community not only survived the hardship but emerged with a quiet and calm peace that characterizes a mature and confident community at present. In this case, adversity tested and then tempered the mettle of this community, and residents now reside in a Love Valley they believe can offer them something they cannot receive in the outside world: community that cares; community that is interconnected; community that allows and supports the essential humanity and being of its residents. Currently, the old dream of a religion-based society is barely present; the belief that society must be reformed hardly receives mention; but community exists as strongly as ever.

Immediately following the rock festival, Love Valley took on another persona for some time. The cowboys did not disappear, but the streets of the town looked less like a scene from Dodge City and more like a hippie commune. And in a sense, Love Valley became a retreat for the counterculture vision brought to the Valley by the festival. During the months following the festival, there were experiments in communal living that expanded the town's own experiment in community living. For the "longhairs" (as they were called by some) or "freaks" (as they called themselves) who settled in Love Valley following the festival, the town became the realization of their vision of social utopia, a communal experiment that allowed a great deal of freedom of expression of counterculture values.

The hippies who settled in Love Valley embraced the utopian vision undergirding the town because it correlated with their own vision of social reform—a social message formulated on an underlying religious vision. Thus, the 30 to 40 festival-goers who remained did so because to them Love Valley corresponded to the same impulse it represented for many of the others who were attracted to the little town. Love Valley

Fig. 12. The entrance to Love Valley, Main Street. Note the two traffic rules: the sign to the right of the entrance forbids cars, while the sign on the left post reads, "DO NOT RUN HORSES ON STREET." Photograph by author, 1997.

embodied social reform, religious and spiritual vision, and communal utopia. For a while, tepees and longhairs were more abundant in the streets of the Valley than six shooters and cowboys, but the vision of the longhairs was similar to that of the idealists who founded and inhabited the town. The experiment continued, although in a different guise.

* * *

"Tepees and Longhairs"[2]

The late summer sun plastered the valley without mercy, but inside the tepee, a young woman sat transfixed by her work, oblivious to the heat generated by her crude replica of the skinned cones that dotted the Great Plains a hundred years earlier. Her body bent over a broken sewing machine as her hands expertly turned the wheel, and her eyes keenly observed the bobbin and the stitches of her sewing. Her task was a laborious one, for she was forced to manually manipulate an electric machine with a disabled motor. At other times, the seamstress embroidered by hand a myriad of designs sewn into worn and faded denim. Her artist's eye produced some of the most beautiful embroidery work in the Valley.

As Pam brushed back a stray strand of hair with a sweaty wrist, she thought how pleasant the task was to perform. She did not consider the wearisome repetition to be tedium. Living in a tepee in Love Valley, time and effort took on different dimensions—one had time to cultivate and enjoy a fire on a winter's evening, or to bake a cherry pie in a wood stove, or to read Shakespeare when there was other work to be done, or to embroider beautiful fantasy art work onto worn-out blue jeans. There were no cherry pies lately because of the heat, but when the weather was cool, Pam's old Army surplus stove produced pies crafted with as much aesthetic care as was her embroidery. The old stove was one Andy Barker had given her. It was little more than a space heater with a specially designed stove pipe. Just above the firebox was a little double chambered box. The smoke from the stove pipe circulated through the outer chamber (before going up the chimney) and heated the inner box as an oven. The temperature inside the box would go to 500 degrees easily, and the wood heat was perfect for baking Pam's cherry pies. Her mouth watered at the thought of the pastries, but she knew it was too hot in the tepee to heat the stove for a pie. Nonetheless, she could not help but glance at the odd-looking contraption from which her imagination produced the sweet aroma of a fresh baked pie.

Often Pam's work was interrupted by strangers who would wander into the tepee thinking it to be some type of exhibit rather than a habitation. On such occasions, Pam graciously welcomed her guests and related to them the history and significance of the tepee.

The tepee provided a comfortable but spartan life. There was only cold water piped inside and this produced a major inconvenience in the winter because heating water became an everyday chore. Yet, the tepee's inconvenience encouraged a natural simplicity that matched the easygoing nature of its inhabitant. Perhaps even more inconvenient was the access to an old refrigerator that served the tepee. Pam bought the appliance from Andy Barker for $15, and it sat about 15 feet from the tepee door beside the light pole where it was plugged in. The old compressor regularly shut down and required a good hard kick to the bottom of the machine on the right side to start the cooling cycle again. Many a night Pam had been awakened by that awful noise the compressor made when it shut down, and many a night Pam had trudged out into the dark night to give the ancient cooler a good boot.

The tepee was constructed from scrap materials that were salvaged after the rock festival in 1970. In fact, most of the lumber used in the tepee came from the dismantled stage, and the tepee was built on the abandoned site of the historical musical event. The architecture of the tepee was interesting in and of itself. The tepee boasted a second floor, a sleeping loft accessible by a small ladder. Above the loft, at the very top of the tepee sat perhaps the most unusual and important piece of construction in the whole building. A wagon wheel held the tepee together at its pinnacle. While building the structure, the need for a stabilizing device presented a unique problem. Andy Barker solved the problem by taking a wagon wheel from one of the wagons in town. The wagon wheel performed admirably in supporting the structure, but failed to keep out the rain. Chicken wire, fiberglass, coats and coats of paint, and a polyethylene moisture barrier finally weather-proofed the tepee.

Pam kept one item in the tepee that appeared to be an antique and was quite functional and important. An old typewriter sat on a fruit box along the wall of the tepee. A friend of Andy Barker gave Pam the typewriter. It was quite old even then and printed a few letters above the lines, but it allowed Pam to carry on her correspondence from P.O. Box #1 at the Love Valley Post Office. Pam also used the typewriter to write short fiction and newspaper articles. Pam was working with the paper as a reporter covering court cases.

Pam's exposure to the courtroom sparked an interest with her that eventually led to a decision to enter law school. Pam's decision to become a lawyer surprised everyone. Ellenora simply replied, "Who would've thought it" when Pam informed her that she was going to study law. But the decision probably surprised no one any more than it

Fig. 13. The Love Valley Post Office building. The Post Office is no longer in operation. Photograph by author, 1997.

did Pam who had once looked with suspicion at lawyers who represented "the establishment."

Pam's memories of those Love Valley days are pleasant ones. She arrived at Love Valley an idealistic graduate student in English literature from Berkeley and quickly became a part of a post-sixties counterculture's last gasp at changing the world. She fell into a town that exhibited a tremendous sense of community, not just among the hippies and leftover festival-goers but among all the residents of Love Valley. Living in the tepee, her basic needs were simple, her dwelling was little more than dry and cozy, she lived a spartan life, but she lived a life that was happily carefree. Even so, the idealism that characterized those days also took a beating at times. When she would walk down the streets of Statesville and receive horrified looks because of her hair or clothing, when a merchant would watch her and her friends like a hawk to make sure they did not shoplift, or when a shop owner would refuse to accept her check out of distrust, Pam's spirited optimism about human nature was challenged. While she and her friends thought they were representing the best in human nature by trying to share the message of human cooperation, she seemed to meet fear and suspicion everywhere.

But then there were the times when someone would offer an act of benevolence and restore Pam's faith in her philosophical approach to life. A local dentist treated her on a moment's notice without concern for payment; local bike shop owners held an expensive bike for Pam without a down payment when she offered them her grandmother's opal ring as collateral; and, of course, there were the Barkers, who adopted the two dozen or so leftovers from the rock festival as their own and cared for them until, one by one, they left or started working. These people restored Pam's idealism in human nature and the dream of the "new generation."

Pam's integration into the community did not always proceed effortlessly. For example, when Pam first met Joe and Velma Ponder, she realized they were worlds apart. Joe was a World War II veteran who made saddles and performed circus stunts on weekends; Pam was a California graduate student who spouted peace and brotherhood. The Ponders looked at her and her compatriots as if they were aliens from another world speaking unknown languages. Nevertheless, Pam learned, as did the Ponders and the rest of the residents of Love Valley, that in many ways they already spoke the same language; they already sought the same things; they were trying to build a "Great Society" that had been promised but was increasingly disappointing and failing.

Residents of Love Valley began to question the possibility of social reform when feelings of mistrust and fear ran high in the small North Iredell community surrounding Love Valley. After the rock festival, the nearby residents who disapproved of the festival and its results banded together to insure that no more such events would come to Love Valley. Part of the plan to block any such possibility involved ridding the neighborhood of any and all leftover hippies who might decide to take up permanent residence in the community. The North Iredell community called a meeting at Central School to discuss how to get rid of the hippies in their community because of the fears and rumors of drugs, immorality, and anti-Americanism. Pam and some of the other residents of Love Valley caught wind of the meeting and showed up, much to the obvious discontent of some North Iredell locals. At one point during the meeting, Pam had the chance to speak on behalf of many in Love Valley. She tried to convince the crowd that Love Valley was not a drug haven for outlaws and rebels. Others echoed her sentiments, and by the end of the meeting, minds had been changed and moods altered. Finally, one of the leading opponents to the new North Iredell neighbors stood up and withdrew his opposition.

There were others who shared this time in Love Valley, among them musicians who often treated the residents of Love Valley to a free concert. After such a concert, Andy Barker would sometimes drive around in an old Army surplus weapons carrier he kept around the Valley and pile a bunch of hippies on it. The lot of them would go riding out across the mountains (as if they were on some kind of hay ride) hanging on to the sides of the weapons carrier to see the midnight moon. The irony of 20 or so hippies being escorted by a middle-aged cowboy, singing anti-Vietnam songs while bouncing along on a machine built to cart weapons of destruction was impossible to miss but at the same time typical for Love Valley.

A group of these new residents learned that the Allman Brothers Band was going to record a live album at the Fillmore East in New York City and set out for New York with no transportation and little money. This was no problem for a bunch of adventurous young adults in the early seventies—they hitchhiked the 600 miles from Love Valley to the Big Apple. Once they arrived in New York, the group caught up with the Allman Brothers Band at their suite and stayed with other friends there.

In a sense, the longhairs were a tourist attraction that captivated the imagination and inspired the soul. To describe them as free and independent spirits would be simply to make an understatement of an old cliché. Their spirit was ubiquitous and embodied the spirit of Love Valley, the spirit of unbridled idealism, high aspirations, community service and involvement, and the hopes for a reformed social order. The longhairs channelled those aspirations and goals through a variety of pursuits. Pam directed hers to a legal career. But somewhere inside the lawyer's polished exterior is a hippie wearing hope on her sleeves and exhibiting the same innovative vitality that created, maintained, and sustained Love Valley.

* * *

Pam was not the only hippie to live in the Valley in the early seventies. For the first couple of years following the Rock Festival, long-haired young people were a common sight in Love Valley. In fact, Andy Barker himself became one for a little while. He did not grow his hair long; however, in the aftermath of the controversial festival, he found himself living on the other side of the mountain, raising vegetables, collecting honey for market, and living a contemplative life like some modern-day Thoreau or his younger contemporaries who found other ways to escape the modern rush to outrun life. And for a little while, this group of young people constituted one big family under the supervision of their so-called "benevolent dictator," Andy Barker.

The months following that hot July weekend in 1970 were less eventful than the three days of the festival, but no less interesting. The longhairs who stayed intended to help clean up the awful mess left behind by the festival goers. However, pretty soon, many decided to remain and live an alternative lifestyle in a place they felt would accept their experiments with communal living. Nevertheless, many residents surrounding Love Valley did not share Love Valley's openness to these alternative lifestyles and opposed the addition of the new residents. The controversy continued for another 18 months to the extent that Andy Barker disconnected his telephone in order to fend off daily threatening phone calls. For a while, the town was a curious mixture of hippies, tie-dyed clothing, cowboys, western boots, and SBI agents in suits, crawling around in the dust and mud searching for fledgling marijuana plants left behind by the concert goers. The SBI agents eventually left after a big bonfire destroyed the last vestiges of marijuana in Love Valley. The freaks eventually left, most of them gone by 1972. But the cowboys endured, and so did Barker.

Some of the hippies who had attended the festival bought property in the area. They even tried their luck at rodeo—it might have been the only rodeo with ponytails as well as ponies and tie-dyed clothing as well as leather chaps. Some of the Allman Brothers Band members spent time in Love Valley as a retreat. But as the Allman Brothers hit the big time, they were on the road more and more and were in Love Valley less and less.[3]

The rock group, Flood, settled in Love Valley and made the town its base for a while. They became local favorites, played and practiced in the town, cut a record about Love Valley, and eventually moved on to Atlanta to do some recording. Perhaps Flood summed up the longhair attraction to Love Valley best in their promotional literature. In a promotional poster, the band presented themselves as searching for answers to life. The band's search attracted them to Love Valley. According to Flood, "Searching brought us to Love Valley—a communion with mountains and minds. Here we are learning and growing; striving toward a spiritual and human understanding, we believe is basic in all mankind. . . . We must tear down the walls. . . . Walls around our nation, our cities. But first ourselves. For all to receive—All must give."[4]

The Flood band echoed the unofficial creed of Love Valley, and according to one member of the band, some of the band members were searching for some kind of spiritual meaning during their sojourn at Love Valley. This is why they felt a peculiar kinship to the Love Valley experiment.[5] This spiritual undertone took on an overt religious sense that was demonstrated by the origin of their name from Psalm 90, which they used as their official motto and which they reprinted on their promotional literature: "They are as asleep . . . a thousand years are but as yesterday . . . carriest them away as with a flood."[6]

Flood wrote songs and performed for a Love Valley audience until they were able to branch out. Some of their music, including part of a rock opera the group wrote and performed, was recorded by a fledgling new company, Love Valley Records, started at Love Valley to accommodate and promote its new residents. One song the group recorded, "Love Valley, U.S.A," expressed the para-religious idealism shared by the post-rock-festival inhabitants of Love Valley, and it described the utopian vision many longhairs felt concerning their adopted town.

The song, "Love Valley, U.S.A.," began with a slow a cappella rendition of the traditional tune, "Down in the Valley," with a slight change in the words: "Down in the Valley, Love Valley so high,/Lift your head up now, cause we're gonna fly."

After this introduction, the tempo changed to upbeat rock with gospel flavor. The story of the song chronicled the journey of someone down on his luck searching for the "promised land" where he could make his home. He ran into a "brother" who gave him a hand by telling him of a place "where the mountains and the heavens meet," where "rewards would never cease." The place, of course, was Love Valley, U.S.A., the U.S.A. added to symbolize the universal acceptance of the town for all and to suggest the town was representative of the ideal American community. The young man made his way to Love Valley and was greeted there with open arms, fed a meal by his gracious hosts, and asked to express his opinion of the town and its people. The verses of the song were followed by the chorus, "I found hope, I found peace, In Love Valley, U.S.A."

According to Don Berg, the Flood band member who wrote the song, the song expressed the utopian ideal as envisioned not only by Andy Barker but also by the counterculture representatives who settled there in the early seventies, and the song expressed the experience most of those festival goers had at Love Valley.[7] Love Valley was envisioned by many of the counterculture settlers as a religious utopia (note the overt religious language and imagery throughout) that served as a haven for the downtrodden and outcasts. The town was pictured as a community that fed the hungry, cared for the homeless, and then demonstrated respect for them by allowing their input into the community. This, of course, was virtually what happened with the town's care for and acceptance of the longhairs who came to the community during the festival. And this is Love Valley as one band member, Rory Knapton, remembers it. Rory, or "Rabbit" as he was known then, remembers being fed and cared for by "Ma" and Andy Barker and still cherishes their tolerance and kindness.[8] This religious utopia was described as the "promised land . . . where the mountains and the heavens meet," and the song all but designated the community as God's kingdom on earth. In any event, one of the favorite tunes of the band, and the town's unofficial theme song, aptly expressed and reinforced the utopian theme that did not fade during the controversy of the early seventies but rather was expressed through a different language with different faces. The idealism of the 1954 founding of the community was perhaps at its greatest point during the most difficult period of the town's existence.

Love Valley, U.S.A.
by Don Berg[9]

> Down in the Valley, Love Valley so high,
> Lift your head up now, cause we're gonna fly.
> Leaving from Atlanta
> Don't know where I'm bound,
> Searchin' for the promised land
> Carryin' what I own, lookin' for a home,
> Tell me brother can you lend me a hand
> Told me 'bout a place up in North Carolina,
> Where the mountains and the heavens meet.
> Said it was a long road and the travellin' may be hard
> But those rewards would never cease.

Chorus:
I found hope, I found peace,
In Love Valley, U.S.A.
I found hope, I found peace,
In Love Valley, U.S.A.

Went up to the city limits down on my luck
Looking for the man in charge.
Little Joe sent me to Mayor Andy Barker
Who greeted me with open arms.
He said, "Son, you're lookin' down and
I'd like to show you 'round,
but first let me give you a meal.
And when you've had the time to think things over
I'd like to know what you feel."
Chorus:
So if you're on the roam,
And you're lookin' for a home,
People come along with me,
Back into a Valley in North Carolina,
With the land and the sky and the trees.
Chorus:

Of course there were drifters who made their way through Love Valley before, during, and after the festival. Some became legendary among the freaks who stayed behind after the festival. One such figure was known as Psychedelic Joe, who became a bit of a folk hero to the festival crowd at Love Valley. Many of those who knew him still speak affectionately of Psychedelic Joe and see him from time to time.[10]

Another wanderer showed up on Andy Barker's doorstep right before the festival, helped Tonda and David work on the event, and decided to stay on afterwards. He and a group of eight or nine others bought a farm after the concert and set up a group commune adjacent to Love Valley. The group members grew organic vegetables, kept horses, and lived in a farm house. They considered themselves "Jesus freaks," they were intelligent and articulate, and they established their commune as a religious group seeking an apocalyptic end to the present evil age. One member explained the coming end as the reason the group had established itself near Love Valley: "One thing nearly everybody—the freaks—in the valley share is a belief that a very bad era is coming. That there will be major earthquakes and other catastrophes, that California and New York will slide into the oceans, that there will be more wars and a great deal of inhumanity and evil. . . . It's based on the Bible and some other signs, and will last until the Age of Aquarius goes out."[11] Other longhairs who did not share the apocalyptic vision of the commune were very religious as well, attended the Love Valley Church faithfully, and traded in their drugs in order to "get high on life and nature."[12] At least they traded in the hard stuff—among the freaks, even the Jesus freaks, marijuana use still seemed to be generally acceptable.

The commune fell apart when they could not make the mortgage payments on the farm, and their leader went on to become a traveling evangelist. One of the members of the group married the leader and went with him. One moved to Florida to show horses, another married a member of the group and moved to Maine to build a cabin and start a farm and cabinet shop. Still another moved to Jamaica, bought some remote land, and intended to set up a farm.[13] The members of the commune went their own ways, but each took a bit of Love Valley with them (either agricultural knowledge, cabinet-making skills, or religious fervor they obtained during their sojourn at Love Valley). In many ways, their stay at the Valley provided them the skills and direction they needed to get on with their lives.

There were many free spirits who lived in the Valley because, for a while at least, they found an enclave where society's prejudices and restrictions seemed to be relaxed, a place where honesty seemed to outweigh hypocrisy and where they could find themselves. This was perhaps understood more clearly by Andy and Ellenora Barker than anyone. The Barkers encouraged the longhairs to stay even in the face of continued community opposition because, in Ellenora's words, "It's like Andy's said all along, that these young people just needed to find themselves. And they've been here finding themselves, finding a place to go, and direction. We've just been going through a period of unrest."[14] And most of them did find themselves, moving on in due time with renewed ideas, hopes, and goals. That there was an overt religious orientation to many of the hippies who stayed seems more than simply coincidental. It is as if the utopian dream of Barker was sensed by a segment of the 75,000 who shared a vision of religious utopia. These were among the ones who stayed, and the underlying spiritual vision of Love Valley was adopted by those hippie spiritualists themselves.

Some who stayed and moved on did not find themselves accidentally but through the concerted efforts of many Love Valley residents. In particular, the Barkers "adopted" many of them and offered them a boost. During a time when Barker's social and political goals were destroyed, he and Ellenora refocused their idealism toward the microcosm of the counterculture that found itself in the Barker living room.

* * *

In a matter of a few minutes, Ellenora could transform a seemingly bare kitchen into a feast serving two dozen. She did not know how many would sit at her table that particular evening, but then she rarely did. The young people began to filter in slowly as the smells of a baked picnic ham wafted from her stove to the street outside. Some of them helped by setting plates or washing the pots as Ellenora finished with them; others began to chat as more arrived; men and women collapsed on the big sofa, exhausted from a long, hot day's work tearing siding off an old farm house, laying brick for a foundation, or reconstructing a building in the middle of town. All were kept busy with one of Barker's projects, and at the end of the day, all would gather together at the Barker's common table. There were 21 that particular night—the Barkers fed them because they had little money, except the money Barker paid them for work in the valley. They were working, for room and board and a little cash, but more important, for the trade skills and life experiences of communal existence in Love Valley.

The scene was repeated three times a day (breakfast, lunch, and supper), seven days a week with one exception. Everyone knew that on Sunday evening the Barker household was off limits. A few hours after church was the only time the Barkers reserved for themselves, and the hippies who otherwise congregated in their house at anytime respected the sacred hours on Sunday evening.

All the meals around the Barker table were boisterous affairs, resembling a cross between a family gathering and a Woodstock reunion, but it was supper that generated the largest crowds and most interesting conversation. Supper gave this makeshift family a chance to catch up on the progress of the day. Barker checked on the status of work projects he had assigned that morning, projects that were designed more to keep everyone busy or to teach trade skills than to actually accomplish anything. The young people used the time to catch up with each other, to report to "Ma Barker" (as Ellenora was affectionately known to her adopted family), or to discuss current events that were of interest.

After supper, some of the guests went on about their business, but invariably, a dozen or so would settle into the Barkers' living room to sift through magazines and newspapers. These papers were the only contact most of the young people had to the outside world, and articles in them would invariably lead to a "rap" session that would often extend into the early hours of the next morning. The topics of these "rap" sessions were predictable: Nixon, Vietnam, politics, police brutality, the New Age revolution. All of these discussions and more enraptured

Barker's hippies and anyone else who might wander into the Barkers' house during these late-night vigils.

The next morning, after a hearty breakfast, Barker formed groups and assigned work projects. Early on, after the initial cleanup from the rock festival was accomplished, Barker divided the hippies who stayed into various groups with different specialties or tasks. For example, there was a carpentry crew, a stone masonry crew, a woodworking crew, an agricultural crew, etc. Barker coordinated work from Love Valley and surrounding areas, and the hippies provided reliable work crews. The stone masonry crew called themselves "Stoned Inc.," and they planned to carry the training they received from Barker into a business venture after the Love Valley experience. The carpentry crew renovated several structures, including an old farmhouse for a retired couple in Virginia, some of the women drove dump trucks from the rock quarry to construction sites, and all the crew members went about their work in a diligent manner without the anxiety of job security or advancement. They said they simply wanted to do a good job and to enjoy life while doing it.[15] One of the members of the carpentry crew summed up their attitude by describing Love Valley as a place where people could work together and have fun.[16]

An element of the communal life of the longhairs that cannot be ignored was the religious context of their existence. A simple Christianity was evident in many who stayed on at Love Valley. They attended church and tried to follow the golden rule in all their dealings. In fact, this reductionist Christianity formed the basis for their "hippie philosophy," and the Love Valley experiment of a community founded on religious and spiritual values played a large part in attracting the "Jesus freaks" to stay in the first place. As a result, many times the hippies would be found abandoning their paying jobs to help a farmer get in hay before the rains or to help an elderly couple make repairs on their home. For a while, Love Valley was infused with an extra dose of goodwill, and Barker's utopian idealism was expressed with a hippie slant.

The rock festival may have threatened to destroy the town, but it failed to destroy the Love Valley task of social reform and utopianism. Rather, for a while, the Valley of Love embraced a group that was dispossessed, if not rejected by society. In an atmosphere of openness, diversity, and acceptance, the flower children who are now a distant reminder of an all but forgotten counterculture found peace and hope and substance in the revolution that gave rise to their protest. The acceptance and love from a community, which had every reason to reject the new rock festival residents, expressed once again the driving force behind the town, the utopian ideal and experiment.

* * *

In time, tensions with the surrounding community eased, although threats leveled at Barker continued to such a degree that by January 1971, he resigned his post as mayor and retired from his position as president of Love Valley Enterprises. He became a bit of a hippie himself. Retiring from public life and pursuing the contemplative life, he moved to a farm (Horseshoe Ranch) on the other side of the mountain to read, paint, grow vegetables, and build furniture. With Barker's resignation, Jet, Andy's son, succeeded his father as president of Love Valley Enterprises while just a teenager. Jet's dream of succeeding his father and continuing the Love Valley experiment was beginning to come true, but it seemed that Jet's vision differed somewhat from his father's. Jet directed much of the rebuilding and revitalization of the Valley after Barker's retirement, and Barker praised his son's efforts.[17] In fact, many of those in the town praised the young man's ability to manage the affairs of the town following what was the most turbulent period of Love Valley's history. To mount a successful revitalization effort after the fallout of the rock festival required an incredible talent and mature vision that Jet so clearly demonstrated. Soon, the news from Vietnam and Hurricane Celia eclipsed the Love Valley Rock Festival, and by the summer of 1972, only four or five hippies remained and the rodeo enthusiasts and horse lovers were beginning to return. And Barker's self-imposed exile was anything but permanent.

Once on the other side of the mountain, Barker was far from fading out of sight. In fact, his temporary isolation perhaps heightened his idealistic impulse even further. Not long after mayor Barker's resignation, a curious reporter caught up with the exiled founder of Love Valley. He found Andy and Ellenora living in a 135-year-old log cabin on an isolated farm with no phone, no TV, and an outhouse. The setup seemed perfect for the contemplative life, but Barker, who prides himself on being a "doer," was showing signs of boredom. After restoring the log home, Barker found himself with little to do. The vegetable garden and bees took only a few spare moments of his time. So he turned his attention to the old outhouse and set out to make his privy more comfortable. Inside the otherwise nondescript outbuilding was a throne room that could have been designed for royalty. The floor was carpeted with thick pile carpet, while air conditioning, heating, and exhaust controls were within easy reach. Books lined the back wall, and various types of lamps provided ample light for the inquisitive visitor. Barker even claimed to have plans to cover the commode seat with mink.[18] The eccentric Barker was making news even in his retirement.

By his own admission, any man who spent his spare time remodeling an outhouse must be bored, and Andy Barker was bored in retirement. By 1973, Barker was back in the middle of the action, his name appeared in the 1972 edition of *Personalities of the South,* he was planning rodeo events and other promotional activities for Love Valley, and he entered the 1973 mayoral election and won. For the most part, people with names like Hoss and Arizona populated the streets again rather than the hippies. Nevertheless, the communal life and counterculture ideas of Love Valley's longhaired residents changed the Valley, and vestiges of their legacy lived on after most had left.

The four or five hippies from the rock festival who stayed beyond 1972 attracted others. A community known as Weird Acres became the home for those who decided to retire from society. In the early seventies, some lived in tents or built small cabins, watched for UFOs, and raised children.[19] Other hippies remained and established an artisan community in the town. Soon arts and crafts shops rivaled the leather shop for revenues. This new artisan community has remained, more or less, to the present and is the closest tie Love Valley maintains to the events of the early seventies. In any event, the introduction of all forms of arts and crafts helped Love Valley rebound from the lean years of 1970-1972 and transform itself from a ghost town to a once again bustling western town with an artsy twist.

One art form that had been around Love Valley for some time but that was revived in the early seventies was blacksmithing. Blacksmiths toured the country as experts, but were in short supply in the 1970s. One showed up at Love Valley with an old leather apron, a ten-gallon hat, and his blacksmithing tools and went to work. His work was all but a lost art that was preserved in the Valley.[20] Other crafts and arts that became part of the seventies artisans revival at Love Valley included pottery, weaving, metal sculpture, woodwork, leathersmithing, silversmithing, and macrame. The interest was so great that the artisans in Love Valley were able to open a cooperative shop for display and to host an annual arts and crafts show. By 1975, Love Valley had organized a community arts council granted by a charter from the secretary of state. Even hot air ballooning became an art form, and while not a part of Love Valley, a nearby business, Balloon Works, began to flourish and attracted the attention of the artisan community just up the road.

The Community Arts Council of Love Valley, Inc. was chartered as a nonprofit organization to promote traditional and experimental arts and crafts.[21] The council was so successful that it was able to spark a crafts revival in the area that resulted in numerous shows and the attraction of established artists to Love Valley. From custom jewelry, to sculpture, to weavers, to hand-built homes, for a while, Love Valley was known as an "artist haven," and this new identity insured the presence of longhairs in the community for some time. Nevertheless, the revival of arts and crafts became a way for town residents to reorient their direction and to live down the rock festival. One news reporter commented that it was no coincidence that Love Valley sponsored only art "shows," not "festivals."[22]

* * *

The 1970 Love Valley Rock Festival opened a new era of Love Valley's history and in the process nearly destroyed the town. By the middle of the decade, however, Love Valley had rebounded from the bad images of the festival but had not completely recovered from that one weekend in July. Still, more than 25 years after the fact, Valley residents, Barker included, would rather not talk about the festival and the hardships associated with it, and they are still sensitive about being known as the place where the rock festival took place. Nevertheless, through it all, the town and its leaders persevered and managed to maintain the idealism upon which the town was based. Somehow, they redirected that idealism into positive avenues, and the town was able to survive, prosper again, and rebuild an image that would endear itself to neighbors, or at least ease suspicions about the place.

8

Tragedy and Triumph

The Love Valley Rock Festival in 1970 was followed by difficult years for the people of Love Valley. For the first five years subsequent to the event, the folks of Love Valley were preoccupied with trying to understand what happened, with coming to grips with the repercussions of the event, and with explaining the outcome and changes. For another five years following that, Love Valley tried to recuperate from the adverse effects suffered from the publicity surrounding the festival. For years, the population of Love Valley slowly but steadily dwindled before reaching a low point around 1974, when decline stabilized and began to turn around. Finally, by the 10-year anniversary of the festival, much of the hullabaloo generated by the event had subsided and the population of the Valley once again began to increase. By 1985, the population of the town had rebounded to its pre-festival number, and the town had regained a sense of normality as a cowboy and arts community. However, by 1985, transition was inevitable, and the long political reign of Andy Barker was beginning to draw examination.

One conspicuous result of the rock festival was the removal of Love Valley from the public eye for years. The residents and promoters of the Valley took a low profile for a while and were determined to return the image of the town to its pre-festival status. During the decade following the festival, a real effort was made to regain the western image of the town and to reemphasize that the community was nothing more than a quiet place where families could live and have fun. As a result of the bad publicity received in the early seventies and as an offshoot of the attempt to recapture the western image of the town, the utopian urge to transform society was muted. Although not absent, philanthropic activity and social reform causes were less publicized out of fear of raising suspicions once again and out of nervousness that anything mildly associated with social reform would be interpreted as a counterculture resurgence from a community that had become known for drugs and hippies rather than reform and cowboys. Nevertheless, the utopian impulse did not disappear but energy was diverted inward to psychic healing and support, and Love Valley entered a protracted period of utopia in the psychosocial sense.[1]

The one exception to this reluctance to pursue social reform in public was the gubernatorial aspiration of Andy Barker. Two failed campaigns for governor in 1976 and 1984 recalled the former attempts to use the utopian community's values as a base for a broader social and political reformation movement. Beyond these two forays in the political realm, Love Valley turned inward during the years after the Rock Festival. The result of this isolationism was that from about 1975 to the present, Love Valley changed very little. Most of the town's effort was directed to regaining its pre-festival image as a cowboy town and as an enclave of nineteenth-century values based on the family unit; reestablishing a stable community of about 75 to 100 residents that would be self-supporting; and strengthening the sense of community that had been a source of support and strength for residents. Goals two and three have been realized; however, Love Valley continues to be an enigma for those outside the community with people still not knowing quite what to make of the little mountain town.

To create stability and a positive image, Love Valley has focused only on two promotional ventures since 1975. The rodeo and the crafts shows now define activities in Love Valley, and the town has regained its status as a western town for horse buffs. The town still looks like a movie set, but few people wear guns now, except on big rodeo weekends, and the cowboys are somehow different, muses Andy Barker. "It used to be in the old days in this town, the guests were rougher and tougher than they are now. Now they come in Winnebagos and want water, power and toilet facilities right where they are. They used to sleep in tents, blankets, barns, sleeping bags or just wherever they could."[2] Nevertheless something binds together the old-timers and the new breed of cowboy and that is the common love of horses, and on most weekends in the summer, one will see innumerable trailers up and down highway 115 headed for the Valley and its miles of trails through the surrounding mountains. The town bustles on weekends during the season, but is quiet during the week, and its current understated stability represents a triumph of recovery after a tragic public relations fiasco in the early seventies. In fact, this move from tragedy to triumph probably best describes Love Valley from the early seventies to the present.

With little change occurring during this time, the one item that characterizes the town is its seemingly disproportionate allotment of tragedy and disappointment. Not only was Barker's dream of becoming governor bitterly shattered, but a series of tragedies affecting the Barker family and the community at large tested the mettle of the town. The

Fig. 14. Shops along Main Street, Love Valley. When Love Valley was developed, the rule was all buildings must look 100 years old. Note the wooden sidewalks and hitching posts. Photograph by author, 1997.

hard times made the community even stronger and closer. Even though the utopian vision of social reform was waning, the utopian aspiration to create a town with communitarian values was stronger than ever. In fact, many residents of the town describe the sense of community as the primary reason for their living in Love Valley. Tragedy did not create the community, but it did help to solidify it and bring it to the attention of those who experienced the deep sense of neighborliness that now seems to define the town. Every tragedy, no matter how deep or disrupting, was accompanied by a triumph of community. This chapter attempts to chronicle the sense of closeness through adversity as it developed from the late seventies to the present by focusing on two areas: political defeat and disappointment, and personal/communal tragedy.

Political Disappointment and Recovery

From 1975 to the present, the indefatigable Andy Barker saw his political fortunes slowly change. Even though he realized one of his stated dreams, to build a working western town, Barker had failed to realize his political goal, to occupy the governor's mansion in Raleigh, North Carolina. In order to alleviate this unfulfilled dream, Barker launched a bid for the state's highest office in 1976 and then again in 1984. He did not run for governor in 1980 because of family and personal obligations. During these years, Barker corresponded with Democratic dignitaries; nevertheless, his campaigns for the gubernatorial post faltered badly, and it became quickly apparent that Barker's dream of being governor would not be realized.

Barker mounted his bids for the governor's post with little money or organization but with a highly developed platform that continued some of the social themes that had emerged earlier in his political forays. Barker stated that he was determined to run a different kind of campaign, that he did not want to buy the office, and that he felt he could win the race simply by appealing to the people and by supporting a more democratic platform than his opponents. However, Barker soon learned that mass media appeal was crucial to be elected to anything beyond Love Valley. The results of Barker's maverick campaigns included resounding defeats at the polls but not in his spirits.

Barker's gubernatorial platforms in both 1976 and 1984 were reminiscent of his Jeffersonian Democrat and Populist ideologies that drove his earlier political ambitions. Barker described a Jeffersonian Democrat, and indeed himself, as "a democrat who was reared by republicans."[3] His self-admitted streak of conservatism was apparent by his position on issues confronting North Carolina. In preparation for the 1976 gubernatorial primaries, "The Smoke Signal," Love Valley's newspaper, devoted an entire issue (eight pages) to Barker's platform. In the issue, Barker outlined an economic development plan, an education plan, and a philosophy on taxation and the state budget, and he commented on a variety of issues such as roads and insurance. To understand Barker's political philosophy, it is worth briefly discussing his ideas—ideas he claims are finally (in the nineties) being considered seriously by state leaders.

Barker's 1976 platform[4] consisted of three major themes focusing on governmental reform, educational effectiveness, and economic development. In developing and outlining the platform, Barker called for an elected citizens' review commission to monitor the necessity, effectiveness, and productivity of state government. His reform slogan was "Money's Worth in State Government," and Barker appealed to the sensitivity of tax-paying voters. Second, Barker insisted on the necessity of a second elected review commission to monitor "Effectiveness in Education." Third, Barker pushed for greater state investment in and promotion of North Carolina tourism, commerce, industry, and retirement living as a way of providing a broader tax base for the state coffers.

Barker's emphasis on governmental reform stemmed from his late-seventies dissatisfaction with politicians who he thought had lost touch with the voting public. Barker called for a stringent evaluation of how tax dollars were spent as a way of increasing the efficiency of state government. His ultimate goal was to seek a tax cut without cutting vital programs by providing greater efficiency and accountability. Among other things, Barker outlined a plan that would alleviate tax inequities by providing alternatives to the state tax system. For example, he suggested raising the state exemption on estate tax and a possible repeal of the intangibles tax. Beyond the tax question, Barker supported the development of alternative energy sources as a challenge to public utilities who possibly had too much influence in Raleigh, and he suggested the formation of a state auto insurance company to set standards for and provide competition to private companies that had profited from unfair insurance laws. Barker's whole premise in his reform of government was to challenge corruption at the state level and to challenge the then current proposal for "zero budgeting," a method that Barker believed would lead to much waste and over estimation in preparing state budgets.

Barker's passion about education and concern for educational reform made up the second major portion of his platform. Barker called for effectiveness in education and suggested establishing a review board to insure progress. As governor, Barker promised to push for educational accountability at all levels, and he proposed to explore the use of alternative methods and technologies to reinforce learning. However, the crux of his reform platform was not experimentation but a return to basics and vocational training. Barker believed that by combating illiteracy and joblessness, education would turn out productive graduates rather than dropouts who placed greater strain on welfare, court, and prison systems.

Last, in order to promote economic development, Barker unveiled a six-point plan to revitalize North Carolina tourism, industry, and commerce. His plan was based on the premise that improving government and education would automatically attract more people to North Carolina; however, real growth would depend on effective promotion of the state nationally and even internationally. The old promoter in Andy Barker had not died away but was being redirected to the political field. Barker encapsulated other issues, such as port and road development and prison reform, under the general heading of economic development, and he put together a complex, yet very practical, platform.

Andy Barker did not come close in 1976 or in 1984 (when his platform was virtually unchanged) to winning his party's nomination. Nevertheless, Barker claims his highly developed platform influenced some state leaders in those elections, and he believes his ideas are still cropping up in Democratic circles in the nineties. Thus, Barker views his failure to win office as a triumph—a triumph of idealism if not position.

Nevertheless, Barker's political defeats in his attempts at state office did not adversely affect his political standing in the town. Love Valley continued to elect Barker to the post of mayor, and the town continued to be defined by Barker as much as by anything. So high was his popularity through the late eighties that he was once elected to the mayor's post without even running. In 1987, Barker decided not to run for mayor of Love Valley to allow new faces and ideas to lead the town,[5] and his name was absent from the ballot. Only one candidate ran unopposed for the seat, yet in a grassroots movement, the citizens of Love Valley mounted a write-in campaign for Barker that garnered almost 68 percent of the votes cast for mayor.[6] Thus, in a demonstration of strong political force within Love Valley, Andy Barker was elected to his twelfth term as mayor of the town. Nevertheless, after the 1987 election, Barker's influence began to teeter, at least his stronghold on the mayor's post was questioned.

Before his twelfth term ended, Barker announced his retirement in June of 1989, and even though he had tried to retire from municipal office before, this time he vowed his retirement would be permanent. Barker's health had deteriorated in a bout with skin cancer, and he retired in order to undergo surgery and spend more time with his family.

His surgery was a success, Barker eventually returned to the local political scene, and Barker today is still cancer free. In the meantime, a replacement was sworn in to fill the vacant spot created by Barker's retirement. The 1989 race for mayor was in disarray, with no names on the ballot. Finally, the town elected Buddy Price mayor in a write-in campaign. This time, Andy Barker received no write-in votes.

The late eighties perhaps witnessed the greatest change in the history of Love Valley with the exception of the Rock Festival years. For one of the few times in the town's history, Andy Barker was not directly in charge of the town's decision making. The changes tested loyalties, friendships, and political resolve so much so that Barker decided to make another run for the office of mayor in 1991. Barker ran against the incumbent Buddy Price. At issue were two items: how best to tackle the town's water problems, and how best to govern the town. There seemed to be little difference between the two candidates. While Barker suggested the two had differing governing styles, Price suggested that he shared Barker's vision of maintaining the character and tradition of Love Valley.[7] Surprisingly, the race was not close, and Price defeated Barker with 65 percent of the vote. Only four years after electing Barker through a write-in campaign, the voters of Love Valley rejected Barker as their mayor.

Observers and residents tried to assimilate the significance of this transition of leadership. The election signalled the need for change in the small town, or perhaps it reflected the changing population of Love Valley itself. The Barkers and the Ponders were practically all that was left of Love Valley from the era before the Rock Festival, and the 1991 mayoral election reflected the changing face and interests of the town's population. Barker took the disappointment in stride and vowed to bring his up and down political career to an end. But with a sheepish grin on his face, he did not discount the possibility of future ventures into the political realm: "Who knows," said a wistful Barker, "the Democratic party might draft me yet to run for governor."[8]

Barker's defeat did not signal an end to his popularity and staying power. In July 1993, the town gave a parade in honor of the founder and former mayor of the community, and the following November, the town once again elected Andy Barker mayor. Barker's name did not appear on the ballot, but he was elected in a write-in campaign that garnered him almost 60 percent of the vote. Barker remains mayor to the present.

* * *

Personal Tragedy and the Triumph of Community
The posters were everywhere.

SEE JOE PONDER . . .

Be the first to see Joe Ponder lift a live 500 lb. Mule
with his teeth, then climb a ladder with the mule, lifting it three additional feet! A WORLD'S RECORD!
See Joe Ponder bend a steel rod between his teeth
Watch Joe Ponder pull a Pilot tractor and trailer with his TEETH
Witness Joe Ponder drive 5" steel spikes through 2" wood with his BARE HANDS
Watch Joe Ponder lift a beautiful woman on a swing with his TEETH

See Joe Ponder perform the dangerous DEATH SLIDE

Joe Ponder was going to perform some of his stunts at Love Valley for the public to try to get his name in the *Guinness Book of World Records* and *Ripley's "Believe It or Not!"* Joe, the owner and operator of Ponder Leather Company in Love Valley was a bundle of pure strength. A former navy boxing champ, Joe had always been strong, but he developed some unusual strengths and talents when he began to rehabilitate his neck muscles following an automobile accident in 1970. After developing unusually strong neck and jaw muscles, he began to do stunts in his spare time, when he was not making leather saddles or on the road driving a truck. He still works out habitually in the dusty little gym he maintains in the back of the leather shop, and the robust saddle maker remembers his stunt days fondly, except for one episode.

For the show on May 14, 1978, Ponder planned and executed several stunts. He set a new record by lifting a 500-pound mule with his teeth using a harness and mouth piece he had designed for such purposes. After lifting the animal, Ponder was able to walk up three stairs, thus astounding the crowd. Later in the afternoon, Ponder lifted his wife, Velma, who sat in a swing, using the same mouth piece and harness and even pulled a 32,000-pound tractor-trailer rig with his teeth. But as amazing as these feats of strength were to the crowd, most bristled with anticipation as Ponder built up to the main event, something he called the "death slide."

May 14 was to be the public debut of Ponder's new stunt. Using the mouthpiece and harness assembly used in his stunts, Ponder planned to suspend himself from a cable using only his teeth and slide 50 feet on the cable from one pole to another. The cable was suspended 35 feet off the ground. The crowd gathered quietly around as Ponder mounted the

35-foot pole and attached his mouthpiece assembly to the suspended cable. Love Valley was, for a moment, a circus, and the same atmosphere of the most daring circus acts prevailed in the streets of the town. There was anticipation of great danger, yet there was the assurance that no harm would come, because, after all, the crowd had already witnessed Ponder lift 500 pounds with his teeth and mouthpiece.

The crowd waited anxiously as Ponder situated himself and pushed off, and a loud cheer went up as he began to soar through the air. Suspended by his teeth with outstretched arms, Ponder's body position mirrored the crucifixion and the large crosses he had sewn onto the front of his stunt outfit. Suddenly, a loud crack like a gun shot cut through the cheers of the crowd and the spectators gasped with horror as Ponder fell to the ground. The mouthpiece had snapped, Ponder did not realize he was hurtling toward the ground, and he landed square on his legs. Another pop on impact signalled the compound breaks to both legs and ankles. His feet were somehow still attached to his legs, but the connection was tenuous—his feet were simply hanging (no bones left connected) by muscles and flesh. Ponder felt no pain, but the extensive nature of his injuries left some sick to their stomachs.

Ponder was rushed to the hospital where he was treated for compound breaks, torn ligaments, and a broken jaw (26 bones were broken). The "death slide" had almost turned deadly, yet, within a month Ponder was able to talk and joke about his exploits. Relieved that his stunt had not produced a broken back or worse, Ponder credited his good fortune to his religious faith and to the support of people in his community, Love Valley. With the help of neighbors, he began rehabilitation and was confident he would recover fully. He joked about some of his more interesting stunts: lifting giant pumpkins, pulling freight train cars, and lifting two models who had been crowned Miss Nude World and Miss Nude America, all with his teeth. Ponder was determined to build a better mouthpiece for future stunts and was quite proud that his teeth survived the accident.

And Ponder, with the help of his friends and neighbors, did make a comeback. By July 1980, Ponder once again was lifting donkeys, leopards, and women and pulling trucks with his teeth. However, in the 1980 show, the "death slide" was conspicuously absent from the program, probably a result of Velma's dissatisfaction with Joe's hobby and the better part of Joe's good sense. Ponder continued to conduct stunts for years to come, even performing stunts in a wheelchair in 1985 after undergoing surgery to repair his ankles.

Today, Joe Ponder lives a more sedate life, preferring to run the leather company with Velma and to work out in his gym. Ponder runs his company the way he did his stunts—his way! Like other businesses in Love Valley, Ponder's company is not regulated by regular hours. He's open when there is a customer. But Ponder's laid back style of business has produced the most successful and long-lived business in Love Valley. There since 1960, Joe Ponder the man and Joe Ponder's work are as much a part of the history of the town as anything or anyone else, save the Barkers. Ponder himself is almost a permanent fixture in town politics, serving on the town council for most of the town's history. But even Ponder admits he does not define the town. Rather, the town defines who he is. Without the help of his neighbors and the support of his community, Ponder believes he would not have overcome his own personal tragedy and might not be producing the best saddles this side of the Mississippi.[9]

"Jet"[10]

In early August of 1981, Ellenora Barker spoke with her son, Jet, by telephone. The conversation was not unlike any such call between mother and son, except this one was punctuated by the undercurrent of Jet's lingering illness. Mother and son talked casually, and Jet seemed particularly optimistic about his condition and about his plans. Jet reassured his mother, convinced her not to worry, and indicated that he would be fine and looked forward to seeing her. The conversation ended on a positive note.

Jet's call marked the last time he talked to his mother. Afterward, he busied himself with making arrangements for his wife and children. Then, not long after Ellenora had spoken with her son on the telephone, the phone rang again at the Barkers' Love Valley residence. August 2, 1981, ended a long and painful struggle for Jet and his family, when the 29-year-old heir to Love Valley died in the afternoon of that day. That day brought to a culmination the pain and struggle that Jet had endured since the end of 1979 when the most pressing thing on Jet's mind was to build a home for his family on the land he had purchased in Youngsville—that and the painful knot in his stomach.

The tragedy began to unfold in January of 1980.[11] Jet, who had spent most of his years in Love Valley, fell in love while in Raleigh and moved there after his marriage to the former Cynthia Sanders. By 1980, Jet and Cyndy had two children, Jetter Andrew Barker, IV (Drew) and Victoria Allison (Tori), had purchased land in a small town north of Raleigh (Youngsville), and had begun to build a home in Youngsville. The young couple and their children were living the dream of all those who wish for happy homes. Jet worked hard at his construction skills and was determined to build a good life for his family as a building contractor in Raleigh. Before his death, Jet established himself as a nationally known expert in passive solar construction. Shortly after the discovery of Jet's cancer, he was hired as a solar construction consultant and was traveling across the country to consult on passive solar techniques while he supported his family, built his home, and battled his cancer.

Jet was working on the foundation of his home when the pain in his abdomen became debilitating. Exploratory surgery in early January uncovered a huge malignancy. Ironically, Jet's home loan was approved on the same day as his surgery. One day in January 1980 saw the fruition of both the means by which Jet could realize his dream of building his own home and the presence that threatened to take away that dream. Jet went into surgery hopeful because of the good news about the construction loan, but when he awoke after surgery, he learned the extent of his disease.

As soon as he was able, Jet continued to work on his family's home, determined to finish the house before his disease made it impossible for him to work. His ability to work was impeded every three weeks by the chemotherapy and the terrible sickness that accompanied it. Nevertheless, Jet continued doggedly and eventually finished the foundation of the home. The foundation came from rock that Jet had quarried at Love Valley and transported to Youngsville in a pickup truck, and the symbolic significance was lost on no one: the dream of Love Valley had been transferred to Jet's own dream for the life and home he was building for Cyndy, Drew, and Tori. The work continued amid financial, physical, and emotional anguish. The once robust man, who was six feet, five and weighed over 200 pounds, was beginning to show the destructive effects of his illness. Nevertheless, on into 1980 he worked, vowing to finish the house and doing most of the work himself.

The reach of Jet's benevolence surfaced during the difficult times of illness as friends from all corners reached out to him, Cyndy, and the children. In June of 1980, Love Valley and the Southeastern Rodeo Association hosted a benefit rodeo to raise money in support of the Barkers. The event was a success, and to Jet, this gesture from the SRA was an expression of friendship forged through the years. But to those who knew Jet, no amount of assistance could repay the man for his kindness and caring nature.

After the rodeo, Jet returned furiously to the construction of his home. By the end of July, he had framed the house, completed the roof, and almost completed the siding. His hope was to have his family into their home by Thanksgiving. Jet built every cabinet, counter, wall, and door, using building materials that he had timbered himself or salvaged from antique homes. Jet finished his home a sick and dying man. He was able to live in his home for only one month, but by providing shelter for his family, he did all he could in a hopeless and helpless situation. He provided them security and something he could not have, a future.[12]

When Jet died, his friends and family were devastated. It seemed impossible and so unfair that this young man, so full of life, energy, and ambition, could be struck down by an unseen foe. The local obituary quietly remembered the deeds of his life, the schools he attended, the company he owned, and the family he left behind. But the real testimony to this young man's life came not in the obituaries but in the heartfelt eulogy, written and spoken by his brother-in-law David both at the memorial service in Wake Forest and at the funeral in Love Valley. David's words eloquently summarized feelings that were so hard to express but that so accurately described Jet for those who knew and loved him. On a late August afternoon, on a silent hill overlooking Love Valley, as loved ones gathered by the Love Valley Church, David eulogized his brother-in-law and friend.

Jet's goals were to finish his family's home and to see his children grow up. He finished the house, yet even though he could not watch his children grow to maturity, one gets the feeling that the indelible mark he left on them in his short time as father continued long after he passed from this world. Raising those children on her own after Jet's death was a difficult and lonely task for Cyndy, yet it was one made easier by Jet's love that survived his death. Jet embodied the best of the spirit of Love Valley, and his death highlighted a life built on a courageous vision of family and community responsibility. Through the years, Jet's reach still touches Cyndy, Drew, and Tori, as well as the many friends and family Jet's life touched through the years.

Jet's illness and death were tragic for his family but also left an unforgettable impression on Love Valley itself. Jet and Tonda had been part of the town since its inception, and many people identified Jet with Love Valley. Everyone from those cowboys who had watched Jet grow up on the streets of the town or on the back of a horse to Jet's friends from the Love Valley rock era mourned his death, and with Jet Barker's passing, a bit of Love Valley passed, too.

The late seventies and eighties witnessed political disappointment for Barker, Jet's death, Andy Barker's cancer, political upheaval in the town, and quiet, almost imperceptible change. But the hard times and tragedies of the era were multiplied in a tragic event that rudely interrupted the lives of Love Valleyites in the early months of 1991.

On Wednesday, February 13, 1991, North Iredell and Love Valley were rocked by the news that a long-time friend of the Valley had shot and killed a local dairy farmer.[13] By the weekend following the shooting, friends had gathered in Love Valley to raise bond money for their friend and to arrange for his defense. The Barker household became the unofficial center of operations during the hectic and frantic weekend. Supporters drove for hours to the Valley to help their long-time friend. Confusion over events marked the gathering; rumors and uncertainties defined the tragedy. However, friends in Love Valley demonstrated their loyalty in a close-knit community by bonding in the aftermath of the tragedy.

Eventually, the charge of second-degree murder was brought against the accused by the state, the defense contended that the shooting was an accident, and the accused entered a plea of not guilty. The defendant claimed that he did not think the shotgun was loaded, that he only intended to scare the victim with it, and that the gun discharged accidentally when he swung it at the victim. The defendant was not acquitted but found guilty of the lesser charge of involuntary manslaughter and given a three-year suspended sentence with supervised probation. The defendant expressed his remorse for the whole incident. In a painful moment of recollection, he told me his story of what happened, and expressed his gratitude for the support he received from his Love Valley neighbors.

Two families and their friends were victimized by these events, and for some, healing began almost immediately and was demonstrated in the Love Valley Church the Sunday following the shooting. In that service, the focus was forgiveness, and the parson intimated that forgiveness embodied the essence of the Love Valley community.[14]

Following the tragic events of early 1991, a long-time friend of Love Valley faced tremendous adversity. In May of 1991, C. A. (Jack) Laws watched his dream go up in smoke. The stained-glass business he and his wife, Helen, had built together burned, and in the process, the Lawses lost over a half a million dollars in orders and work. At the time, Laws was in his mid-seventies. Faced with the monumental task of rebuilding, retirement crossed his mind. But he had wanted the business to continue with his children, and he had obligations to fill orders with several churches. The Lawses rebuilt. With grit and determination, they and their employees worked in makeshift quarters or even outside and rebuilt the business.[15] The creators of the beautiful stained glass windows in the Love Valley Presbyterian Church, the couple who had contributed so much to the early years of Love Valley's history, demonstrated through their own courage and perseverance those qualities that Love Valley has come to embody through the years. Through tragedy, their will was tempered, and they emerged triumphantly stronger than before

—strengthened and energized by a sense of responsibility and dogged optimism.

Love Valley has endured these and other tragedies through the years but, like Helen and Jack Laws, has refused to allow the tragic to destroy the unbridled optimism that built and continues to sustain the town. The utopian vision, the communitarian values, the unrelenting desire to create a social haven of good will continues to uphold the town even during its darkest moments, and to the extent that the town is sustained by its own strong sense of community, the utopian vision endures and turns tragedy into triumph. A rock festival, an injured stuntman, failed aspirations, the death of family and friends, life-threatening illnesses—all tragic events, faced collectively, and overcome through the triumph of the human spirit. Not the spirit of one lone champion who faces the world's injustice and triumphs over evil—not the superhuman spirit of the heroes we construct from imagination and hope—but rather the spirit that is undergirded by community, by a collection of wills that together support and brace one another. This collection creates a whole that is much greater than simply a sum of its parts, and this, more than any-thing, accounts for the dogged persistence of the little utopian cowboy town in the woods of northern Iredell County. Triumph comes from tragedy because as the rock band Flood reminded Love Valley, "many waters cannot quench love, neither can the floods drown it" (Song of Solomon 8:7).

9

Maturity and Community

Love Valley in 1997 does not look so different than it did in the early sixties, and if you ask most of the residents there, they would suggest that Love Valley has never changed much. To a certain extent, they are right. Love Valley still symbolizes many of the same ideals and attitudes that it has always embodied. Yet, to a lesser extent, they are underestimating the degree to which the little town has changed, not in any observable way, but in small, gradual, imperceptible movements that have produced the Love Valley of the nineties. The political leadership has changed, the residents have changed, and people have moved, but these are not the changes of importance. Rather, those small gradual alterations have to do with maturity and stability. Perhaps for the first time in its history, Love Valley is standing still. After more than 40 years, Love Valley has reached a state that finally allows rest—rest for its founder, his family, and the residents who still walk the streets of their western dream.

What would one find on those streets in Love Valley in the nineties? The following scenarios and colorful characters will give the reader some idea of what to expect on the dusty streets of Love Valley.

Arizona[1]

The old coal stove churned out heat relentlessly as Ellenora somehow managed to shove coal into the hungry beast while making sure her guests were even better fed. A lazy drowsiness settled in on the visitors who were relaxing around the dining room table after finishing a warm lunch. One could not imagine a cozier setting than sitting around Ellenora's table (a table that will and often does seat 24) with the coal stove working away while the cold January winds whipped through the stables and around the house. Andy Barker puffed contentedly away at his pipe while Ellenora quietly began to clear and clean the table. Arizona washed down the last bite of his pound cake with a swig of hot coffee, looked sheepishly at his inquisitor, and continued, "Yeah, I just came back from over at weird acres, and it reminded me of the time me and my cousin . . ." Another story began as his listener drifted in and out of consciousness, totally content with the world, with his full belly, and with the warmth he was receiving on a cold, bitter winter afternoon.

Until a recent move, Arizona had lived at Love Valley off and on for many years and had seen it through almost as many trials as its founder, Barker. He remembers the old timers D. L. Morris and Jack Harris. He remembers all the difficult times, controlling outlaw motorcycle gangs and drugs during the rock concert. He remembers all the antics he and his cousin enjoyed during his years in Love Valley. But most of all, Arizona remembers the trail—the riding trail and the trail of the cowboy—a trail of life that, for Arizona, is marked by simplicity. "The simple life is better," opines Arizona. "Why, even plumbing gives problems. I sometimes think we were better off before we had indoor plumbing and running water."

Arizona cuts a tall profile and always sports blue jeans, a plaid shirt, and a red bandanna. He epitomizes Love Valley with his ways of independence, and he probably has more sweat equity in the place than anybody except the Barker family. Until he moved, Arizona could be seen all around Love Valley cleaning up trash after a rodeo weekend; repairing fences on the north side of the stadium; building a new stall in the stable; chucking wood from the old furniture shop to the back of a waiting pickup truck; or perched high upon his stallion, ready to lead a young couple on a three-hour trail ride back through the woods surrounding the town. But during a short break from his labors, Arizona looks contemplative and speaks of the wonders of the trail. His voice grows distant, his eyes narrow and then widen, and he speaks poetically about the trail, repeating and quoting verse and talking about how different the world seems from atop a horse.

According to Arizona, those who ride the trail are lost to the wonders of nature and in Thoreau-like rapture can lose themselves to the vision of the world from horseback. One can see it in Arizona's eyes and hear it in the echoes of mystic, muted voices from Love Valley's past. And so, the dream of a cowboy lives on in a man named Arizona.

Tonda Barker[2]

Tonda does not live in Love Valley any more. Nevertheless, a look at the town in the present would be incomplete without a retrospective look at her life. For, in many respects, Tonda's life is Love Valley, and Love Valley owes much of its life to Tonda. Love Valley is as it is today thanks in large part to the first born of the Barker household.

From the time she moved to Love Valley as a six-year-old until shortly after her marriage and the Love Valley Rock Festival, Tonda's life was dominated by the town, her parents' dedication to it, and her own investment in helping her parents' dream become a reality. Even though Tonda no longer lives in the town (and has not since the early 1970s), in many ways she is still living Love Valley. The town made such an indelible impression on her that she will likely never escape its impact on her life. Yet, she has, in turn, influenced the town to a degree few realize.

From the earliest days of the town in the fifties, Tonda competed with Love Valley for her parents' affections. As a result, growing up in the Barker household meant growing up in a hurry. By the time she was eight, she ran her own concessions business in Love Valley, and by her twelfth birthday, she ran single-handedly a western wear store on the streets of Love Valley. Her precocious entrepreneurial savvy demonstrated the cowboy spirit of Love Valley. Tonda became a tough, independent young lady before she was dating age. And the same young lady who was running a successful business could also pick cotton and ride horses with the most hardened North Iredell cowboys. She was a champion barrel racer and a judge in horse shows across the Southeast.

At first glance, it may appear that a cowboy town would be the ideal romantic place for a youngster to grow up, yet early years in Love Valley were tough. Not only did Tonda have to fend for herself much of the time and grow up faster than most kids her age, but she also had to deal with a total life change at the tender age of six, when she was removed from a comfortable, suburban life in Charlotte and placed in a cabin with no water or latrine facilities. The move turned her world upside down.

To add to the difficulties of moving from a pampered childhood to a cabin in a rural community, she never seemed to fit in with her cohorts. Families in the area were suspicious of the Barkers, and children often voiced those suspicions directly to the Barker children. To her classmates, young Tonda was just a city girl whose father entertained dignitaries and celebrities.

But difficulties in transition and in fitting in were not the most traumatic memories for this child of Love Valley. Her father made a lot of enemies through the years, and it was difficult for this little girl to deal with people hating her father. Her eyes still mist over when she talks about an attack after a horse show that left her father bleeding from a head wound. The 10-year-old Tonda watched several men jump her father and threaten to kill him. Neither was it easy for the little girl to deal with her father's role as justice of the peace. She would lie awake many nights, listening to the fights with drunken rowdies he and the sheriff would haul in for sentencing. Yet for all the pain she endured, for all the sacrifice expected of her, for the loss of her childhood, Tonda

Fig. 15. Tonda Barker Smith in Love Valley as a teenager. Love Valley photo archives, used by permission of Andy Barker.

emerged an independent and self-assured woman whose impact on the town continues today.

No one faced the challenge of building a utopia with more strength and courage than did Tonda. And today, when she visits the town, she can survey its streets with pride, because she, as much as anyone, built Love Valley. Tonda is a child of Love Valley, but even more so, she has and still does give it life. The town owes much to that youngster with the strawberry colored hair who could ride with the best of them and who still beams as she walks the streets of the town.

Grandchildren[3]
The Barker grandchildren have grown up visiting Love Valley, but they have not outgrown their love for the place. They find themselves in

Love Valley on weekends, during the summer, and on holidays from school. They are not around as much as they were when they were younger, but when they come, they bring with them the spirit of youth that once dominated and energized the town.

Ellenora Barker described that spirit by relating a story from one brisk but unseasonably warm day in late December a few years back. The grandchildren migrated to the valley during the break between Christmas and New Year's Day. Late that afternoon all the grandchildren piled into the back of Barker's pickup truck. They were anxious to ride their horses before supper (each grandchild has a horse that they broke as colts), but first they had a small errand to run. What looked like an open air tour of town was actually a mission to help a neighbor. The kids were being ushered by Barker to the other side of the valley to haul and stack wood for a neighbor who had run out during the last cold spell. They managed to get their ride in before dark, but in the process these young adults continued the spirit that initiated the town's utopian impulse.

Tori was the first to hop into the back of the truck. Then a vivacious teenager, Jet and Cyndy's daughter carried herself with the confidence and pride that came from competing as a track athlete, as a member of the AAU basketball team, and from her modeling experience, an outgrowth of Tori's natural beauty. Later Tori was to be honored as the most valuable player on her high-school volleyball team and as the recipient of the Highsmith Award, an award recognizing the most outstanding student at her high school. Tori's ambition, resolve, and determination were evident even then and will allow her to realize her goals that at present include a career in fashion design. Tori, the youngest of the Barker grandchildren, was in the truck first and urged her brother and cousins to join her. A boundless bundle of uninhibited energy, this youngster provided the same spirit for the group she provided for the rodeo crowd during barrel races.

Her cousin, Angela, jumped in beside Tori. Angela is Tonda and David's daughter who, in her twenties, has inherited her mother's beauty and savvy. Before graduating from Southern Seminary College in Buena Vista, Virginia, Angela served as Student Government Association president and received the Joyce O. Davis Scholarship for leadership and involvement. Angela graduated from Salem College in Winston-Salem in 1993 and was the type of student who makes her college proud. She has since taken a bit of Love Valley's benevolence into her career as a counselor for at-risk youth and their families. Wise and mature beyond her years, Angela provided an interesting contrast to her younger cousin in the truck bed beside her. Her careful tutoring and refinement balanced the youngster, and one got the feeling that Angela was the intellectual energy of the group—the logical grounding that balanced Tori's passion.

Jeff, Angela's older brother by one year, was third into the bed of the truck. This senior member of the group cut a handsome profile and exuded authority. It was clear that the others admired his accomplishments. He has since graduated from Presbyterian College in Clinton, South Carolina, married Kim, a fourth-grade schoolteacher, and is now overseeing his own construction company, Johnson-Smith Concrete Contractors, in Charleston, South Carolina. Even then, his cousins expected such accomplishments, and Jeff had become a leader to them. As the eldest grandchild, for a while it seemed that Jeff would someday inherit Andy's title as patriarch of Love Valley. However, Jeff's career interests took him in different directions. Nevertheless, Jeff was still the leader of the group, and the others looked to his example and were hesitant to act without him.

Drew, Jetter Andrew Barker, IV, Tori's older brother, was the last to climb into the rear of the truck. He hoisted an imposing frame up over the tailgate, the same frame he used to rope calves and to sack quarterbacks. Drew completed the group, together they created a group in which each one complemented the other. Tori provided the group with spirit and passion. Angela gave the group intellectual strength. Jeff provided leadership and focus. And Drew provided physical strength and dreams. Drew's dreams have now led him to own and operate J. A. B. Construction, making Drew the fourth Jetter Andrew Barker to be in the construction business. Even then, Drew was the dreamer of the group, and years ago, his dreams tied him inescapably to Love Valley and its future.

"Drew, would you like to help me park cars?" The words still echoed in Drew's head. This was the first indication he had received that he might realize his own dream—a dream that was born and had matured during summers spent at Love Valley. The words possessed a magical quality. With excitement, Drew calmly replied, "Of course, Granddad." Andy replied nonchalantly, "Well, get your gear and meet me down by the lot."

Drew returned to his room and carefully strapped on his holster, admiring the hand-tooled leather and fine craftsmanship characteristic of Ponder's leather shop. His fingers caressed the buckle as he snapped it into place. Which gun would he carry? Drew boasted a fine collection for a boy of fourteen. Many of the guns were his father's, others were gifts from his granddad, some were tokens of appreciation from his grandfather for a job well done. Finally, Drew settled on the Colt that Andy had given him a few days earlier for helping him finish up a job at his shop. Drew carefully selected the Colt, checked its chamber to make sure it was loaded, admired the gun he had so dutifully cleaned that morning, and slowly slid it into place by his side. The weight of the gun felt good in its holster and somehow expanded Drew's already sizeable frame that he had inherited from Jet. Finally, Drew took his hat from its peg, planted it squarely on his head, and then tilted it slightly to one side. Drew stepped back, looked at himself in the mirror, and smiled.

Standing at the end of town, Drew peered through the trees and down the steep slope to the vacant field where he and his granddad would direct traffic and park cars. There would be hundreds of cars that evening full of spectators who had come to see the rodeo, and he was charged with keeping order when the crowds started to arrive so that each person could park within walking distance of the arena. There was his granddad down below, standing by the gate, a figure who stood silently proud, no doubt recalling the years and memories of Love Valley in those few quiet moments before the cars would start arriving. Drew stood up straight and walked confidently down the hill to join his grandfather in those memories.

Andy smiled at the approaching boy, he reminded him so much of Jet—he had Jet's stature and his intimidating stare. He had even inherited Jet's stride—the stride of confidence that marks a boy's passage into manhood. With Drew's short walk across the field to join his grandfather, the two closed the distance between generations through the man who bound them together—a man who was father to one and son to the other. Andy thrust his hand forward, and Drew shook it firmly.

The first arrival barreled down the dusty entrance to the parking area as the two men broke their grasp. "You take it," Andy said, and Drew stepped forward to take his place, a poised confident man at 14—a man who would have made his father proud. He was living a dream that had directed his ways for some time—a dream that had passed from his granddad to his father and now to him. From a distance it was hard to tell the two apart—Jetter Andrew Barker, Jr., the dreamer and the builder, and Jetter Andrew Barker, IV, the future.[4]

* * *

The Love Valley Presbyterian Church, the cornerstone of the community from the beginning, has seen seasons of growth and decline through the years. Lately, many members sense a renewal in process because young people have begun to involve themselves in the life of the church in a uniquely Love Valley way. It is not unusual to see several youth selling concessions during rodeo weekends. Invariably, they wear white aprons upon which they have sewn a horse and the words Love Valley Presbyterian Church. All their profits go to the church, and to a church with a budget as small as the Love Valley church, their contribution is significant. Renewal symbolized by these young people is felt by many in the congregation. This renewal is, for some of the town's residents, a return to the Love Valley of old, with the focus squarely on church, the young, rodeo, and family entertainment.

When the Reverend Wayne Dixon came to the church around Easter of 1993, he brought with him an exuberance unusual for a retired minister. That excitement produced a growing membership of young couples and families and a continuation of the emphasis on lay ministry and voluntarism. The church depends on the voluntary efforts of its members as seen in the service of Mr. Walter Tilley, the first person one sees at the Love Valley Church. Mr. Tilley is a retired Navy chief petty officer who served during the Korean and Vietnam conflicts. He is currently an officer and a member of the Honor Guard at a local VFW Post and is active in veteran's affairs.[5] Mr. Tilley serves Love Valley with the same honor and dedication he holds for his country. He has served as the water commissioner and town board member as a volunteer, giving many of his hours in severe weather to keep the town water system in working order. He calls himself the "pseudo-sexton" of the church, and he takes care of the grounds, the graveyard, and the buildings. Tilley also arrives early each Sunday morning to start the worship music that plays over the loud speakers of the church. "Pseudo-sexton" or not, Mr. Tilley is one of the most valuable lay leaders in the church who keeps things running when there is no preacher, and even when there is.

* * *

On most weekends, the streets of Love Valley are filled with horses, cowboys, and riders in blue jeans and western attire. However, the curious and amused make their way to the town as well. These visitors are easily recognizable by their bermuda shorts and topsiders, which provide a strong contrast to jeans and boots. Rather than a cowboy hat, these visitors sport baseball caps; rather than guns, they shoot with cameras draped around their necks. Yet, for some reason, these day trippers do not feel out of place and their presence is accepted as a matter of course. The unofficial motto of Love Valley seems to be that everyone is welcome, horse lovers and curiosity seekers alike, and that philosophy extends to the most obvious tourist.

Most of these visitors invariably find their way to Ponder's Leather shop, a trademark of the town and a fixture in Love Valley lore. Ponder is widely known for his leather work and craftsmanship, and his shop has become a minor museum of sorts. The main attraction is difficult to determine. Is it the crafts, the machines, or simply Ponder himself? Regardless, a trip to his shop is an experience in itself.

As the tired visitor makes her way to the front of the leather shop, she notices how attractive the old clapboard building appears. Ponder's shop is one of the largest buildings on main street, for it houses inventory, work space, and machinery, plus a few added attractions one would not associate with the leather business. In addition, it is also one of the neatest and tidiest buildings in Love Valley. The care the Ponders take in maintaining their business reflects the care that goes into their craftsmanship. Red, white, and blue banners stretch the length of the building to celebrate the Fourth of July weekend. Signs advertising the shop are accompanied by a diagram describing how to custom fit a saddle to an individual rider. The boards creak softly under her weight as she walks toward the front entrance. Two horses are tied in front by the hitching post.

As she walks into the shop, she is greeted with a big hello and an offer to help. Upon stating her intention of browsing, Ponder himself offers to show her around. He leaves his apprentice working diligently away on the latest project (a beautiful saddle being crafted for a client in Montana) and he changes hats for a short while—the craftsman becomes museum curator.

"Over here you will see some of the smaller items . . . belts, knapsacks, saddle bags, and the like. These are more like off the rack items in a clothing store. The real tailor-made items are in the back room here." Ushering his visitor into his showroom, Ponder weaves his way through saddles costing several hundred dollars (some of them thousands). His round face beams, and the muscles in his short, stocky body flex a degree harder as he surveys the room and its contents. His pride is undefinable, inexhaustible, and enviable.

The tour continues with an introduction to the art of leathercrafting and the history of saddle making. Then Ponder turns the corner and his eager listener is treated to another side of the artist. Off to one side of his shop is a gymnasium where Joe works out regularly. Since his boxing days in the Navy and his stunt man days that nearly ended his life, Ponder has trained his body by hoisting tons of iron around a musty, dark room. In his own makeshift gym, he boasts a wide variety of equipment and machines, including some special equipment he designed to strengthen his neck muscles for the stunts he did years earlier.

As Joe demonstrates some of the equipment, he points out a large poster on one of the walls, which reads, "The Association of Oldetime

Fig. 16. Joe and Velma Ponder outside of the Ponder Leather Co. Circa late '70s. Love Valley photo archives, used by permission of Andy Barker.

Barbell and Strongmen: An International Iron Game Fraternity, Organized 1982." Joe claims the fraternity includes some 500 members and promotes the sport of weight lifting as a mind and body activity. Joe uses this opening to espouse his own philosophy about the sport. "To me, lifting weights is much more than simply a physical exercise. For example, take this steel rod." Joe reaches around behind him as he talks and pulls out a steel rod that has been bent into the shape of a pretzel. "I watched a man bend this rod with his bare hands, and that cannot be done with simple brute force. You see, lifting weights helps you to focus on the relationship between the mind and body, and through concentration and meditation, you can overcome the limitations of the physical body. My personal belief is that you can exert the infinite powers of the mind over the limited powers of the body. That's what allows some men to bend steel bars, some men to overcome disease, and some men, me for example, to lift and pull massive weights with my teeth."

As he continues to philosophize, Joe points out the evidence of his beliefs: on the back wall are pictures depicting various "strongmen" (including himself) performing all sorts of feats that defy explanation. There is a black and white photo of Joe in mid-flight of his "death slide;" there is a color poster of Joe pulling a double tractor-trailer rig with his teeth (and beneath the poster is one of Joe's business cards, which reads, "Pulling for Jesus Christ"); there are pictures of Joe's exploits as they have been captured for *Ripley's "Believe It or Not!"*

Joe invites his visitor to see his inner sanctuary, the place where he collects and gathers his inner strength. Off to one side of the gym is a small door that leads to his dry sauna. Joe's visitor cautiously steps into the room, which is slightly larger than a closet. In the cramped quarters, she can barely turn around, but she can move around enough to take in the unique ambience of this spiritual sanctum. The entire room is enclosed with stained glass (from Lawses' stained glass studio) and the result is a mystical glow that floods the room with outside light filtered through colored lenses. In one end of the chamber is an elevated reclining couch. The couch is situated to face a stained glass wall depicting the praying hands and Jesus embossed upon a cross. "This is my meditation place," says Joe. "You see, I draw my strength from meditating upon the Christian mystery, but all faiths draw strength from meditation as well." This is where Joe fuses the connection between mind and body—in his sauna/chapel/meditation chamber.

After showing his visitor his swimming pool, jacuzzi tub, and plans for his strongman museum, to be called "Joe Ponder's Centurion Crusade Museum," the tour is over, and Ponder escorts his visitor back to the door. He loves showing folks around and is proud of his little shop in

Love Valley. As his visitor leaves, two men amble in to chat with Joe. Sometimes his shop serves as a gathering place for residents. Joe greets them and invites them in for a spell—it makes one wonder when Ponder finds time to make those beautiful saddles in his shop.[6]

* * *

On hot summer days, the place to seek relief from the heat is the saloon. The establishment offers everything one might imagine a saloon to offer—cold beer, a pool room in the back, a stage for live music, and a huge dance floor. The building that houses the saloon once served as the town's main dance hall, and dancing, at least on the weekend, seems to be the main attraction.

On weekends, the place is packed with men and women dressed in their finest western wear and $300 boots. More often than not, country music provides the beat for the dancers and blasts over the PA system when there is no live entertainment. The energy is high, the laughter is loud, and the crowd is boisterous.

Not everyone is dressed in western garb, and the ones who are not sometimes feel a bit awkward. At the very least, jeans are mandatory for a minimal level of comfort. For the most part, the patrons of the saloon reflect the attitudes of Love Valley in general. They cherish rural life and hold strong to values centering on family and community. These are the people one would like to have around when hard times come, for their love of country music and good times is undergirded by big hearts.

* * *

Ellenora wipes sweat from her brow. The kitchen is stifling hot. The Barkers always keep the house "cozy" with the old coal burning stove, but when you add to it the cook stove running at full tilt for 24 hours straight, the house gets about as hot as one can imagine in November. Ellenora has been faithfully watching over her turkeys for a day, and she has already prepared over 100 pounds of the gobbler since the day before. Every year she must bake a little more, because every year the number of people who come to Thanksgiving supper increases.

Ellenora opens the oven door as another blast of hot air greets her with the aroma of baked turkey and herb dressing. When she finishes basting the golden-brown bird, she once more turns her attention to the loaves of homemade bread ready to be popped into the oven. At the same time, she gives her attention to the pots simmering on the stove top. Ellenora is a master cook, and she is used to feeding large crowds of cowboys, hippies, or whoever else might show up on the front stoop. Nevertheless, she still gets a little overwhelmed when Thanksgiving comes. Every year since the Barkers moved to Love Valley, the church has sponsored a Thanksgiving supper for the community. Practically everyone in the town who is available attends, and many from the surrounding North Iredell community participate as well.

Often over 100 people attend the Thanksgiving meal, and the tiny fellowship hall of the church is hardly suited for more than 50. Gay Burr helps make the feast a success. Gay and her husband, Benny, own the boarding stables in town, and like the other residents, they contribute their time and talents to every aspect of community life. This attitude of civic responsibility will continue for at least another generation. Their son, Thomas, once planned and refurbished the exterior of the church as a scout project. Love Valley belongs to the people of the town, and they, together, make it a communal exercise. It is people like the Burrs who make the exercise a good one.

As Gay organizes the kitchen, she notices that already baked goods, pots and pans, and jugs of iced tea have been dropped off for consumption and use later at the supper. It goes without saying that the food at these meals is indescribably good, but the real treat of Thanksgiving in Love Valley is the gathering of the community for a meal. Even during the years when Love Valley and the surrounding communities were at odds, Thanksgiving supper still went on and people from around the area still gathered to share table with their neighbors.

On Thanksgiving Day, the afternoon and evening are a bit chaotic, but by supper time, all the food is prepared and delivered, the tables are arranged and decorated, the church is open and welcoming, and the people began to gather, some by car, others by foot. The table is sumptuous with turkey and dressing surrounded by every sort of vegetable and casserole imaginable. Everyone who attends brings a covered dish and with Ellenora's turkey and bread, there is more than enough for three times the number of people who actually attend. Bowls of steaming mashed potatoes with butter are flanked by green beans seasoned with ham. Sweet potato casseroles are arranged around the perimeter of the vegetables to add color to the main dishes. The hungry diner finds homemade cranberry sauce, baked apples, corn pudding, country ham biscuits, sweet preserves, pickled beets, black-eyed peas and ham, cornbread and yeast loaves, and an old favorite, persimmon puddin'. Persimmon puddin' is hard to come by these days and for the most part is a rare delicacy that appears at such special occasions as family reunions and holiday gatherings. This Thanksgiving there are three different persimmon puddin's: one dark in color, one light, and one somewhere in between. Most people will sample all three but will be unable to say which is their favorite. Persimmon puddin' bridges the gap between the main meal and the dessert table, and this year's collection of pies and cakes is only surpassed by the county fair. Apple pies with fresh Brushy Mountain apples, pound cakes that are moist and just a bit sad in the middle, pecan and chess pies, coconut cake, chocolate cake, cherry and peach cobblers only begin the list of sweets. The adventurous will fill a plate with desserts and may even go back for a second helping of their favorite—some opt for more persimmon puddin' instead. All of this is served with plenty of sweet iced tea and hot, strong coffee.

The feast is hard to imagine except for those who have attended a family reunion or gathering, because in reality, the Thanksgiving meal is a big family homecoming embracing a whole community. And the community is the key to the whole gathering—the food is simply an excuse for getting together. Old friends share memories and talk about recent problems; family members catch up with each other; new acquaintances are sparked; the men go to a corner and talk about hunting while the women clean up after the meal, each complimenting the other on a particular dish or creation; the children play; and the feeling of well-being makes one believe that an old-fashioned Thanksgiving is still an option in a world that rarely sees families taking the time to sit at the table without a television blaring in the background. But at the Love Valley Presbyterian Church, community is the thing, and the Thanksgiving prayer uttered before the meal reminds one of the reason for the celebration in the first place.

The Thanksgiving meal symbolizes the communal aspect of Love Valley as well as anything. Joe and Velma Ponder, Andy and Ellenora, the Barker grandchildren, Mr. Tilley, Gay and Benny Burr, Harry and Juanita, and other friends and family understand the bond. Alice Gordon is there joking about being Andy's favorite sister (she is Andy's only sister). Tonda's quiet strength undergirds the whole scene—her life was Love Valley, and perhaps no one has lived it more than she. There are others there too—those who cannot be seen but who are present nonetheless. "Doc" Morris lives on through the stories being told over in the corner; Mama Jib's exuberance for life can be felt in every heart; and, yes, Jet is there, too—in every part of Love Valley, Jet is there. They are all family—the Love Valley family.

10

Conclusion
Love Valley—Utopia and Mythic America

In chapter 1, I suggested that Love Valley is a utopian community. In this chapter I will build on that claim by focusing on those characteristics of Love Valley that are utopian in nature. Love Valley is utopian because it exhibits traits that commonly characterize experimental communities, especially religious communities from the nineteenth century. Nevertheless, Love Valley does not fit the mold of the familiar nineteenth-century millenarian religious utopia that was often organized to create the kingdom of God on earth or to usher in the kingdom. Such communities, for example the Oneida Perfectionists, were religiously oriented, as Love Valley is; however, Love Valley departs from this portrait of utopia in that it is not millenarian. Likewise, Love Valley never patterned itself after communistically organized groups that demand surrender of personal property and high-demand group orientation and boundaries. While Love Valley has always emphasized shared responsibility and resources, it has never organized on the concept of economic resources nor has it created unyielding social boundaries. Rather the boundaries have remained quite fluid through the years and demands have stayed lenient, probably characteristics that have allowed Love Valley to survive for more than 40 years.

This lack of adherence to some traditional models of utopian communities does not mean that Love Valley is not such a community, it simply does not fit some of the traditional forms for past utopian experiments.[1] However, if one means by utopia an intentional community organized around utopian ideals, a community that "is not a perfect place, but [has] the aspiration to create one;"[2] if one means creating "alternatives to established society . . . and attempts to realize unique ideals, dreams, and aspirations;"[3] if one means operating on the belief that "only in intimate collective life do people fully realize their human-ness;"[4] then Love Valley does constitute a utopian experiment and community. This, of course, is the bedrock of this study: Love Valley might not fit some of the conventional notions about what does or does not constitute a utopian experiment; however, in its intentions, in its organization, and in its existence, it embodies utopian ideals and aspirations.

As a working definition of Love Valley's brand of utopianism, the following are suggestions and models. Love Valley residents themselves often refer to their community as an outgrowth of the American enterprise. This places Love Valley generally in the context of an American community that sees itself continuing the American experiment as the community perceives it. The underlying premise of most American utopias and most studies on American utopianism is that "from the very beginning Americans have dreamed of a different, and usually of a better world"[5] and have been committed to social change, to the "feeling of freedom from traditional limitations"[6] imposed by established society. This type of independent idealism lies at the heart of Love Valley's utopian ideals and is expressed in the community's symbolic act—the re-creation of frontier virtue, independence, and freedom through the reconstruction of a nineteenth-century frontier community. In this community based on the frontier model, Love Valley represents an experimental society where community cooperation is established to preserve individual fulfillment and personal attainment.[7]

* * *

American utopian experiments often hold certain characteristics and attributes in common. Following is a brief discussion of 12 items that are common to many American utopian experiments and that distinguish Love Valley in one way or another. I have attempted to describe some common traits and to suggest how Love Valley might exhibit or refute such characteristics.

1. *Charismatic leader.* John Egerton notes that many utopian communities are "initiated by a single individual who [has] an idealistic vision, a strong personality, and a large public following."[8] Charismatic leadership usually defines the purpose and nature of the community, and the success of communities often depends on the ability of the leader to articulate his or her vision to a significant number of committed individuals. Love Valley has its own charismatic leader, Andy Barker, who from the beginning has defined the nature and direction of the community. Barker, in one way or another, has steered the direction of the town, and like other charismatic leaders, he began his experiment based upon commitment to an idealistic vision of society. More than 40 years after the establishment of Love Valley, Andy Barker is still mayor of the town and continues to direct the community.

2. *Relationship between economics, religion, and politics.* One theory concerning the establishment of alternative communities suggests links between economics, religion, and politics. Brian J. L. Berry argues that economic depression gives rise to religious millenarian expectation and experimental utopian building in response to nervousness about the health of capitalism. The utopian reaction to this perceived faltering is to separate from society and to build an alternative social and economic order.[9] This theory is instructive for the Love Valley story. While there is no certain link to economic crisis in this story, certainly the dynamics described here apply. Love Valley is in many ways a reaction to a perceived social and moral faltering in a competitive society. The Love Valley response creates an alternative society through a religious vision and a political entity and power base.

3. *Good versus evil.* The preceding characteristic establishes an oppositional relationship between the utopian community and society at large. As Rosabeth Moss Kanter has noted, this relationship is based upon the premise that the community represents the "good" that has been lost to the "evils" of larger society.[10] The charismatic leader generally perceives the community to be necessary because of defects within society. The vision of the community is based upon remedying those defects. Love Valley is no exception to this rule. Andy Barker founded the community at least in part to recapture wholesome values that he thought had been lost by larger society. Furthermore, many of the residents moved to Love Valley to participate in a community focused on virtue.

4. *Inherent optimism.* The good versus evil scenario is not fatalistic with utopian communities, because many utopias operate from an inherently optimistic outlook. This is particularly true of the nineteenth-century American utopias such as the Oneida Community.[11] The underlying theory views human beings as basically good and humanity as perfectible, while society exists as a culprit that causes discord. The goal of utopian communities, therefore, seeks to reinstate a natural but lost harmony between the individual and oneself, between individuals and others, and between the individual and God.[12] Utopias reject the larger culture as that which causes discord and exist to reestablish natural relationships through "restructuring social institutions."[13] This belief in the perfectibility of human beings, of human relationships, and of society itself constitutes utopian optimism.

Love Valley exhibits this optimism at every stage of its history. In the beginning, Andy Barker founded the town on the church and Christian ideals with the belief that before ruptured human and societal relationships could be repaired, one's relationship with God must be restored. Furthermore, Barker's unwavering confidence in the human spirit and in human ability reflects the dominant creed of the community and lies behind Love Valley's tolerance and openness. During experimental periods, Love Valley sponsored work projects and job skills training for young people from impoverished backgrounds, for juvenile delinquents who were rehabilitating, or for the post-rock concert hippies who populated the Valley for a few years. The optimistic philosophy initiating these projects assumes that individuals need only a fair chance to become successful and productive citizens in a reformed society. This inherent optimism undergirds Barker's outlook and acceptance of individuals and his theory concerning societal reform.

5. *Back to the land.* According to Kanter, one way to reinstate proper relationships with oneself, with one another, and in society as a whole is to "return to the land" and to rediscover harmony in relation to nature.[14] With contemporary utopian experiments, this often stems from a rejection of the chaos associated with urban life, where lack of community creates anonymous individuals, in favor of the perceived tranquility of a rural existence, where community exists to bind people together. Love Valley's founder began this community with just that philosophy in mind. Barker moved his family from Charlotte to the country to try to recapture rural values he believes are rooted in a nineteenth-century agrarian lifestyle. One of the purposes in styling Love Valley after a cowboy community is to recapture a rural atmosphere as a protest against urbanization. The re-creation of the frontier village represents the attempt to recapture American life as it appeared before industrialization and urbanization. The Love Valley lifestyle sponsors the "back to the land" motif at various points in its history, particularly in its sponsored wagon trains, its extensive riding trails, and its sixties back-to-nature and counterculture era.

6. *Unity of body and mind.* According to Kanter, utopian experiments sometimes attempt to reinstate proper relationships by drawing a direct connection between physical labor and psychic wholeness.[15] This utopian value has been expressed most clearly through communities such as the transcendentalist experiment, Brook Farm.[16] In Love Valley, labor has always been valued, at times as the key to psychic wholeness. This quality came to the forefront during community sponsored labor experiments meant to rehabilitate individuals or to help residents with a fresh start. The connection of mind and body appears even more explicitly in the eccentric philosophy of Joe Ponder as it was presented in chapter 9.

7. *Accidental location.* Often, the location of utopian experiments is not so much the result of careful planning as it is fortuitous circum-

stances and availability of land. For example, Egerton points out that the three Tennessee utopian experiments, Nashoba, Rugby, and Ruskin, did not settle in Tennessee consciously but rather "almost by accident . . . as an incidental choice of available land."[17] This characteristic calls to mind the stories surrounding Love Valley's location. Andy Barker had formulated a vision of his community but had made no formal plans until he happened upon some land during a business venture. He came about the land quite by accident and then set plans into motion to purchase the land for his community. Understanding this haphazard way of locating Love Valley, and indeed many utopian communities, dismisses questions concerning whether or not the community is situated in an advantageous location. In Love Valley's case, the accidental location of this town helps to answer the obvious queries about why one would build a western cowboy town in the rolling hills of Appalachian North Carolina.

8. *Order.* Since utopian experiments are founded partly on the premise that society exists as chaotic, it is not surprising that a high degree of order would be imposed on these alternative communities to overcome societal chaos.[18] High order has been a cornerstone of the Love Valley community and is, perhaps, best expressed in its model of frontier justice and high-handed imposition of law and order. The days when Justice of the Peace Andy Barker maintained law and order by patrolling the streets of Love Valley with a sawed-off shotgun are in the past; nevertheless, the principle of frontier justice remains firmly rooted in the Love Valley ethos.

Order in experimental communities usually extends beyond strict social control and even affects the physical layout of such communities. Some communities show a high degree of physical order in the way buildings are arranged in relationship to one another and in the way social space is inhabited and divided.[19] This type of strict physical order exists in Love Valley and is best seen in the careful planning of the frontier village. Barker and town planners were careful to maintain a nineteenth-century motif to the village even to the point of insuring that buildings appear to be at least one hundred years old. Perhaps the best expression of physical order imposed upon the town can be seen in Barker's unilateral decision to move the town to an alternative site after it had been planned, built, and arranged. Barker's decision was based upon reasons of organization and physical control.

One of the most obvious ways physical order is maintained is through the arrangement of ceremonial space within the community. A study of architectural arrangements provides intimate insight into the values, activities, and beliefs of communities.[20] For example, the Shaker community's highly functional buildings, including worship space large

Fig. 17. The Love Valley Rules. Photograph by author, 1997.

enough to house communal worship and dance, immediately come to mind when focusing on physical order.[21] Architectural order and ceremonial space constitute extremely important entities for Love Valley. The church, which still stands overlooking the Valley, was the first permanent building erected at Love Valley and illustrates the founder's wish to establish his community on Christian principles. Other buildings, such as the dance hall, the saloon, the jail, and post office have played important roles at various times during Love Valley's history. Perhaps the most highly ceremonial space in the community is the rodeo arena, which continues to define a certain aspect of the community's existence. All of these spaces are ceremonial, they reinforce the cowboy town motif, and they are efforts to impose physical control on the community in one way or another.

Finally, order in utopian communities exists often in the form of highly structured and planned community activities. Kanter points out that in many communities, order is imposed when "leisure time, entertainment, social activities, and opportunities for artistic self-expression are planned and included in the schedule."[22] Especially in the early years, Love Valley leaders carefully planned leisure and social activities that reinforced the system of values built into Barker's vision. Wagon trains, country fairs, square dances, rodeos, badman competitions, parades, and "wholesome entertainment" in general have been part of the Love Valley planned activity schedule for the members of its community. The infamous Love Valley Rock Festival itself was an attempt to plan and conduct an activity that would be "wholesome" if given proper supervision and support. Still today, craft fairs, rodeos, and other activities allow the community opportunities for self-expression and entertainment.

9. *Personhood.* A common utopian value might be described as high respect for the personhood of members in the community, a feeling of group intimacy engendered through common experiences or common identification. Sometimes utopian communities encourage this feeling of personhood through shared property or economic cooperation and often reinforce these feelings of shared experience through group rituals.[23] Personhood as a value, respect for others, and feelings of closeness with members of the community have always constituted important group beliefs for Love Valley. From the beginning, personhood was espoused in Love Valley's unofficial religious code (the golden rule), through the common cowboy identification (which virtually every resident adheres to in one form or another), and through group rituals that bond members of the community together (ranging from church services, to Thanksgiving community dinners, to the rodeos that come to Love Valley).

10. *Family.* Either as the fundamental unit of community or as the dominant threat to community, family usually is a central focus of utopian communities. Some communities, based on Fourierism, attacked the traditional institution of nuclear families because of the negative results of exclusive sexual relations.[24] The Oneida Community is a prime

example of this type of community. Other communities accepted the family as a basic social unit, but they experimented with different forms of familial arrangements. As a result, some utopian arrangements focus on alternatives that experiment with the complementary relationship between family and social structure.[25] Love Valley falls into the latter category and promotes a community that strengthens and preserves the family unit as the primary social unit.

Many utopian experiments in the twentieth century have fostered interesting notions about the family because the family unit has been in flux for much of this century.[26] Love Valley encourages a vision of the family in response to the seeming instability of the family unit and has from the beginning sought to reinforce and restore the traditional family through the promotion of family activities, especially in the early years. Later in its history, some Love Valleyites experimented with new ways to think about extended family including alternative groups and communes within the community in the early seventies. In any event, the family unit has been and still is integral to Love Valley, and through the years, the Love Valley experiment has responded to the redefinition of gender roles in the family unit, the perception that the nuclear family is no longer the central unit of American society, the awareness that the extended family is breaking down because of differentiation of economy and geographical mobility, and the growing reality of single parent households. Love Valley's response to these issues has varied at different points in its history, but the family has remained a constant priority.

11. *Communitarianism.* Utopian communitarianism exists in a wide variety of forms ranging from cooperative communities with shared assets to simply close-knit groups with a strong community orientation. In most cases, utopian communitarianism is not communism but "a system in which reform is attempted through small communities."[27] Arthur Bestor describes utopian communitarianism "as a lever to exert upon society the force necessary to produce reform and change."[28] In addition, Bestor argues, utopian communities are not escapist, as many of their critics claim, but rather reforming, seeking to make their communities a light and beacon to the future.[29]

This description of communitarianism communicates well Love Valley's driving force. Andy Barker always conceived of Love Valley as a small community that would exist as an example and in an activist manner to reform the larger society. Some characteristics of communitarian groups do not fit Love Valley. For example, only rarely have sharing of finances and resources occurred, and boundaries between members and nonmembers have always been quite fluid as opposed to the strict boundaries often found in these communities.[30] Nevertheless, the Love Valley experiment has been communitarian from the start and still maintains strong community traits. This collectivist impulse serves to critique individualistic concerns, and this creates some interesting connections to perceived Jeffersonian and Populist ideals inherent in the political leanings of town leadership.

Nevertheless, Love Valley's communitarian self-understanding is best described by its unofficial creed. Ideologically expressed, and religiously conceived, Love Valley's creed is "Do unto others as you would have them do unto you," the golden rule. Practically expressed through the everyday functioning of the town, that creed is understood by the residents of the town and is articulated by Andy Barker. The underlying belief is that citizenship requires responsibility; therefore, citizens must give time, effort, and support to other members of the community. Doing unto others becomes the primary means of supporting the community and provides the means by which communitarian life supports a network of helpful relationships. Individualism, perceived as insular, is tempered in the context of a community existing on a covenantal ideal. In such a community, one's actions necessarily affect the lives of neighbors and friends.

This utopian ideal, which is lived out in concentrated form in the microcosm of Love Valley, is present at every stage in its history: in the promotion of Love Valley as a tourist attraction, the idea is to provide a means for achieving a community lifestyle; in its philanthropic outreach, Love Valley attempts to extend its vision of societal accountability; in its political leanings, Love Valley attempts to spark a Jeffersonian vision of a government in covenant with its people; in its religious underpinnings, Love Valley re-creates the best of the Puritan vision of a society founded upon religious principles and divine covenant; in its unwavering acceptance of people from all walks of life, Love Valley allows a vision of a nonexclusive social structure; in its survival through hardship and tragedy, Love Valley demonstrates that the communitarian ideal works, at least in microcosm.

Nevertheless, the residents of Love Valley believe that their town is not simply an isolated microcosm. Contrary to the assumption of many sociological and political critiques and despite the evening newscast that continually reminds one that lack of community responsibility threatens to undermine American society, Love Valley prods one to believe that the covenantal ideal between individuals and society still exists. Many expect to find this ideal in rural communities across the country. This covenantal standard still exists in Love Valley and one would guess elsewhere as well.

12. *Utopias are perceived as deviant.* Many utopian communities are perceived by the larger society as deviant groups involved in aberrant behavior. Many times such charges come from fear, ignorance, suspicion, or simply dislike. Alternative communities initiate these feelings because they critique the status quo and are, thus, threatening. Some communities are undermined by this opposition while others attain social acceptance by becoming less alternative and more mainstream. Love Valley is no different—it has been perceived as deviant for most of its history. From the beginning, some of Love Valley's neighbors have reacted to the community with distrust, suspicion, and opposition. While such feelings reached a peak during and after the 1970 rock festival, they have never completely disappeared, yet Love Valley has been able to survive this opposition for more than 40 years.

These 12 characteristics do not exhaust the traits exhibited by American utopian experiments, but they are representative and shed light on the Love Valley experience in one way or another.

* * *

In addition to examining the dominant characteristics of utopian communities, one can categorize groups by type. In her insightful study, Rosabeth Moss Kanter suggests that in America there exists "three kinds of critiques of society [that] have provided the initial impulse for the utopian search: religious, politico-economic, and psychosocial."[31] I will use Kanter's typology to suggest that Love Valley has constituted each of Kanter's main types of societal critiques at various points in its history, and the history of Love Valley can be considered or examined in relation to the dominant type of critique that existed at various times and that led to various activities and emphases.

Kanter describes the three utopian types as societal critiques based on "religious and spiritual values," political or economic processes, or "psychosocial growth."[32] Kanter argues successfully that these three impulses roughly correspond to the three main historic periods of communal development in America (from early periods to the middle of the nineteenth century, during the 1820s-1840s, and during the 1960s).[33] Her framework provided me a clue and vantage point from which to study Love Valley. Kanter's categories provide a helpful structure that describes three waves of development in Love Valley's history.

During the early years of development in Love Valley, the religious vision of Andy Barker dominated the founding and philosophy of the community. Later, Barker used that religious philosophy to build the community into a political unit to seek political reform in the larger society. Finally, after the 1970 rock festival, Love Valley, staggered by criticism and bad press surrounding the festival and losing any political clout it had gained during the sixties, focused more on the community and psychosocial growth of its members. It is important to note that Love Valley has never been exclusively one or another type of community described above, rather certain themes and impulses of each of these types have dominated at various periods of development and through various community-related activities. Nevertheless, even when Love Valley was dominated by the desire for political reform, that desire was instructed by the dominant religious philosophy of the founder, and both the political and religious ideologies undergirded a strong sense of community support and concern for the holistic well-being of the community's residents. All the elements have been present throughout Love Valley's history with certain ones coming to the forefront during crucial points in the development of the community.

Following is an examination of how Love Valley fits Kanter's three categories.

1. *Religious critique.* The earliest American utopias, such as the Shakers and later the Oneida Community, were founded on religious principles, spirituality, and often biblical models. These communities "criticized the evil and immorality of the surrounding society" and offered the "possibility of human perfection through conversion to the more spiritual life" of the utopia.[34] For example, John Humphrey Noyes's theology was developed not so much to legitimize plural marriage in the Oneida Community as it was to describe the human path to perfection, to holiness, and to a "reconciliation with God."[35]

Often, these religious communities exhibited greater longevity than their secular counterparts. For example, statistical tabulations for nineteenth-century groups demonstrate the remarkable staying power of religious groups as opposed to secular communities. Almost one-third of the secular groups failed after the first year of existence while only 8 percent of the religious groups did not see their second year. After 10 years, five of six secular groups no longer operated while three-fourths of the religious groups still continued. Finally, hardly any of the secular-based groups lasted for 25 years, while two-thirds of the religious groups still functioned after a quarter of a century of existence.[36] It is not clear why religious utopias of the nineteenth century lasted longer. One would assume that a clearly understood philosophical center to which community members pledged their allegiance would create a greater commitment to the survival of the alternative community and viewpoint. If this is the case, such a religious cornerstone might help account for Love Valley's continued existence.

The desire to build a religious community, which would lead to a more spiritual life for the inhabitants and would allow for the striving for human perfection and holiness, permeated Andy Barker's initial impulse to build his Christian community. Barker wrote, "tonight I'm thinking and planning . . . my western town. . . . I know that with Him, my purpose and complete faith, anything is possible. My part of the bargain is to build a town, a Christian Community with clean recreation and strive to help people know more about God and His outdoors."[37] Barker acted upon this vision by building first a church and then a community around the church. From the beginning, the purpose of Love Valley was to provide a spiritual haven from the larger society.

Another characteristic common to religious utopian communities is a charismatic leader with a spiritual vision, a vision often crystallized by some significant event. The leader then becomes the spiritual leader of the community. Love Valley also exhibits this trait through Andy Barker's own religious vision and through the respect he and his family enjoy when they enter the Love Valley Presbyterian Church.

2. *Politico-economic critique.* Religious utopias seldom focus simply on spirituality but tend to extend a religious vision to one of societal reform. Alfred Braunthal points out that "among religious thinkers, insistence on societal change has frequently become an element of the quest for salvation."[38] Thus, religious utopias often spill over into the political and economic realms to create reform in society. This gives rise to Kanter's second type of utopian critique, the politico-economic.

The politico-economic impetus in utopian communities historically developed in response to the "dislocation, mechanization, overcrowding, and poverty" associated with the Industrial Revolution and focused on ideas and political theories. These communities focus on the perfectibility of human society and try to redress the evils created by the existing social and political system.[39] Often this leads to communities organized around economic cooperation and socialist experiments.

Love Valley never experimented with economic cooperatives, except on very limited bases early on and in subgroups in the early seventies, and of course, this community did not develop immediately following the Industrial Revolution. Nevertheless, Love Valley and its leaders did operate on the premise that society is perfectible through political activism and sought to overcome social and economic ills through involvement in political activity and social reform. Love Valley's activities along these lines can be seen in early experiments to attain economic self-sufficiency, to provide job training for economically distressed groups, through Barker's own political activity and philosophy, through efforts to restructure institutions such as the educational establishment, and through social reform throughout Love Valley's history.

As Barker has served as Love Valley's spiritual leader, so has he loomed as the unavowed political power and representative of the residents in Love Valley. The first and foremost testimony to this is Barker's almost uninterrupted tenure as mayor of the town and the base of support the town provided him during his gubernatorial runs. Nevertheless, by the time the fallout of the 1970 rock festival was over, it was clear that Barker had lost any widespread political clout he might have otherwise garnered, and the active period of Love Valley as a politico-economic unit of reform slowly subsided. At the same time, the rock festival itself brought a period of crisis to the community, followed by a series of individual crises suffered by high-profile members of the town. The result was an intense need for psychic healing and support within the community, and Love Valley's energies refocused on psychic wholeness through Kanter's third type of utopian critique, the psychosocial.

3. *Psychosocial critique.* Many of the communal experiments of the 1960s and 70s originated from the psychosocial responses to "alienation and loneliness, both social isolation and inner fragmentation."[40] Such groups (like Synanon) promote psychological wholeness by creating and maintaining support structures focusing on "self-actualization" and "personal growth."[41] While Love Valley has no formal structures in place at the present to promote psychic wholeness, the community has provided support structures through extended family units and communes, through providing opportunities for self-actualization, and through psychological and emotional support in times of individual or community tragedy. Since the 1970s, Love Valley has existed largely as a community that provides psychosocial wholeness and integration to its residents and visitors, a quality most members of the community express and believe is absent in larger society.

At present, the religious idealism that permeated Love Valley's early days is present but muted; the political activism that was such an important part of much of Love Valley's activities is limited to local politics and the mayoral and town council elections. The social reform directed at educational and recreational institutions all but vanished with Love Valley's counterculture element in the late sixties and early seventies. What is left is a quiet community that has experienced hardship and struggle, that still is a popular gathering place for many outside of the community, that serves as a haven from the complexities of modern life for residents and visitors, and that embodies the best of the psychosocial communities through a strong community orientation and support structure for friends and community members.

* * *

This conclusion places Love Valley in the context of American utopian communities. I have noted 12 common characteristics of American utopian communities and three different types of communities with their emphases and directions. My premise is that Love Valley exhibits all of these main characteristics and resembles each of the three types of utopian communities at various points in its long history. Yet one cannot classify Love Valley neatly as any one type or as exhibiting any dominant characteristic over the others. Above all, Love Valley's utopianism is unique, shaped by the vision of its founder, by its dominant ideology, by its distinct community awareness and commitment, and by its unique ambience and character.

Love Valley's brand of utopianism is unique. As the community enjoys its fifth decade of existence, it is perhaps less alternative than it was during the turbulent years of its maturation, but it is no less eccentric. Where Love Valley will go in the decades to come remains uncertain; who will lead the community in the future raises interesting questions and possibilities; the town's relationship with surrounding communities continues to evolve. These questions and issues remain unanswerable for the present, but one can easily imagine that Love Valley will continue to do what it has done for more than 40 years: explore the human spirit and attempt to provide opportunities for seeking and realizing human potential.

Although many of the utopian characteristics of Love Valley tie it to utopian communities that flourished in the nineteenth century, Love Valley is a community of the twentieth century—a community that in many ways maintains strong ties to the counterculture of the sixties. Some scholars argue that twentieth-century idealistic communities are qualitatively different from the nineteenth-century utopias, yet Love Valley exhibits characteristics of both twentieth century communities and those of the last century. This is where Love Valley's uniqueness qualifies it as an unconventional utopian community. Love Valley is a twentieth-century community built along the lines of vision of the nineteenth-century symbolic American West. Thus, Love Valley re-creates a nineteenth-century myth of America based on a twentieth-century, counterculture model. The picture of Love Valley as "mythic America" defines Love Valley as utopia in all its uniqueness and eccentricity.

First, Love Valley resembles the type of twentieth-century utopia described in terms of the counterculture. Just as utopianism was replaced by progressivism (leading to widespread social engineering) at the end of nineteenth century, the latter part of the twentieth century (beginning especially in the sixties) witnesses the challenge to progressivism in a new flourish of utopian idealism.[42] These countercultural utopian ventures that were initiated in the sixties, arose out of "'cynical realism'" rather than from the "buoyant optimism" of the nineteenth century.[43] The result of these trends has led some to view twentieth-century utopias as reacting negatively against society rather than as positively for optimistic reform for the future.

There is some validity to this perspective. Many nineteenth-century Christian utopian experiments operated on the premise of millennial expectation and preparation. Accordingly, they exhibited a basic optimism in their attempt to realize the kingdom of God on earth and the perfection of society. On the other hand, many twentieth-century utopias, in particular counterculture, retreat from larger society out of a recognition of, or belief in, the failures of the social order. Often these communities look to the past for examples of social models that work better while nineteenth-century communities were future oriented in their attempt to escape the Old World and create a new one. Twentieth-century communities often nostalgically search the past for simpler, better, less complicated models of social organization.

Love Valley constitutes a unique combination of both. Like the countercultural communal movement, Love Valley mounted its initial social protest at least in part from a pessimistic view of the contemporary social order. Nevertheless, Love Valley never operated out of cynicism, but like the nineteenth-century movements, based its social reform on a basic optimism about the perfectibility of society and tried to provide a model for larger society. In this sense, Love Valley is future oriented and forward looking. Yet, Love Valley also looks to the past with a great deal of nostalgia for its model of the perfect society and for its basic reform philosophies. This is symbolized by its existence as a nineteenth-century cowboy town. Thus, Love Valley is both forward looking and nostalgically oriented, searching for the right combination to provide for the perfectibility of humanity and society.

Above all, whether Love Valley has looked backward or forward, it has been outward reaching, attempting to use its utopian base to provide a haven and model for social reform of society at large. Love Valley's history remains remarkably replete with examples of its openness to the outside world. This community never instituted closed or even strict boundaries. In fact, through its history, the boundaries that define this community have fluctuated and evolved but always remained open to the outside. Perhaps this as much as anything can account for the community's resiliency through conflict and controversy and its ability to survive for more than 40 years. Love Valley's staying power is a result of its flexible boundaries and its ability to secularize its vision. The original predominantly religious vision has been muted through the years, and this secularization of the experiment has allowed Love Valley to acculturate, to adapt, and to change in the face of opposition.

Along with this adaptation has also come some loss of the reforming tendencies found early on in Love Valley history. In some ways, Love Valley exists now as an alternative community rather than as a reforming community. Such shifts have characterized other utopian experiments, as Paul Gaston has demonstrated in reference to Fairhope.[44]

Finally, Love Valley's uniqueness reveals itself in its very character as a Christian, cowboy town. As an alternative society, this designation is perhaps as creative and unusual as any community's. The designation "Christian, cowboy" carries all the symbolic imagery associated with Christian idealism and benevolence and with frontier optimism and opportunity. As its final claim to utopia, Love Valley creates a mythic time and space wherein is housed its vision of society. It is in this creation of a mythic America that Love Valley creates its unique utopia.

* * *

Love Valley as Mythic America

Love Valley as mythic America operates as all myth operates—it provides access to truths about human nature and human society. In the case of Love Valley, it serves this purpose in at least four ways. Love Valley offers a vision of mythic place, mythic time, benevolent empire, and communitarian town. These four elements make up the mythic elements of Love Valley.

Love Valley as Mythic Place

Sense of place describes much more than merely space and boundaries, although space and boundaries help define place. Sense of place includes all those things that locate people in a particular bounded space but also includes those things that ground people to their essential humanness. Sense of place is that quality of living that defines life and relationships, sanity and wholeness, and, ultimately, death and dying. Sense of place is expressed in Willa Cather's picturesque descriptions of the desert Southwest; in Lee Smith's portraits of Appalachian hills and hollers; in Ernest Hemingway's streets of Pamplona; in a young mother's mournful glance toward the horizon pointing home; in a farmer's peaceful walk through the fields; in a cowboy's lonesome trail. Sense of place is what ties one to ancestry, to nature, to other people, and to the earth. Sense of place defines life. Because sense of place extends beyond boundaries, it includes more than geography and the certainties of surveyed space. As such it transcends physical boundaries and cannot be recognized by landmarks or property lines. It is, rather, universal and infinite, it is inhabited by all and by no one, it is mythic in that it grounds one to the source of ultimacy. Love Valley, as mythic place, does this by recreating a cowboy town that is far separated from the frontier spatially but is the frontier in the mythic sense.

When Andy Barker set out to build Love Valley, he did not try to literally re-create the "Old West," rather, he was trying to discover the "Old West" and the virtues the myth of the West recalls. The frontier town, as it exists in Love Valley, may be a recognized township in North Carolina; it may be a working and self-sufficient town; however, to the extent that it grounds those who live there and those who visit there to something far more remote than a North Iredell community, it is a mythic town that creates a sense of place for those who feel the mystic pull of its remote setting. As mythic place, Love Valley grounds one in the truths that lie behind the ideal of the frontier myth—courage, virtue, autonomy, heroism, and the indefatigable human spirit.

Love Valley's sense of place is periodically reinforced through mythic reenactment in the primary ritual space of the town, the rodeo arena. In the drama of rodeo, the utopian impulse of Love Valley is ritualized, and the myth of origins of the utopia is remembered through a combination of southern and religious ideology and participation in the cowboy persona. This ritual space insures that even if utopia is not realized in community, it is remembered through ritual, and through this mythic activity, Love Valley's sense of place is experienced communally.[45]

Love Valley as Mythic Time

Nostalgia is yearning for a lost place or time, and in the case of Love Valley, it is a yearning for a lost America—an America defined by its innocence; an America that exists before the twentieth century and perhaps beyond time itself. Love Valley re-creates a mythic time—a time that perhaps never occurred but that remains fixed in consciousness as elemental, paradigmatic, and cherished. By definition, in Love Valley the time is mid-nineteenth century; however, the time could be any time that is defined by the utopian vision of wholesomeness and virtue.

When Barker started Love Valley, it was with the intention of providing a solution to the problems of society by re-creating a setting he believed existed before those problems plagued the contemporary world. Thus, in the beginning, the emphasis was on "wholesome entertainment" and on alternative activities that were supervised and provided "clean

Fig. 18. Two riders on a rainy, muddy July the Fourth weekend. Photograph by the author, July 1992.

fun." Barker's clue to "wholesome activity" was in the past, and he started Love Valley on the premise that contemporary life, particularly urban life, had destroyed much of what was virtuous and good. Building Love Valley on the model of the mid-nineteenth century was Barker's way of nostalgically searching for a lost time, a mythic America without the problems of poverty, anxiety, and hatred that seemed to him to plague twentieth-century America in such concentrated doses.

Many who live in Love Valley and who visit to ride the trails or simply stroll the streets participate in Barker's vision of a mythic time in America's past. This is not a time bound to any span of years but is the same time that some social commentators allude to; it is the same time that American artists have captured in so many paintings of homespun virtue and life; it is the same era celebrated by patriotic remembrances of our country's founders and those who have sacrificed to preserve the union; it is a time that perhaps has never existed outside of our collective consciousness, and the point of Love Valley is to allow one timeless connection to mythic time.

Love Valley as Benevolent Empire

America in the latter half of the nineteenth century gave rise to numerous voluntary societies, utopian groups, missionary organizations, religious institutions, and political policies that tried to mobilize resources, people, and funds to provide a better life for all people through "disinterested benevolence."[46] Education, temperance, suffrage, and workers' rights were all seen as avenues for building the benevolent empire, a society defined by good will toward all people, by equal opportunities for all people, and by the realization of the golden rule. The individual issues and the strategies for achieving goals may have differed, but the fundamental energizing force was the same for many of the benevolent societies of the nineteenth century: One should exercise civic and community responsibility to reach through and beyond the community in order to build a more perfect society. The authors of the sociological study *The Good Society* recognize this impetus to social responsibility as that which provides substance to individual freedom.[47]

Love Valley, too, has sought to create a benevolent empire reminiscent of the utopian experiments of the latter nineteenth century and of the social vision of *The Good Society*. Barker's social vision is based upon the golden rule, the idea of civic responsibility, and the faith that political and social institutions can work to bring about the "good society." For years, Love Valley has been involved in philanthropic ventures that reach well beyond the boundaries of the town. Based upon a nineteenth-century religious vision that the kingdom of God can be established on earth through benevolence and philanthropy, Love Valley offers itself to the world with a "God Bless" printed on its sign and an outpouring of community good deeds. Love Valley has attempted to operate as a "benevolent empire" through philanthropy at institutional, political, and social levels—philanthropy that has been extended through the years to the sick, the poor, and the homeless.

Love Valley as Communitarian Town

Community is the operative word in trying to unravel the complexities of Love Valley. One would be hard pressed to find another town that relies so heavily on a strong sense of community responsibility. In a sense, this story of Love Valley has been an examination of the role social responsibility can play in the establishment and maintenance of communities. Likewise, Love Valley's founders assume that such community standards are rare in American life today. This examination is a glance at, as Barker would say, Jeffersonian democracy in action.

In 1985, a group of sociologists published a book titled after a phrase Alexis de Tocqueville used to describe the social mores and principles of American life. *Habits of the Heart*[48] forces readers to take a close look at American social institutions, political theory, and individualistic philosophy. The authors took their cue from the monumental work of Tocqueville, *Democracy in America,* whose nineteenth-century analysis of a young democratic country still informs twentieth-century Americans on the role of democracy in society. Like Tocqueville, the authors of *Habits of the Heart* focused on family, religious, and civic life in America as keys to "the maintenance of free institutions."[49] And like Tocqueville, the authors looked with mixed feelings at individualism and warned that unrestricted individualism may in fact threaten to undermine freedom. Thus, the authors of *Habits of the Heart* examined the relationship between private and public life to focus on "those cultural traditions and practices that, without destroying individuality, serve to limit and restrain the destructive side of individualism and provide alternative models for how Americans might live."[50] The models they describe provide a framework for understanding Love Valley, for Love Valley itself is an alternative model for how Americans might live that seeks to balance the destructive effects of individualism by a strong commitment to civic and community responsibility.

As a final reflection on Love Valley as alternative social structure, one might look at a few characteristics of alternative models from *Habits of the Heart* and compare them to the distinctive qualities of Love Valley. Without attempting to be exhaustive, a few comparisons come to mind.

First, Tocqueville's work warned that unregulated individualism and self-interest would produce isolationism and privatization to such a degree that Americans could lose touch with public life altogether and risk sacrificing the freedoms based upon the political and public sphere. To combat this isolationism, Tocqueville suggested voluntary participation in civic organizations and political institutions so that individuals would play an active role in defining public life.[51] Voluntarism and civic participation would serve as bridges between the private and public spheres of life and would ensure the survival of a citizen's free participation in establishing and maintaining public policy. This view of Jeffersonian democracy in action fits the model established by the town of Love Valley under the leadership of its own self-avowed Jeffersonian, Andy Barker. Tocqueville even described the agrarian life centered in the township as the model for this type of active participation in public life to assure the common good. The town functioned as "a moral grid" that balanced individual self-interest by "collective well-being."[52] This, perhaps, is as apt a description of the role Love Valley plays as any. Love Valley is a town where, at its best, active participation of citizens helps maintain the collective well-being rather than individual self-interest.

Tocqueville's idealized vision of American democracy was grounded in the small community where citizens lived interdependently rather than independently, where each individual performed a vital role for the survival of the community, and where that role was recognized and supported by the community. The authors of *Habits of the Heart* characterize this vision of America as mythic and supportive of collective meaning.[53] These persistent American myths give one insight into the values that continue to be important to many people, if only in idealized form. It is in this way that Love Valley operates at the mythic level, by providing a working model for the tension Americans feel between individual self-interest and communal responsibility and by basing that tension on the model of the religiously enlightened social vision. In this way Love Valley reflects at least one myth of America.

Love Valley and its residents value individualism as evidenced by the town's mythic hero, the self-reliant cowboy or frontier pioneer. Nevertheless, this individualism is not the type of self-interested utilitarianism that the authors of *Habits of the Heart* describe. Rather, it is more akin to the biblical or civic individualism where individuals see themselves as part of an organic whole, an ecosystem, where their individuality is dependent on the proper functioning of the community.[54] In Love Valley, this has been demonstrated time and time again throughout its history: the insistence on establishing the town on a religious base; the goal of reaching out to the larger community through civic action and social programs; the emphasis on philanthropy; the acceptance of the counterculture in the face of great opposition; the binding together when one of their own faced trouble. All of these activities highlight the tension, the dialectic, between private and public that exists in Love Valley.

Even the town father of Tocqueville's vision of America and *Habits of the Heart* is present in Love Valley in its attempt to establish a township of civic voluntarism. The town father exists as the quintessential nineteenth-century man whose individual striving for success is balanced by his concern for and service to his community. The town father exerts authoritarian leadership and serves to ensure the economic well being of the community. His authority, as the model goes, is possible because of the family structure and a wife who provides support emotionally and through service to the community in the way of clubs and charitable organizations.[55] The town father model so fits Andy and Ellenora Barker that one might think the authors had them in mind when describing the model. That Barker has, for most of his career in Love Valley, exerted authoritarian leadership in the town is indisputable. That his leadership was directed primarily toward the economic betterment of the town also seems to be the case. In addition, Ellenora has provided a limitless source of support, not only emotionally, but through her volunteer efforts with organizations sponsored by or associated with the town. Her tireless efforts to help community members through voluntarism fit the town father model perfectly. The result is a "first family," so to speak, that embodies the aspirations, the goals, and the hopes of the town to such an extent that they have surrendered their identities to the community. The Barkers make up such a first family, both literally and figuratively, and they are the first family of Love Valley.

Finally, Tocqueville's vision of nineteenth-century America included mention of religious and political tendencies toward egalitarianism. Religion, beyond its private nature, constituted one of the chief means for Americans involving themselves in the public life of the community. Thus, religion was where the intersection of the private and public realms would likely take place in an egalitarian mode with the goal of seeking the public good over private success. Religion exerted a political force that often included a populist emphasis on the ordinary person, and it helped form a priesthood of citizens as applied in the secular as well as religious realms to ensure equality and benevolence in the community.[56] In Love Valley, it is sometimes difficult to decipher where religion leaves off and where politics begins. From the very beginning, Barker's vision of the town was built upon a religious base that sought to incorporate the golden rule in all areas of public life. In other words, Barker's religious vision intersected with his political aspirations to seek

Fig. 19. Andy and Ellenora Barker, founders and "first family", of Love Valley, on main street of the town in late 1997. Photograph by the author.

the common good for the community. Furthermore, Barker's political stance as mayor, as candidate for state office and governor, and as political reformer was always one infused with populist leanings or, in his words, "Jeffersonian democracy." In any event, his stance, both political and religious, was one where the ordinary citizen would be vitally involved in community life on a voluntary basis and would receive full equality within the community as a result of that participation. And, of course, Barker's vision, at least for a fair portion of the town's history, became Love Valley's.

These comparisons are not meant to suggest that Love Valley is an ideal town or the utopia its founder wanted it to be. It certainly has seen an abundance of trouble and controversy in its day. Rather, these examinations suggest that Love Valley exists as a unique town that constitutes a utopian experiment. It is a mythic town in that it represents and embodies some of the things that some people believe America should be and could be. And to this end, Love Valley provides access to a truth like only myth can.

* * *

This story began with the dream of Andy Barker, and it ends with the Barkers' hope and optimism for the future and for children. The ideals of this utopian experiment, benevolence, communitarian virtue, religious mores, and family values, continue in the enterprise of Love Valley, U.S.A.

Notes

Chapter 1

1. David Kimbrough, *Taking Up Serpents: Snake Handlers of Eastern Kentucky* (Chapel Hill: University of North Carolina Press, 1995), pp. 7-8.

2. William Lynwood Montell, *The Saga of Coe Ridge: A Study in Oral History* (Knoxville: University of Tennessee Press, 1970), pp. viii, xviii, as quoted from Kimbrough, *Taking Up Serpents,* pp. 7-8.

3. Robert N. Bellah, Richard Madsen, William M. Sullivan, Ann Swidler, and Steven M. Tipton, *Habits of the Heart: Individualism and Commitment in American Life* (Berkeley: University of California Press, 1985), and Robert N. Bellah, Richard Madsen, William M. Sullivan, Ann Swidler, and Steven M. Tipton, *The Good Society* (New York: Alfred A. Knopf, 1991).

4. Such a method is suggested by Lyman Tower Sargent in "Utopia and the Family: A Note on the Family in Political Thought," *Dissent and Affirmation: Essays in Honor of Mulford Q. Sibley,* ed. Arthur L. Kalleberg, J. Donald Moon, and Daniel R. Sabia, Jr. (Bowling Green, OH: Bowling Green State University Popular Press, 1983), p. 106. This method is desirable because of the multiplicity of texts and communities. By focusing on themes, one can consult the rich tradition of utopian studies without getting mired down in endless comparisons to other communities.

Chapter 2

1. Arline Brecher, *The Love Valley Thing,* Souvenir Program 1970 Love Valley Rock Festival (Charlotte: Halfway House Publications, 1970), p. 1.

2. Robert N. Bellah, Richard Madsen, William M. Sullivan, Ann Swidler, and Steven M. Tipton, *The Good Society* (New York: Alfred A. Knopf, 1991), p. 12. The authors also argued in *Habits of the Heart* (Harper & Row, 1985) that individualism and autonomy without communal responsibility can be a destructive force in American life.

3. See Bellah et al., *The Good Society* (New York: Alfred A. Knopf, 1991). In *The Good Society,* the authors argue that civic responsibility can balance individualism only through institutions. See p. 12.

4. Rosabeth Moss Kanter, *Commitment and Community: Communes and Utopias in Sociological Perspective* (Cambridge: Harvard University Press, 1972), pp. vii-viii.

5. Portions of this chapter appeared in Conrad Ostwalt, "Love Valley: A Utopian Experiment in North Carolina," *North Carolina Humanities,* vol. 1, no. 1 (Fall 1992), pp. 101-108. The story of Barker's foxhole vision is based on Barker's account of his envisioned community. This story is also related by D. L. Morris, unpublished manuscript, chapter 1. Morris's manuscript is housed in the Appalachian Collection at Appalachian State University.

6. Arline Brecher, "How Love Came to the Valley" in *The Love Valley Thing* (Charlotte: Halfway House Publications, 1970), p. 3. See also D. L. Morris, unpublished manuscript, ch. 2, p. 2. Andy Barker related this story to me on several occasions.

7. Andy Barker letter to mother, 1 February 1945. As reproduced by Morris, ch. 1, p. 4. The accuracy of the contents of the letter was verified by Andy Barker.

8. Sidney E. Mead, *The Lively Experiment: The Shaping of Christianity in America* (New York: Harper and Row, 1963).

9. This is Barker's self-descriptive phrase.

10. Brecher, p. 3.

11. Andy Barker suggested this as the rule for the Rock Festival, Brecher, p. 12.

12. Lyrics to the "Love Valley Song" are reproduced here by permission of Loonis McGlohon.

Chapter 3

1. See Rosabeth Moss Kanter, *Commitment and Community: Communes and Utopias in Sociological Perspective* (Cambridge: Harvard University Press, 1972) for her discussion of religious utopia.

2. This story is based upon an actual event as told by Andy Barker in an interview, 26 February 1991.

3. "Iredell Acres Purchased for Resort Ranch," *Statesville Record and Landmark,* 27 March 1954: 5.

4. "Down in Iredell," *Statesville Record and Landmark,* 30 March 1954: 1.

5. D. L. Morris, unpublished manuscript, ch. 2, pp. 8-9.

6. Jim Taylor, "Dude Ranch Shaping Up in North Iredell Valley," *Statesville Record and Landmark,* 4 June 1954: 1, 8.

7. "Iredell Dude Ranch Stages First Annual Stampede," *Statesville Record and Landmark,* 6 July 1954: 6.

8. "Letters to the Editor," *Statesville Record and Landmark,* 27 August 1954: 1.

9. "Letters to the Editor," *Statesville Record and Landmark,* 28 August 1954: 1.

10. "Letters to the Editor," *Statesville Record and Landmark,* 30 August 1954: 1.

11. Area papers highly publicized the Ambassador's visit as well as the significance of his talks on trade. An international visitor in Statesville was quite an event in 1954.

12. Interview by the author with Andy Barker, Love Valley, NC, 26 February 1991.

13. The following scenarios of the Fair and Fiesta are based on information from "Love Valley Fair Will Benefit Community Scholarship Fund," *Statesville Record and Landmark,* 5 October 1954: 8; "Foxhunters Club Fair Held at Love Valley," *Statesville Record and Landmark,* 11 October 1954: 1; Interview by the author with Andy Barker, Love Valley, NC, 1 October 1991.

14. The following is based on the author's observations of the 30 August 1991 rodeo. Those initial observations were reinforced by subsequent visits to other events including a rodeo as late as August 1997.

15. *The Concord Presbyterian* magazine, 15 August 1956. See also, Morris, ch. 12, p. 3.

16. "Valley Church Is Presbyterian," *Iredell Morning News,* 4 September 1956.

17. This story was related by Andy Barker during an interview on 8 October 1991. See also Morris, ch. 12, p. 5. The story was confirmed by Dolphus Allen in an interview from 9 September 1997.

18. The following story is based upon an incident described by Andy Barker during an interview on 1 October 1991, stories collected by several residents from Love Valley concerning the same incident, and Morris's version, ch. 12, p. 6. The story was verified in an interview with Marie Clark, 22 September 1997.

Chapter 4

1. Heath Thomas, "Wild West Reborn in Iredell's Love Valley; Phony or Authentic, It Attracts Thousands," *Salisbury Post,* 13 September 1959: 1B. This quotation is reproduced by permission from the editor.

2. This story is based upon Barker's own account of these events, several newspaper articles describing the move, and Arline Brecher's "How Love Came to the Valley," *The Love Valley Thing* (Charlotte: Halfway House Publications, 1970), pp. 4-5.

3. See "Dream Comes True for Barker," *Statesville Record and Landmark,* 21 May 1960.

4. " 'Love Valley' Is Growing Fast in Popularity," *The Eagle,* 20 May 1959.

5. Ibid.

6. For details about the 1958 parade see, Douglas Eisele, "Festive Holiday Program Slated by Merchants," *Statesville Record and Landmark,* 3 November 1958: 1; "Turkeys to Liven Parade Dec. 5th," *Iredell Morning News,*

13 November 1958: 1; "More than 100 Units Promised for Event; L. W. Gaither Named Marshall," *Iredell Morning News,* 4 December 1958: 1; "Parade 'Gimmicks' Are Promised," *Iredell Morning News,* 4 December 1958: 1; and Douglas Eisele, "Over 200 Units Are Assembled for Spectacle," *Statesville Record and Landmark,* 6 December 1958: 1.

7. The "bullshitter" reference was told to me by Barker in an interview, 8 October 1997.

8. For details concerning the 1959 parade see Fred Rigsbee, "Christmas Parade Plans Shaped," *Statesville Record and Landmark,* 6 November 1959; Fred Rigsbee, "Plans Progress for Big Parade," *Statesville Record and Landmark,* 21 November 1959; "Entries Exceed Record Number in 1958 Parade," *Statesville Record and Landmark,* 30 November 1959: 1; "Thousands Will View Big Event Set for Today," *Statesville Record and Landmark,* 2 December 1959: 1; and Fred Rigsbee, "256 Entries Form Spectacular Show Four Miles Long," *Statesville Record and Landmark,* 3 December 1959: 1.

9. "Thousands Will View Big Event Set for Tonight," *Statesville Record and Landmark,* 2 December 1959: 1.

10. Douglas Eisele, "Grave in Love Valley Offered for Tom Dula," *Statesville Record and Landmark,* 4 December 1958: 1. "Tom Dula's Plight Brings Offer of Iredell Grave," *The Charlotte (NC) News,* 5 December 1958.

11. Ibid.

12. Harry Gatton, "Investigation of Confederate Records Shows Tom Dula's Civil War Service Honorable," *Statesville Record and Landmark,* 10 January 1959: 1. See also Thomas W. Ferguson, *Tom Dooley* (Lenoir, NC: Smith Printing Company, 1959) and John Foster West, *Lift Up Your Head, Tom Dooley* (Asheboro, NC: Down Home Press, 1993).

13. See Ferguson, *Tom Dooley* for the details of Tom's saga.

14. This interpretation of the story largely accounts for Tom's folk hero status.

15. Homer Keever, "In New York Herald: Witness Describes Dula Hanging," *Statesville Record and Landmark,* 15 January 1959: 3.

16. Douglas Eisele, "Wilkes Citizens Want to Keep Dula's Grave," *Statesville Record and Landmark,* 5 December 1958: 4.

17. For the reference of the singing cowboy, see Douglas Eisele, "Wilkes to Keep Dula Grave," *Statesville Record and Landmark,* 8 December 1958. There are hundreds of versions of the ballad, "The Tom Dooley Song." One particular version was found in North Iredell on old yellowed paper, copied by a school girl and was reproduced in an article by Homer Keever, "Dula Ballad Wowed Iredell Long Time Ago," *Statesville Record and Landmark,* 17 December 1958: 13.

18. "Rodeo Group Gets Charter," *Statesville Record and Landmark,* 25 May 1959: 2.

19. See also "Wally Dunham," *The Western Horseman,* October 1963, pp. 26, 97.

20. Ibid.

21. Mimi Howard, "Old West Lives on in Tar Heel State," *The Charlotte Observer,* 23 August 1959.

22. "The Observer Forum, So What's to Love in Love Valley?" *The Charlotte Observer,* 28 August 1959: B3. Reproduced by permission of the editor.

23. See "Letters to the Editor," and "The Forum," *The Charlotte Observer,* 30 August 1959: B2; 31 August 1959; 3 September 1959: D6.

24. Brien Robb, "It's Hog Pasture or Paradise Accordin' to Who's Lookin'," *The Charlotte Observer,* 3 September 1959: D 6.

25. Brien Robb, "It's Hog Pasture or Paradise Accordin' to Who's Lookin'," *The Charlotte Observer,* 3 September 1959: D6. Reprinted by permission of the editor.

26. The runaway bull story that follows is based upon Andy Barker's recollection of the event in an October 1993 interview, upon Brien Robb's article, "Angry Bulls Steal Show at N.C. Rodeo," *The Charlotte Observer,* 7 September 1959, and D. L. Morris's mention of the event throughout his manuscript. See chapter 6, pp. 4-5.

27. D. L. Morris writes at length about such trail rides in his unpublished manuscript. See chapter 14.

28. See Douglas Eisele, "Airport Is Under Construction at Love Valley," *Statesville Record and Landmark,* 4 August 1960.

29. For details of the expansion of 1960-62, see Douglas Eisele, "Love Valley Expansion Set," *Statesville Record and Landmark,* 2 December 1960: 1. Eisele, "Western Town to be Moved and Developed," *The Smoke Signal,* November/December 1960; Eisele, "Love Valley to Become Year-Round Attraction," *Journal and Sentinel,* 4 December 1960; Don Gray, "N.C. Resort Town Is Planning Big Expansion," *The Charlotte Observer,* 21 January 1961: A3.

30. The Fourth of July stories and the race track incidents were based upon the following reports: Douglas Eisele, "Rodeo Tonight, Games Tuesday Among Events," *Statesville Record and Landmark,* 1 July 1961: 3, and Eisele, "Valley Opens Racing Season," *Statesville Record and Landmark,* 12 June 1961: 1. Andy Barker also added his version of events from that weekend.

31. "Love Valley Celebrating 10th Anniversary," *Statesville Record and Landmark,* 25 February 1964: 12.

Chapter 5

1. Andy Barker once attempted a dangerous and daring rescue of a local person who had fallen down a well. Barker had himself lowered into the well to raise the victim.

2. "Love Valley Holds Large Bible School," *Statesville Record and Landmark,* 2 August 1957: 10. Also, telephone interview with Dolphus Allen, 9 September 1997.

3. Alfred McCormack, Jr., "Barker Calls His Love Valley Creation 'A Place for Kids,'" *Statesville Record and Landmark,* 31 May 1961: 3.

4. For information on the Mobility Fund Project, see Bill Fuller, "Behind Lumbees Are Their Old Homes—and Poverty," *The Charlotte Observer,* 22 November 1965: B1; "Hope for Future Eased the Pangs of Leaving Home," *The Charlotte Observer,* 22 November 1965: B1; Heath Thomas, "Lumbees Readjust in Iredell," *Winston Salem Journal,* 7 March 1966: 3; and Heath Thomas, "'Mobility Project' Moves Lumbees from Flatlands to Hills for Jobs," *Salisbury Sunday Post,* 20 February 1966: C1.

5. "Kirby Rancho Opening Set," *Statesville Record and Landmark,* 5 March 1957: 2.

6. "Camp Opening at Love Valley," *Statesville Record and Landmark,* 7 July 1958: 5.

7. For details of the 1959 March of Dimes drive, see "Dimes March Drive Started," *Statesville Record and Landmark,* 6 January 1959: 1; "Dimes March Dance Planned," *Statesville Record and Landmark,* 7 January 1959; "Students to Aid March of Dimes," *Statesville Record and Landmark,* 9 January 1959: 8; "Rural Students Set for Unique Race," *Statesville Record and Landmark,* 14 January 1959: 1; "Troutman Wagoners Fastest Dimes Team," *Statesville Record and Landmark,* 24 January 1959: 1; and "Mothers Take in Over $2,000 for Polio Fund," *Statesville Record and Landmark,* 30 January 1959: 1. See also, "'Blue Crutch Day' on Saturday Begins Iredell Campaign," *Iredell Morning News,* 8 January 1959.

8. For details of the March of Dimes Drive, see citations from previous note 7.

9. "'Moon' to Light Way for Cancer Research," *Statesville Record and Landmark,* 23 August 1961: 3.

10. See "Star to Appear at Love Valley," *Statesville Record and Landmark,* 15 August 1961: 5; "Love Valley Event to Aid Cancer Drive," *Elkin Tribune,* 17 August 1961; "TV Star Taking Part in Cancer Campaign," *Wilson Daily Times,* 15 August 1961; "Television Star Will Aid Drive," *Statesville Record and Landmark,* 26 August 1961: 4; "Cowboy Star Rex Allen Set to Appear at Love Valley," *Salisbury Evening Post,* 3 September 1961: 6C; and "Down in Iredell," *Statesville Record and Landmark,* 4 September 1961: 1.

11. The following story is based on a popular tale around Love Valley. The event that inspired it was reported by Douglas Eisele, "Horse Is Nursed in Living Room," *Statesville Record and Landmark,* 24 March 1960: 16.

12. Ibid.

13. For a treatment of McAlister, see Glenn T. Miller, "Cooperation and

Peace: A. W. McAlister, A Progressive Southern Christian Layman," in *Cultural Perspectives on the American South: Volume 5, Religion,* edited by Charles Reagan Wilson (New York: Gordon and Breach, 1991).

14. Andy Barker interview with author, Love Valley, NC, 19 March 1993.

15. Ibid.

16. Ibid.

17. These stories are told mostly in good humor by those who know Barker, and at least one has been recorded in a written account by D. L. Morris, unpublished manuscript, ch. 10, pp. 3-6.

18. Letter from Syed Amjad Ali to the Barkers, 26 May 1955.

19. Letter from Gerard de la Villesbrunne to the Barkers, 15 April 1963.

20. For details of the Johnson visit see Dwayne Walls, "Vote Democratic, He Tells Crowd," *The Charlotte Observer,* 16 October 1962: 1A, 2A; "Sanford Will Be Here for Johnson's Address," *Statesville Record and Landmark,* 13 October 1962: 1; Douglas Eisele, "Vice President Cites Nation's Strong Posture," *Statesville Record and Landmark,* 16 October 1962: 1-2; and Jerry Josey, "LBJ Has Double Meaning at Rally," *Statesville Record and Landmark,* 16 October 1962: 2. This account also reflects Barker's remembrances of the event.

21. "Love Valley Incorporated," *Statesville Record and Landmark,* 3 April 1963: 1; and "Love Valley Becomes a Town," *The Salisbury Post,* 2 April 1963: 2.

22. "Three Candidates Seek Love Valley Posts," *Statesville Record and Landmark,* 15 April 1963: 7.

23. For details of the candidates and the election, see the following articles from the *Statesville Record and Landmark:* "Phillips Seeks Post in Valley," 10 April 1963: 1; "Three Candidates Seek Love Valley Posts," 15 April 1963: 7; "J. A. Barker, Sr. Runs for Mayor," 18 April 1963: 3; "Women to Make Race for Love Valley Posts," 19 April 1963: 5; "Ponder in Race at Love Valley," 20 April 1963: 4; and "First Town Officials Named in Love Valley," 20 May 1963: 1.

24. Love Valley Town Commissioners Minutes, May 21, 1963, and "Board Holds First Session," *Statesville Record and Landmark,* 22 May 1963: 7.

25. "Letter to the Editor," *Statesville Record and Landmark,* 3 June 1964: 7.

26. See also *The Conductor,* May 1964.

27. "Letter to the Editor," *Statesville Record and Landmark,* 3 June 1964: 7. Reprinted by permission of the editor.

28. "Letter to the Editor," *Statesville Record and Landmark,* 11 April 1963: 15.

29. Ibid.

30. "School Board District Group Hears Dr. Otts," *Statesville Record and Landmark,* 19 April 1963: 3.

Chapter 6

1. "Community Action Plan Sought," *Statesville Record and Landmark,* 22 September 1965: 15.

2. "Heavy Equipment School Sought," *Statesville Record and Landmark,* 10 April 1965: 12. This article outlines the specifics of the school. In addition, Andy Barker provided details and an explanation of his philosophy for the school.

3. Ibid. See also Love Valley Town Commissioners Minutes, 1 September 1965.

4. "Community Action Plan Sought," *Statesville Record and Landmark,* 22 September 1965: 15.

5. "Program Is Initiated for Community Action," *Statesville Record and Landmark,* 9 December 1965: 7.

6. Ibid. See also Love Valley Town Commissioners Minutes, 1 September 1965.

7. "EOA Action Group Meets," *Statesville Record and Landmark,* 15 December 1965: 5.

8. Andy Barker, "Letters to the Editor," *Statesville Record and Landmark,* 11 December 1965: 7. Reprinted by permission of the editor.

9. For information on the Mobility Fund Project, see Bill Fuller, "Behind Lumbees Are Their Old Homes—and Poverty," *The Charlotte Observer,* 22 November 1965: B1; "Hope for Future Eased the Pangs of Leaving Home," *The Charlotte Observer,* 22 November 1965: B1. Heath Thomas, "Lumbees Readjust in Iredell," *Winston-Salem Journal,* 7 March 1966: 3; Heath Thomas, "'Mobility Project' Moves Lumbees From Flatlands to Hills for Jobs," *Salisbury Sunday Post,* 20 February 1966: 1C.

10. "Letters to the Editor," *Statesville Record and Landmark,* 18 November 1965: 18.

11. See "Andy Barker Schedules 'Land Rush' for Labor Day," *Statesville Record and Landmark,* 17 August 1967.

12. See Howard Covington, "Movie Will be Filmed at Statesville," *The Charlotte Observer,* 6 March 1968: 9A; and "Major Studio Plans to Film Movie Here," *Statesville Record and Landmark,* 5 March 1968: 3.

13. See Covington, "Movie Will be Filmed at Statesville," *The Charlotte Observer,* 6 March 1968: 9A; "Major Studio Plans to Film Movie Here," *Statesville Record and Landmark,* 5 March 1968: 3; Jesse Poindexter, "1,000 Prospective 'Extras,'" *Winston-Salem Journal,* 5 June 1968: 4. Photographs in *Statesville Record and Landmark,* 24 September 1968: 1 and 29 November 1968; and Ralph Miller, "The Yankees Are Coming—to Iredell," *Salisbury Sunday Post,* 19 January 1969: C1.

14. Karen Freeman, "'John Brown's Body' Lies A-Molderin'," *The Charlotte Observer,* 2 September 1969: 14A.

15. Harold Warren, "It Warn't Never a Stayin' Jail," *The Charlotte Observer,* 26 September 1969: 3B.

16. The following account was told by Andy and Ellenora Barker, 1 October 1991.

17. See Harold Warren, "Wild West Wins a Vietnamese Cowpoke," *The Charlotte Observer,* 7 April 1970: 1B, 8B; and Steve Hass, "Vietnamese Efforts Stressed," *Statesville Record and Landmark,* 7 April 1970: 1-2.

18. Andy Barker interview with the author, Love Valley, NC, 1 October 1991.

19. Butch Trucks telephone interview with the author, 18 February 1992.

20. John Ogden (pseudonym Henry Porter), "First There Is a Mountain," *Creative Loafing,* vol. 20, no. 31 (28 December 1991): 32, 35.

21. Tonda and David Smith interview with the author, Winston Salem, NC, 7 February 1993.

22. Ibid.

23. "Atlanta Won't Stop Love Valley," *Winston-Salem Journal,* 7 July 1970: 2.

24. Eddie Bradford, "Thousands Arrive for Festival at Love Valley," *Statesville Record and Landmark,* 18 July 1970: 1.

25. Ibid.

26. Jim Maxwell, "Soldier Dies at Festival," *Statesville Record and Landmark,* 20 July 1970: 1A, 8A.

27. "Charge of Assault Filed in Shooting," *Statesville Record and Landmark,* 20 July 1970: 1A

28. Gary Freeze, "Varied Look at Festival," *Statesville Record and Landmark,* 29 July 1970: 8A.

29. I am indebted to many sources for information about the Love Valley Rock Festival. However, the most valuable information came from those who were in the middle of planning and implementing the festival. In particular, Tonda and David Smith spent hours relating stories and personal anecdotes concerning the festival. Except where otherwise noted, most of the information on the festival stems from a 7 February 1993 interview with the couple in their home. Other information comes from conversations with the Barkers, with festival goers, and from countless newspaper descriptions. See also Edward J. Myers, "Tar Heel Woodstock," *The State,* vol. 63, no. 2 (July 1995): 35-36.

30. Freeze, "Varied Look at the Festival," 8A.

31. Ibid.

32. The gang story was told to me in an interview with David Smith, 7 February 1993.

33. Butch Trucks telephone interview with the author, 18 February 1992.

34. See Ogden, p. 35.

35. "Down in Iredell," *Statesville Record and Landmark,* 24 July 1970: 1.

36. For examples of such letters, see the "Letters to the Editor" section from the following editions of the *Statesville Record and Landmark,* 23 July 1970: 2B; 1 August 1970: 7A; 3 August 1970: 5B; and 5 August 1970: 9B. See also Boots Clanton, "Property Owners Rap Rock Festival," *Statesville Record and Landmark,* 20 July 1970: 8A.

37. For examples of letters of support, see the "Letters to the Editor" section of the *Statesville Record and Landmark,* 28 July 1970: 7; 30 July 1970: 7A; and 6 August 1970: 3A.

38. See Norman Cousins, "All Hail Andy Barker," *Saturday Review,* 8 August 1970: 26.

39. Ibid.

40. Ibid.

41. Barker talked freely of his problems with local residents and state investigators. Andy Barker, interview with the author, Love Valley, NC, 8 October 1991.

42. Boots Clanton, "Legal Action Being Sought," *Statesville Record and Landmark,* 21 July 1970: 2.

43. "Rock Festival Bill Presented," *Statesville Record and Landmark,* 22 January 1971: 2.

Chapter 7

1. See Rosabeth Moss Kanter, *Commitment and Community: Communes and Utopias in Sociological Perspective* (Cambridge: Harvard University Press, 1972), pp. 5-8.

2. Most of what follows is based upon interviews with various people who lived in Love Valley during the period following the 1970 Rock Festival. Much of the information is based upon a February 6, 1992, interview with Pam Simon. Other information comes from a February 18, 1992, interview with Butch Trucks, and informal talks with Valley residents. The information on the tepee and the reconstruction of the New York trip are based on interviews with Pam Simon, February 6, 1992, and June 25, 1997.

3. Butch Trucks telephone interview with the author, 18 February 1992. This information is also reflected in Tonda and David Smith interview with the author, Winston Salem, NC, 7 February 1993; and in Dickey Betts interview with Linda Austin, " 'Long Hairs' Go to Work," *Salisbury Sunday Post,* 11 October 1970: C1.

4. From Flood promotional literature. Rory Knapton remembered the Flood credo and suggested that it was similar to the lyrics of a rock opera, "Dear Little Man," that the band wrote. Rory Knapton, telephone interview with the author, 22 September 1997. Material here is used by permission of Mr. Knapton. Mr. Knapton is still playing music with a band called "Wild Blue Yonder."

5. Rory Knapton telephone interview with the author, 22 September 1997.

6. Ibid.

7. Don Berg telephone interview with the author, 25 September 1997.

8. Knapton interview.

9. Lyrics of the song are reproduced by permission of Don Berg, who wrote the song, and of Andy Barker, president of Love Valley Records. The title of the song, "Love Valley, U.S.A," was a phrase that Andy Barker had used since the early sixties to describe his community and had become a popular designation for the town.

10. Pam Simon interview with the author, 6 January 1992. Many of the festival participants I talked to recalled Psychedelic Joe.

11. Harold Warren, "Love Valley Learns to Like Longhairs," *The Charlotte Observer,* 16 May 1971: 6A. Reprinted by permission of editor.

12. Ibid. Reprinted by permission of the editor.

13. Harold Warren, "Love Valley: Now The Longhairs Are Mostly Gone," *The Charlotte Observer,* 9 July 1972: 1C-2C.

14. Ibid. Quotation reprinted by permission of the editor.

15. See Linda Austin, " 'Long Hairs' Go to Work," *Salisbury Sunday Post,* 11 October 1970: C1.

16. Harold Warren, "Love Valley Learns to Like Longhairs," *The Charlotte Observer,* 16 May 1971: 6A.

17. Ibid.

18. Harold Warren, "Here's One Worth Sitting Out," *The Charlotte Observer,* 4 October 1971: 10B.

19. Andy Barker interview with the author, Love Valley, NC, 8 October 1991. See also Brad Schram, "Down Home in Love Valley, NC," *Kansas City Star,* 1975.

20. Alan Marshall, "Hoss Patterson: Restless Cowboy," *Statesville Record and Landmark,* 9 September 1972: 13A.

21. "Love Valley Arts Council Chartered," *Statesville Record and Landmark,* 4 November 1975: 18.

22. See Pam Simon, "Love Valley Rebuilds Image," *Statesville Record and Landmark,* 18 March 1980: 1E.

Chapter 8

1. See Rosabeth Moss Kanter, *Commitment and Community: Communes and Utopias in Sociological Perspective* (Cambridge: Harvard University Press, 1972), pp. 5-8.

2. Interview with Andy Barker by Janice Stutts, "Love Valley, Bucking Broncos Replace Hard Rock Music," *High Point Enterprise,* 6 July 1980. Reprinted by permission of the editor.

3. Andy Barker interview with the author, Love Valley, NC, 8 October 1991.

4. Barker's platform appeared in *The Smoke Signal.* Andy Barker expanded this platform in the October 1991 interviews.

5. Donna Swicegood, "Write-in Vote Selects Barker for 12th Term," *Statesville Record and Landmark,* 4 November 1987: 6A.

6. Ibid.

7. Tracey Thomas, "Founder Tries for Comeback in Love Valley," *The Charlotte Observer, Iredell Neighbors,* 6 October 1991: 1, 6. Price's assessment was expressed during a telephone interview with the author, 9 March 1998.

8. Andy Barker interview with the author, Love Valley, NC, 8 October 1991.

9. For stories about Joe Ponder's stunts see, "Ponder Severely Hurt in 'Death Slide' Fall," *Statesville Record and Landmark,* 15 May 1978: A2; "Mouthpiece Blamed by Ponder for Fall," *Statesville Record and Landmark,* 15 June 1978: B18; and Kate Boylan, "Leather Working: Strong Man Joe Ponder Polishes Laid-Back Business Style," *Iredell Neighbors,* 29 July 1984: 10. Ponder's exploits even won attention in the nation's popular press. See "It's No Place for Dentures," *National Examiner,* 27 June 1978. These stories are also based on an interview with Joe Ponder in October 1992.

10. The following account of the phone conversation is based on Ellenora Barker's account of this event during interviews in late 1991.

11. Much of the information about Jet and his illness comes from two interviews with Cyndy Allison, Jet's wife. These interviews were September 16 and 17, 1997.

12. Cyndy Allison telephone interview with the author, 16 September 1997.

13. The following account is based upon trial testimony, newspaper accounts, and interviews with the accused and others. Some of the interviewees asked to remain anonymous, and I have respected those wishes.

14. The sense of this service is based on a visit and on the transcript of the sermon delivered 17 February 1991 at the Love Valley Presbyterian Church. Scripture references for the sermon are from the Book of Job, chapter 36, and the Book of Ruth, chapter 1.

15. See John Minter, "Fired Up Again: Stained-glass Maker Rebuilds," *Statesville Record and Landmark,* "Iredell Neighbors," 19 February 1992: 1, 4. Also, Helen Laws telephone interview with the author, 17 September 1997.

Chapter 9

1. The following account is based on a series of interviews with a man who goes by the name Arizona during January 1992.

2. The following is based upon an interview with Tonda and David Smith, 7 February 1993.

3. The following is based upon stories told by a proud grandmother,

Ellenora Barker.

4. Ellenora Barker related this incident to me on several occasions.

5. This information was shared with me by Walter Tilley in a letter dated 14 September 1997.

6. This account is based on visits by the author and Mary Ostwalt to Ponder's shop on 4 July 1992 and during October 1992. During these visits, Joe Ponder granted the author interviews.

Chapter 10

1. The task of defining utopia is a complex one, and I am working with a broad understanding of the utopian impulse for my work with Love Valley. Ruth Levitas deals with the difficulties of defining utopia in Ruth Levitas, *The Concept of Utopia* (Great Britain: Syracuse University Press, 1990). See especially chapters 7 and 8.

2. John Egerton, *Visions of Utopia: Nashoba, Rugby, Ruskin, and the "New Communities" in Tennessee's Past* (Knoxville: The University of Tennessee Press, 1977), p. 87. For a full-length study on the Ruskin communities, see W. Fitzhugh Brundage, *A Socialist Utopia in the New South: The Ruskin Colonies in Tennessee and Georgia, 1894-1901* (Chicago: University of Illinois Press, 1996).

3. Rosabeth Moss Kanter, *Commitment and Community: Communes and Utopias in Sociological Perspective* (Cambridge: Harvard University Press, 1972), pp. vii-viii.

4. Ibid., p. 32.

5. Vernon Louis Parrington, Jr., *American Dreams: A Study of American Utopias* (Providence: Brown University, 1947), p. vii.

6. Michael Fellman, *The Unbounded Frame: Freedom and Community in 19th Century American Utopianism* (Westport: Greenwood Press, 1973), p. xiii.

7. See Kanter, *Commitment and Community*, p. 1, for a good working definition of utopia that supports this description of Love Valley. For a discussion of communitarianism, see Christopher Clark, *The Communitarian Moment: The Radical Challenge of the Northampton Association* (Ithaca: Cornell University Press, 1995).

8. Egerton, *Visions of Utopia*, p. 88.

9. Brian J. L. Berry, *America's Utopian Experiments: Communal Havens from Long-Wave Crises* (Hanover: University Press of New England, 1992), pp. xv-xvii.

10. Kanter, *Commitment and Community*, p. 1.

11. Maren Lockwood, "The Experimental Utopia in America," *Utopias and Utopian Thought*, ed. Frank E. Manuel (Boston: Houghton Mifflin, 1965), p. 183.

12. Kanter, *Commitment and Community*, pp. 33, 8.

13. Ibid., p. 8.

14. Ibid., pp. 8, 34.

15. Ibid., p. 49.

16. John Thomas Codman, *Brook Farm: Historic and Personal Memoirs* (Boston: Arena, 1894). See, for example, pp. 3 and 53-56.

17. Egerton, *Visions of Utopia,* p. 88.

18. See Kanter, *Commitment and Community,* pp. 39-41.

19. See Kanter, *Commitment and Community,* p. 42, and Dolores Hayden, *Seven American Utopias: The Architecture of Communitarian Socialism, 1790-1975* (Cambridge: The MIT Press, 1976).

20. Hayden, *Seven American Utopias,* p. 43.

21. See Lawrence Foster, *Religion and Sexuality: The Shakers, the Mormons, and the Oneida Community* (Chicago: University of Illinois Press, 1984), pp. 21-71.

22. Kanter, *Commitment and Community,* p. 42.

23. Ibid., pp. 43, 47.

24. Lyman Tower Sargent, "Utopia and the Family: A Note on the Family in Political Thought," *Dissent and Affirmation,* ed. Arthur Kalleberg et al. (Bowling Green, OH: Bowling Green State University Popular Press, 1983), p. 114.

25. Ibid., pp. 107, 109.

26. Ibid., pp. 114-115.

27. Arthur Eugene Bestor, Jr., *Backwoods Utopias: The Sectarian and Owenite Phases of Communitarian Socialism: 1663-1829* (Philadelphia: University of Pennsylvania Press, 1950), p. vii.

28. Ibid., p. 3.

29. Ibid.

30. Kanter, *Commitment and Community,* pp. 2-3, 52ff.

31. Ibid., p. 3.

32. Ibid., p. 8.

33. Ibid., p. 8.

34. Ibid., pp. 4, 3.

35. John Humphrey Noyes, "Bible Argument," in the *First Annual Report of the Oneida Association,* (Oneida Reserve, NY: Leonard, 1849), pp. 27-28 as quoted in Lawrence Foster, *Religion and Sexuality: The Shakers, the Mormons, and the Oneida Community* (Chicago: University of Illinois Press, 1984), pp. 90-91.

36. Charles J. Erasmus, *In Search of the Common Good: Utopian Experiments Past and Future* (New York: The Free Press, 1977), pp. 143-144. See also Julia Elizabeth Williams, "An Analytical Tabulation of the North American Utopian Communities by Type, Longevity and Location," M.A. thesis, University of Iowa, 1938.

37. Barker letter, 1 February 1945. See D. L. Morris, unpublished manuscript, ch. 1, p. 4.

38. Alfred Braunthal, *Salvation and the Perfect Society: The Eternal Quest* (Amherst: The University of Massachusetts Press, 1979), pp. ix, xi, xiii.

39. Kanter, *Commitment and Community,* pp. 5, 6.

40. Ibid., p. 7.

41. Ibid., pp. 7-8. See also Michael Fellman, *The Unbounded Frame: Freedom and Community in Nineteenth Century American Utopianism* (Westport: Greenwood Press, 1973) for an exploration of trends that would eventually lead to a counterculture critique of society rather than utopian critique. In addition, Keith Melville's *Communes in the Counter Culture: Origins, Theories, and Styles of Life* (New York: William Morrow, 1972) describes how utopian life in the counterculture exists.

42. Michael Fellman, *The Unbounded Frame: Freedom and Community in Nineteenth Century American Utopianism* (Westport: Greenwood Press, 1973), p. xix.

43. Keith Melville, *Communes in the Counter Culture: Origins, Theories, and Styles of Life* (New York: William Morrow, 1972), p. 32.

44. See Paul M. Gaston, *Man and Mission: E. B. Gaston and the Origins of the Fairhope Single Tax Colony* (Montgomery: The Black Belt Press, 1993).

45. See chapter 3 for a description of this activity.

46. For the doctrine of "disinterested benevolence," see Samuel Hopkins, *The System of Doctrines Contained in Divine Revelation Explained and Defended,* 2 vols. (Boston, 1811), I: 465-477.

47. Robert Bellah, Richard Madsen, William M. Sullivan, Ann Swidler, and Steven M. Tipton, *The Good Society* (New York: Alfred A. Knopf, 1991), p. 12.

48. See Robert N. Bellah, Richard Madsen, William M. Sullivan, Ann Swidler, and Steven M. Tipton, *Habits of the Heart: Individualism and Commitment in American Life* (Berkeley: University of California Press, 1985).

49. Ibid., p. vii.

50. Ibid.

51. Ibid., pp. 35-41.

52. For the "moral grid" and "collective well-being" quotes, see *Habits of the Heart,* p. 39. For a discussion of this aspect of Tocqueville's vision of America, see *Habits of the Heart,* pp. 35-41.

53. *Habits of the Heart,* p. 40.

54. Ibid., pp. 55, 83, and 143-144.

55. Ibid., p. 170. See the text and the note for the author's discussion on the town father.

56. See *Habits of the Heart,* pp. 219-229 and 259.

Sources Cited

Ali, Syed Amjad. Letter to the Barkers, 26 May 1955.

Allen, Dolphus. Telephone interview, 9 September 1997.

Allison, Cyndy. Telephone interviews, 16 and 17 September 1997.

"Andy Barker Schedules 'Land Rush' for Labor Day," *Statesville Record and Landmark,* 17 August 1967.

Arizona. Love Valley, NC. Interview, January 1992.

"Atlanta Won't Stop Love Valley." *Winston-Salem Journal,* 7 July 1970: 2.

Austin, Linda. " 'Long Hairs' Go to Work." *Salisbury Sunday Post,* 11 October 1970: C1.

Barker, Andy. Letter, 1 February 1945.

——. "Letters to the Editor." *Statesville Record and Landmark,* 28 August 1954: 1.

——. "Letters to the Editor." *Statesville Record and Landmark,* 3 June 1964: 7B.

——. "Letters to the Editor." *Statesville Record and Landmark,* 11 December 1965: 7.

Barker, Andy. Love Valley, NC. Interview, 26 February 1991.

——. Love Valley, NC. Interviews, October 1991.

——. Love Valley, NC. Interview, 19 March 1993.

Barker, Andy, and Ellenora Barker. Love Valley, NC. Interviews, 1991-1997.

Barker, Ellenora. Love Valley, NC. Interview, Autumn 1991.

Bellah, Robert N., Richard Madsen, William M. Sullivan, Ann Swidler, and Steven M. Tipton. *The Good Society.* New York: Alfred A. Knopf, 1991.

——. *Habits of the Heart: Individualism and Commitment in American Life.* Berkeley: University of California Press, 1985.

Berg, Don. Lyrics to "Love Valley, U.S.A.," early 1970s.

——. Telephone interview, 25 September 1997.

Berry, Brian J. L. *America's Utopian Experiments: Communal Havens from Long-Wave Crises.* Hanover: University Press of New England, 1992.

Bestor, Arthur Eugene, Jr. *Backwoods Utopias: The Sectarian and Owenite Phases of Communitarian Socialism: 1663-1829.* Philadelphia: University of Pennsylvania Press, 1950.

" 'Blue Crutch Day' on Saturday Begins Iredell Campaign." *Iredell Morning News,* 8 January 1959: 1.

"Board Holds First Session." *Statesville Record and Landmark,* 22 May 1963: 7.

Boylan, Kate. "Leather Working: Strong Man Joe Ponder Polishes Laid-Back Business Style." *Iredell Neighbors,* 29 July 1984: 10.

Bradford, Eddie. "Thousands Arrive for Festival at Love Valley." *Statesville Record and Landmark,* 18 July 1970: 1.

Braunthal, Alfred. *Salvation and the Perfect Society: The Eternal Quest.* Amherst: The University of Massachusetts Press, 1979.

Brecher, Arline. "How Love Came to the Valley." *The Love Valley Thing.* Charlotte, NC: Halfway House, 1970. 4-5.

——. *The Love Valley Thing.* Charlotte, NC: Halfway House, 1970.

Brundage, W. Fitzhugh. *A Socialist Utopia in the New South: The Ruskin Colonies in Tennessee and Georgia, 1894-1901.* Chicago: University of Illinois Press, 1996.

"Camp Opening at Love Valley." *Statesville Record and Landmark,* 7 July 1958: 5.

"Charge of Assault Filed in Shooting." *Statesville Record and Landmark,* 20 July 1970: 1A, 8A.

Clanton, Boots. "Legal Action Being Sought." *Statesville Record and Landmark,* 21 July 1970: 2.

——. "Property Owners Rap Rock Festival." *Statesville Record and Landmark,* 20 July 1970: 8A.

Clark, Christopher. *The Communitarian Moment: The Radical Challenge of the Northampton Association.* Ithaca: Cornell University Press, 1995.

Clark, Marie. Telephone interview, 22 September 1997.

Codman, John Thomas. *Brook Farm: Historic and Personal Memoirs.* Boston: Arena, 1894.

"Community Action Plan Sought." *Statesville Record and Landmark,* 22 September 1965: 15.

The Concord Presbyterian 15 August 1956.

Cousins, Norman. "All Hail Andy Barker." *Saturday Review,* 8 August 1970: 26.

Covington, Howard. "Movie Will be Filmed at Statesville." *The Charlotte Observer,* 6 March 1968: 9A.

"Cowboy Star Rex Allen Set to Appear at Love Valley." *Salisbury Evening Post,* 3 September 1961: 6C.

"Dimes March Dance Planned." *Statesville Record and Landmark,* 7 January 1959.

"Dimes March Drive Started." *Statesville Record and Landmark,* 6 January 1959: 1.

"Down in Iredell." *Statesville Record and Landmark,* 30 March 1954: 1.

"Down in Iredell." *Statesville Record and Landmark,* 4 September 1961: 1.

"Down in Iredell." *Statesville Record and Landmark,* 24 July 1970: 1.

"Dream Comes True for Barker." *Statesville Record and Landmark,* 21 May 1960.

Dunham, Wally. *The Western Horseman,* October 1963: 26, 97.

Egerton, John. *Visions of Utopia: Nashoba, Rugby, Ruskin, and the "New Communities" in Tennessee's Past.* Knoxville: The University of Tennessee Press, 1977.

Eisele, Douglas. "Airport Is Under Construction." *Statesville Record and Landmark,* 4 August 1960.

——. "Festive Holiday Program Slated by Merchants. *Statesville Record and Landmark,* 3 November 1958: 1.

——. "Grave in Love Valley Offered for Tom Dula." *Statesville Record and Landmark,* 4 December 1958: 1.

——. "Horse Is Nursed in Living Room." *Statesville Record and Landmark,* 24 March 1960: 16.

——. "Love Valley Expansion Set." *Statesville Record and Landmark,* 2 December 1960: 1.

——. "Love Valley to Become Year-Round Attraction." *Journal and Sentinel,* 4 December 1960.

——. "Over 200 Units Are Assembled for Spectacle." *Statesville Record and Landmark,* 6 December 1958: 1.

——. "Rodeo Tonight, Games Tuesday Among Event." *Statesville Record and Landmark,* 1 July 1961: 3.

——. "Vice President Cites Nation's Strong Posture." *Statesville Record and Landmark,* 16 October 1962: 1-2.

——. "Western Town to be Moved and Developed." *The Smoke Signal,* November/December 1960.

——. "Wilkes Citizens Want to Keep Dula's Grave." *Statesville Record and Landmark,* 5 December 1958: 4.

——. "Wilkes to Keep Dula Grave." *Statesville Record and Landmark,* 8 December 1958.

"Entries Exceed Record Number in 1958 Parade." *Statesville Record and Landmark,* 30 November 1959: 1.

"EOA Action Group Meets." *Statesville Record and Landmark,* 15 December 1965: 5.

Erasmus, Charles J. *In Search of the Common Good: Utopian Experiments Past and Future.* New York: The Free Press, 1977.

Fellman, Michael. *The Unbounded Frame: Freedom and Community in 19th Century American Utopianism.* Westport: Greenwood Press, 1973.

Ferguson, Thomas W. *Tom Dooley.* Lenoir, NC: Smith Printing Company, 1959.

"First Town Officials Named in Love Valley." *Statesville Record and Landmark,* 20 May 1963: 1.

Flood promotional posters and literature. Early 1970s.

Foster, Lawrence. *Religion and Sexuality: The Shakers, the Mormons, and the Oneida Community*. Chicago: University of Illinois Press, 1984.

"Foxhunters Club Fair Held at Love Valley." *Statesville Record and Landmark,* 11 October 1954: 1.

Freeman, Karen. "'John Brown's Body' Lies A-Molderin'." *The Charlotte Observer,* 2 September 1969: 14A.

Freeze, Gary. "Varied Look at Festival." *Statesville Record and Landmark,* 29 July 1970: 8A.

Fuller, Bill. "Behind Lumbees Are Their Old Homes—and Poverty." *The Charlotte Observer,* 22 November 1965: 1B, 7B.

——. "Lumbees Leave Grinding Poverty for a Better Life." *The Charlotte Observer,* 22 November 1965: B7.

Gaston, Paul M. *Man and Mission: E. B. Gaston and the Origins of the Fairhope Single Tax Colony*. Montgomery: The Black Belt Press, 1993.

Gatton, Harry. "Investigation of Confederate Records Shows Tom Dula's Civil War Service Honorable." *Statesville Record and Landmark,* 10 January 1959: 1.

Gray, Don. "N.C. Resort Town Is Planning Big Expansion." *The Charlotte Observer,* 21 January 1961: A3.

Hass, Steve. "Vietnamese Efforts Stressed." *Statesville Record and Landmark,* 7 April 1970: 1-2.

Hayden, Dolores. *Seven American Utopias: The Architecture of Communitarian Socialism, 1790-1975*. Cambridge: The MIT Press, 1976.

"Heavy Equipment School Sought." *Statesville Record and Landmark,* 10 April 1965: 12.

"Hope for Future Eased the Pangs of Leaving Home." *The Charlotte Observer,* 22 November 1965: 1B, 7B.

Hopkins, Samuel. *The System of Doctrines Contained in Divine Revelation Explained and Defended*. 2 vols. Boston, 1811.

Howard, Mimi. "Old West Lives On in Tar Heel State." *The Charlotte Observer,* 23 August 1959.

"Iredell Acres Purchased for Resort Ranch." *Statesville Record and Landmark,* 27 March 1954: 5.

"Iredell Dude Ranch Stages First Annual Stampede." *Statesville Record and Landmark,* 4 June 1954: 6.

"It's No Place for Dentures." *National Examiner,* 27 June 1978.

"J. A. Barker, Sr. Runs for Mayor." *Statesville Record and Landmark,* 18 April 1963: 3.

Josey, Jerry. "LBJ Has Double Meaning at Rally." *Statesville Record and Landmark,* 16 October 1962: 2.

Kalleberg, Arthur L., J. Donald Moon, and Daniel R. Sabia, Jr., eds. *Dissent and Affirmation: Essays in Honor of Mulford Q. Sibley.* Bowling Green, OH: Bowling Green State University Popular Press, 1983.

Kanter, Rosabeth Moss. *Commitment and Community: Communes and Utopias in Sociological Perspective.* Cambridge: Harvard University Press, 1972.

Keever, Homer. "Dula Ballad Wowed Iredell Long Time Ago." *Statesville Record and Landmark,* 17 December 1958: 13.

——. "In New York Herald: Witness Describes Dula Hanging." *Statesville Record and Landmark,* 15 January 1959: 3.

Kimbrough, David. *Taking Up Serpents: Snake Handlers of Eastern Kentucky.* Chapel Hill: University of North Carolina Press, 1995.

"Kirby Rancho Opening Set." *Statesville Record and Landmark,* 5 March 1957: 2.

Knapton, Rory. Telephone interview, 22 September 1997.

Laws, Helen. Telephone interview, 17 September 1997.

"Letters to the Editor." *Statesville Record and Landmark,* 27 August 1954: 1.

"Letters to the Editor." *Statesville Record and Landmark,* 28 August 1954: 1.

"Letters to the Editor." *Statesville Record and Landmark,* 30 August 1954: 1.

"Letters to the Editor." *Statesville Record and Landmark,* 11 April 1963: 15.

"Letters to the Editor." *Statesville Record and Landmark,* 3 June 1964: 7.

"Letters to the Editor." *Statesville Record and Landmark,* 18 November 1965: 18.

"Letters to the Editor." *Statesville Record and Landmark,* 11 December 1965: 7.

"Letters to the Editor." *Statesville Record and Landmark,* 23 July 1970: 2B.

"Letters to the Editor." *Statesville Record and Landmark,* 28 July 1970: 7.

"Letters to the Editor." *Statesville Record and Landmark,* 30 July 1970: 7A.

"Letters to the Editor." *Statesville Record and Landmark,* 1 August 1970: 7A.

"Letters to the Editor." *Statesville Record and Landmark,* 3 August 1970: 5B.

"Letters to the Editor." *Statesville Record and Landmark,* 5 August 1970: 9B.

"Letters to the Editor." *Statesville Record and Landmark,* 6 August 1970: 3A.

"Letters to the Editor and the Forum." *The Charlotte Observer,* 30 August 1959: B2.

"Letters to the Editor and the Forum." *The Charlotte Observer,* 31 August 1959.

"Letters to the Editor and the Forum." *The Charlotte Observer,* 3 September 1959: D6.

Levitas, Ruth. *The Concept of Utopia.* Great Britain: Syracuse University Press, 1990.

Lockwood, Maren. "The Experimental Utopia in America." In *Utopias and Utopian Thought.* Edited by Frank E. Manuel. Boston: Houghton Mifflin, 1965. 183-200.

"Love Valley Arts Council Chartered." *Statesville Record and Landmark,* 4 November 1975: 18.

"Love Valley Becomes Town." *The Salisbury Evening Post,* 2 April 1963: 2.

"Love Valley Celebrating 10th Anniversary." *Statesville Record and Landmark,* 25 February 1964: 12.

"Love Valley Event to Aid Cancer Drive." *Elkin Tribune,* 17 August 1961.

"Love Valley Fair Will Benefit Community Scholarship Fund." *Statesville Record and Landmark,* 5 October 1954: 8.

"Love Valley Holds Large Bible School." *Statesville Record and Landmark,* 2 August 1957: 10.

"Love Valley Incorporated." *Statesville Record and Landmark,* 3 April 1963: 1.

" 'Love Valley' Is Growing Fast in Popularity." *The Eagle,* 20 May 1959.

Love Valley Town Commissioners Minutes, 21 May 1963 and 1 September 1965.

"Major Studio Plans to Film Movie Here." *Statesville Record and Landmark,* 5 March 1968: 3.

Marshall, Alan. "Hoss Patterson: Restless Cowboy." *Statesville Record and Landmark,* 9 September 1972: 13A.

Maxwell, Jim. "Soldier Dies at Festival." *Statesville Record and Landmark,* 20 July 1970: 1A, 8A.

McCormack, Alfred, Jr. "Barker Calls His Love Valley Creation 'A Place for Kids.' " *Statesville Record and Landmark,* 31 May 1961: 3.

McGlohon, Loonis. Lyrics to "Love Valley" song, 1960s.

Mead, Sidney E. *The Lively Experiment: The Shaping of Christianity in America.* New York: Harper and Row, 1976.

Melville, Keith. *Communes in the Counter Culture: Origins, Theories, and Styles of Life.* New York: William Morrow, 1972.

Miller, Glenn T. "Cooperation and Peace: A. W. McAlister, A Progressive Southern Christian Layman." In *Cultural Perspectives on the American South: Volume 5, Religion.* Edited by Charles Reagan Wilson. New York: Gordon and Breach, 1991. 31-44.

Miller, Ralph. "The Yankees Are Coming—to Iredell." *Salisbury Sunday Post,* 19 January 1969: C1.

Minter, John. "Fired up Again: Stained-Glass Maker Rebuilds." *Statesville Record and Landmark,* "Iredell Neighbors," 19 February 1992: 1, 4.

Montell, William Lynwood. *The Saga of Coe Ridge: A Study in Oral History.* Knoxville: University of Tennessee Press, 1970.

" 'Moon' to Light Way for Cancer Research." *Statesville Record and Landmark,* 23 August 1961: 3.

"More than 100 Units Promised for Event; L. W. Gaither Named Marshall." *Iredell Morning News,* 4 December 1958: 1.

Morris, D. L. Unpublished manuscript. [undated]. Appalachian Collection. Appalachian State University. Boone, NC.

"Mothers Take in Over $2,000 for Polio Fund." *Statesville Record and Landmark,* 30 January 1959: 1.

"Mouthpiece Blamed by Ponder for Fall." *Statesville Record and Landmark,* 15 June 1978: 18B.

"Movie Set." *Statesville Record and Landmark,* 29 November 1968: 1.

Myers, Edward J. "Tar Heel Woodstock." *The State,* Vol. 63, no. 2. July 1995: 35-36.

"New Hope Softened Departure." *The Charlotte Observer,* 22 November 1965: B7.

Noyes, John Humphrey. "Bible Argument." In *First Annual Report in the Oneida Community.* Quoted in Lawrence Foster, *Religion and Sexuality: The Shakers, the Mormons and the Oneida Community.* Chicago: University of Illinois Press, 1984. 90-91.

"The Observer Forum: So What's to Love in Love Valley." *The Charlotte Observer,* 28 August 1959: B3.

Ogden, John (pseudonym Henry Porter). "First There Is a Mountain." *Creative Loafing* Vol. 20, no. 31 (28 December 1991): 9-14, 32-36.

Ostwalt, Conrad. "Love Valley: A Utopian Experiment in North Carolina," *North Carolina Humanities,* Vol. 1, no. 1. Fall 1992: 101-08.

"Outlining Plans." *Statesville Record and Landmark,* 24 September 1968: 1.

"Parade Gimmicks Are Promised." *Iredell Morning News,* 4 December 1958: 1.

Parrington, Vernon Louis, Jr. *American Dreams: A Study of American Utopias.* Providence, RI: Brown University, 1947.

"Phillips Seeks Post in Valley." *Statesville Record and Landmark,* 10 April 1963: 1.

"Plans Progress for Big Parade." *Statesville Record and Landmark,* 21 November 1959.

Poindexter, Jesse. "1,000 Prospective 'Extras.'" *Winston-Salem Journal,* 5 June 1968: 4.

"Ponder in Race at Love Valley." *Statesville Record and Landmark,* 20 April 1963.

Ponder, Joe. Love Valley, NC. Interviews, 4 July 1992 and October 1992.

"Ponder to Make Race for Love Valley Posts." *Statesville Record and Landmark,* 9 April 1963: 5.

"Ponder Severely Hurt in 'Death Slide' Fall." *Statesville Record and Landmark,* 15 May 1978: 2A.

Price, Buddy. Telephone Interview, 9 March 1998.

"Program Is Initiated for Community Action." *Statesville Record and Landmark,* 9 December 1965: 7.

Rigsbee, Fred. "Christmas Parade Plans Shaped." *Statesville Record and Landmark,* 6 November 1969.

——. "Plans Progress for Big Parade." *Statesville Record and Landmark,* 21 November 1959.

——. "256 Entries Form Spectacular Show Four Miles Long." *Statesville Record and Landmark,* 3 December 1959: 1.

Robb, Brien. "Angry Bulls Steal Show at N.C. Rodeo," *The Charlotte Observer,* 7 September 1959.

——. "It's Hog Pasture or Paradise Accordin' to Who's Lookin'." *The Charlotte Observer,* 3 September 1959: D6.

"Rock Festival Bill Presented." *Statesville Record and Landmark,* 22 January 1971: 2.

"Rodeo Group Gets Charter." *Statesville Record and Landmark,* 25 May 1959: 2.

"Rural Students Set for Unique Race." *Statesville Record and Landmark,* 14 January 1959: 2.

"Sanford Will Be Here for Johnson's Address." *Statesville Record and Landmark,* 13 October 1962: 1.

Sargent, Lyman Tower. "Utopia and the Family: A Note on the Family in Political Thought." In *Dissent and Affirmation: Essays in Honor of Mulford Q. Sibley.* Edited by Arthur L. Kalleberg, J. Donald Moon, and Daniel R. Sabia, Jr. Bowling Green, OH: Bowling Green State University Popular Press, 1983. 106-17.

"School Board District Group Hears Dr. Otts." *Statesville Record and Landmark,* 19 April 1963: 3.

Sermon Transcript: Love Valley Presbyterian Church, 17 February 1991.

Simon, Pam. "Love Valley Rebuilds Image." *Statesville Record and Landmark,* 18 March 1980: 1E.

——. Telephone interviews, 6 January 1992 and 25 June 1997.

Smith, David. Eulogy. Typewritten copy.

Smith, David, and Tonda Smith. Winston-Salem, NC. Interview, 7 February 1993.

The Smoke Signal. Various issues, 1980s.

"Star to Appear at Love Valley." *Statesville Record and Landmark,* 15 August 1961: 5.

Statesville Record and Landmark, 30 March 1954: 5.

Statesville Record and Landmark, 11 April 1963: 15.

Statesville Record and Landmark, photographs, 24 September 1968: 1; 29 November 1968.

"Students to Aid March of Dimes." *Statesville Record and Landmark,* 9 January 1959: 8.

Stutts, Janice. "Love Valley, Bucking Broncos Replace Hard Rock Music." *High Point Enterprise,* 6 July 1980.

Swicegood, Donna. "Write-in Vote Selects Barker for 12th Term." *Statesville Record and Landmark,* 4 November 1987: 6A.

Taylor, Jim. "Dude Ranch Shaping Up in North Iredell Valley." *Statesville Record and Landmark,* 4 June 1954: 1, 8.

"Television Star Will Aid Drive." *Statesville Record and Landmark,* 26 August 1961: 4.

Thomas, Heath. "Lumbees Readjust in Iredell." *Winston-Salem Journal,* 7 March 1966: 3.

——. "'Mobility Project' Moves Lumbees from Flatlands to Hills for Jobs." *Salisbury Sunday Post,* 20 February 1966: 1C.

——. "Wild West Reborn in Iredell's Love Valley; Phony or Authentic, It Attracts Thousands." *Salisbury Post,* 13 September 1959: 1B.

Thomas, Tracey. "Founder Tries for Comeback in Love Valley." *The Charlotte Observer: Iredell Neighbors,* 6 October 1991: 1, 6.

"Thousands Will View Big Event Set for Tonight." *Statesville Record and Landmark,* 2 December 1959: 1.

"Three Candidates Seek Love Valley Posts." *Statesville Record and Landmark,* 15 April 1963: 7.

Tilley, Walter. Letter to the author, 14 September 1997.

"Tom Dula's Plight Brings Offer of Iredell Grave." *The Charlotte (NC) News,* 5 December 1958.

"Troutman Wagoners Fastest Dimes Team." *Statesville Record and Landmark,* 24 January 1959: 1.

Trucks, Butch. Telephone interview, 18 February 1992.

"Turkeys to Liven Parade Dec. 5th." *Iredell Morning News,* 13 November 1958: 1.

"TV Star Taking Part in Cancer Campaign." *Wilson Daily Times,* 15 August 1961.

"Valley Church Is Presbyterian." *Iredell Morning News,* 4 September 1956.

"Valley Opens Racing Season." *Statesville Record and Landmark,* 12 July 1961: 1.

de la Villesbrunne, Gerard. Letter to the Barkers, 15 April 1963.

Walls, Dwayne. "Vote Democratic, He Tells Crowd." *The Charlotte Observer,* 16 October 1962: A1-A2.

Warren, Harold. "Here's One Worth Sitting Out." *The Charlotte Observer,* 4 October 1971: 10B.

——. "It Warn't Never a Stayin' Jail." *The Charlotte Observer,* 26 September 1969: 3B.

——. "Love Valley Learns to Like Longhairs." *The Charlotte Observer,* 16 May 1971: 6A.

——. "Love Valley: Now the Longhairs Are Mostly Gone." *The Charlotte Observer,* 9 July 1972: 1C-2C.

——. "Wild West Wins a Vietnamese Cowpoke." *The Charlotte Observer,* 7 April 1970: 1B, 8B.

West, John Foster. *Lift Up Your Head, Tom Dooley: The True Story of the Appalachian Murder That Inspired One of America's Most Popular Ballads.* Asheboro, NC: Down Home Press, 1993.

Williams, Julia Elizabeth. "An Analytical Tabulation of the North American Utopian Communities by Type, Longevity and Location." M.A. thesis, University of Iowa, 1938.

Wilson, Charles Reagan, ed. *Cultural Perspectives on the American South: Volume 5, Religion.* New York: Gordon and Breach, 1991.

"Women to Make Race for Love Valley Posts." *Statesville Record and Landmark,* 19 April 1963: 5.

Wright, Kenneth David. Love Valley, NC. Interviews, Summer 1993; North Wilkesboro, NC. Interview, 8 October 1997.

Index